Signifying without Specifying

Signifying without Specifying

Racial Discourse in the Age of Obama

STEPHANIE LI

RUTGERS UNIVERSITY PRESS

NEW BRUNSWICK, NEW JERSEY, AND LONDON

LIBRARY OF CONGRESS CATALOGING-IN-PUBLICATION DATA

Li, Stephanie, 1977–
    Signifying without specifying : racial discourse in the age of Obama /
Stephanie Li.
        p. cm.
    Includes bibliographical references and index.
    ISBN 978–0–8135–5143–2 (alk. paper) — ISBN 978–0–8135–5144–9
(pbk. : alk. paper)
    1. American literature—21st century—History and criticism.   2. Race in
literature.   3. Post-racialism—United States.   4. Politics and literature—United
States—History—21st century.   5. United States—Race relations.   I. Title.
    PS231.R33L5   2011
    810.9'3552—dc22

                                                                    2011001102

A British Cataloging-in-Publication record for this book is available
from the British Library.

Frontispiece: Kara Walker, From *Notes on Hope*, 2008, 2009. Cut paper and
collage, one from a set of 7: 8.25 × 10.25 in. (21 × 26 cm). Courtesy of the artist
and Sikkema Jenkins & Co., New York.

This volume incorporates parts of my article "Performing Intimacy Using
'Race-Specific, Race-Free Language': Black Private Letters in the Public Sphere,"
from *South Atlantic Quarterly* 109, no. 2, 339–356. Copyright 2010, Duke
University Press. Reprinted by permission of the publisher.

Visit our Web site: http://rutgerspress.rutgers.edu

Manufactured in the United States of America

For Dinah

CONTENTS

PREFACE

When I was in the second grade, my teacher announced that our class was going to hold a science fair. She explained that the best way to come up with a topic for our projects was to ask a question that we could not answer. I remember how easy it was to think of questions: Why does the sun shine? Can animals think? What happens when we dream? For a brief time, I thought I might become a scientist like both my parents, but the project I chose proved that having the answer to a question does not mean you understand the problem it poses. I decided to research the question: why do people have different color skin? Most of the students in my Minneapolis elementary school were white. There were a few black kids and an even smaller number of Asians. I knew that I was not like any of them, and skin was the obvious difference, although color did not always set me apart; in the winter I was as pale as most of my classmates.

For my science project, I learned about melanin and how dark skin protects against ultraviolet radiation. I learned that groups of people living in different parts of the world developed melanin quantities according to their exposure to the sun. My father helped me construct three papier-mâché heads, which I labeled "African," "Asian," and "European" as if the parents of my classmates might be unfamiliar with these key varieties. My mother had once explained to me that in the Midwest people look like they are all cousins; she did not have to mention that they were not our cousins.

Most of my cousins lived in Monterrey, Mexico, where my mother was born. The youngest of seven, she was the only one in her family to make her life in the United States. She met my father while pursuing a Ph.D. in pharmacology at Upstate Medical University in Syracuse. The only son of third-generation immigrants from China, he was born in New York and does not consider himself Asian so much as strongly attracted to Chinese restaurants. After they both finished their graduate work, they moved to Minneapolis, where I was born.

Words like "race," "culture," and "ethnicity" are words I learned at school, not at home. My parents practiced their own version of what Toni Morrison calls "race-specific, race-free language" and which I understand as the language of intimacy. It is the language spoken when one's race is both known and irrelevant, that is, irrelevant because it is known. This was the language I craved as a child, hoping that, if I knew the secret to skin colors, its difference might become meaningless.

My science project did little to unravel the meanings attached to various skin colors or to explain why such meanings abide. But the concerns that prompted my first foray into science are ones that I still grapple with today. Now, however, I see the question differently: not why do people have different color skin, but what does this difference signify? This is a book fundamentally concerned with race and its representation in contemporary American discourse. But just as my second-grade science project was less about skin color than about how to understand my own difference from others, below the surface, this is a book about intimacy and the language we might use to express the paradox of how we are both different and the same.

ACKNOWLEDGMENTS

My thanks begin where this project began, with Grant Farred's invitation to me to submit "something on Morrison" for the *SAQ* edition on "Thinking Black Intellectuals." I am grateful both for Grant's confidence and for his helpful feedback on what would become the seed of this book. I also thank the friends, colleagues, and students who have shared my enthusiasm for Obama and the still pregnant promise of his presidency.

This book owes its existence to the support and commitment of Leslie Mitchner, who saw the manuscript through its many evolutions. Early on she became the audience I needed to keep writing.

I am especially grateful to Karla Holloway for her incisive and demanding comments on early drafts. Her rigorous commitment to the manuscript simply made it better.

Morrison's term, "race-specific, race-free language," names the language of my parent's home, a home I carry within me. Sara Antonia and Jonathan Li are responsible for all the words I speak and write. And my thanks to Dinah Holtzman who understands those words, both spoken and unspoken.

Signifying without Specifying

Introduction

When then Senator Barack Obama announced to a crowd of thousands in February 2008, "We are the ones we've been waiting for," few knew that the line referred to a poem by African American poet June Jordan.[1] Instead commentators either thrilled with the power of his commanding oratory or puzzled over the nuances of this peculiar proclamation. It was at once an empowering reiteration of the hope and change vested in Obama's historic campaign and a strange indictment. Why have we been passively waiting when the country is in shambles—fighting two seemingly endless wars, our international reputation in collapse, the stock market teetering toward recession? However, even if we had only been waiting, allowing other powers to wreck havoc on the economy, the environment, and society at large, Obama seemed to promise that this wait was over, not because he had arrived, but because we had finally recognized our own power to change. With its strange syntax, the phrase, "We are the ones we've been waiting for," glosses over the constitution of its own subject. Who is this "we"? There is an additional silence embedded in Obama's borrowed line, an assumption that change has occurred without an explanation of what that change is or how it transpired. But spoken from the man who would become our country's first black president, the change was obvious as was the implicitly multiracial "we." Demonstrating a rhetorical move characteristic of his campaign, Obama gestured toward race without speaking race. The junior senator, whose intellectualism has been nearly as energizing as his race, echoed a type of coded racial discourse emblematic of twenty-first-century literary texts.

"We are the ones we've been waiting for," Obama proclaimed, not the more easily conceived, if less rousing, "I am the one you've been waiting for." Instead the conflation between the glowing politician and the nation that would elect him nine months later anticipated the widespread self-congratulatory calls of his victory. Obama's win was not his alone, but evidence of how far the country had come in its evolution on racial matters. Journalists reporting the news of election day 2008 could not hide their joy. Many Republicans conceded that despite their loss, Obama's victory signaled a new day in American race relations: the country was at last post-racial. It was a term attached not simply to our new president, but, like his inspiring campaign "we," it encompassed all of the United States. As Richard Cohen wrote in the *Washington Post*, "It is not just that he is post-racial; so is the nation that he is primed to lead . . . we have overcome."[2]

What have we overcome to become post-racial? What brave new world has arrived to end our long wait? The editorial page of the *Wall Street Journal* declared on the morning following Obama's win that post-racial connotes the promise of a vision made true, the end of racism: "One promise of his victory is that perhaps we can put to rest the myth of racism as a barrier to achievement in this splendid country."[3] Here, as in many subsequent descriptions of Obama, race is an inconvenient myth, an obstacle that we have at last surmounted because the highest office in the land is open to a member of a historically maligned community.[4] But as the very term "post-racial" indicates, race and racism are oddly conflated here such that the demise of the latter heralds the irrelevance of race-specific discourse.[5] No one suggested that Obama's victory signaled the arrival of a post-racism age. Persistent disparities in housing, health care, education, and other opportunities among racial groups make such a claim absurd. Instead, post-racial implies a more disturbing conclusion: racism can be ended only through the destruction of race as a meaningful category of identity.

If Obama is proof that America is at last post-racial, then, at the moment in which he became president, his blackness ceased to be a site of dynamic change and possibility; instead, his race settled into a static mark of transcendent identity. Fred Moten, distinguishing between the "lived experience of the black and the fact of blackness," notes that life exists in "the unstable zone" between these poles, a "zone, made available to us by the broken bridge of mistranslation."[6] The fact of Obama's blackness overwhelmed his lived experience as a black man, transforming the mark of blackness into a convenient fetish of righteous triumph rather than a signifier of multiplicity and resistance. Mistranslations proliferate with alarming force around our new president, none more powerfully than the illusion of a "post-racial" America. Post-racial here becomes a term of appropriation, a way for a black man to become emblematic of a national fantasy where all enjoy equal opportunity. It is another iteration of the misguided aspiration for "color blindness," a way to ignore both the historical legacy of race and its abiding influence on all aspects of social life.[7] The false premise of Obama's post-raciality leads to a disturbing silence about how race continues to operate in the public sphere. Although Obama never identified himself as post-racial, he certainly benefited from rhetoric that promised a new kind of racial harmony, one heavily vested in symbolic import if not comprehensive change. Noting the instability of meaning attached to our future president, David Roediger observed, "representations of the Obama campaign reflect an overwhelming desire to transcend race without transcending racial inequality, as well as the impossibility of doing so" (*How Race Survived U.S. History*, 217).

Post-raciality implies an escape from race and thus the end of racial oppression. However, even the first documented use of the term "post-racial" demonstrates the troubling merger between race and racism that characterizes its current usage. At a 1971 conference in Durham, North Carolina, President of Duke University Terry Sanford spoke of creating a "truly post-racial society" in the development of a newly industrialized South unmarked by segregation. Yet Philip D. Carter, a *Washington Post* journalist covering the conference, observed that no reference to race was made in the conference's official document.[8] Presumably, a "truly post-racial society" would have no need to mention race at all. Consistent with so many other declarations of post-trends like post-feminism, post–civil rights or post-identity politics, the current allure of post-raciality demonstrates that a prefix does not negate the social conflict it modifies. David Hollinger indicts the "many 'posts' of our time" as a lazy form of critical engagement by noting, "'Posting' is often a way of repudiating a preceding episode rather than building upon it and critically refining its contributions" (*Postethnic America*, 5). We are decades away from the battle for civil rights that defined the 1960s, but equal rights are hardly a guarantee for all Americans. While the "post" of post–civil rights may refer to historical developments beyond the 1960s, it also signifies the fantasy that we live in a truly egalitarian society, a rhetorical ruse that quells the necessity for further social change. Similarly, if we live in a "post-feminist" age, the work of feminism may be assumed to be complete.[9] The urge to identify "post-" moments of social development reflects a desire to be done with the complicated legacies of oppression and inequality that still plague our nation. This totalizing gesture implies the fulfillment of liberty and justice for all, the promise of an ideal America at last made true, as if the wrongs of any nation can be neatly surmounted with a prefix.

We live in a time of new racial meaning, but it is not post-racial. When W.E.B. Du Bois proclaimed, "the problem of the Twentieth Century is the problem of the color-line" (*The Souls of Black Folk*, v), he did not have to specify what he meant by the color-line because segregation so clearly defined early twentieth-century race relations. During his lifetime, the color-line could be drawn geographically around specific neighborhoods and housing projects, physically on bus floors and train cars, and politically between those who championed a segregated America and those who worked for integration. Du Bois's color-line designated injustice, and, although it was not always free of ambiguity, it largely separated the privileged from the oppressed. The color-line still exists today, but it is no longer a simplistic divide between those with power and those without it. A black man can be president, another can be attorney general, and a Latina woman born in the Bronx can sit on the highest court in the land. These achievements might suggest that Du Bois's color-line has been so fundamentally reconfigured as to be meaningless. Might we at last retire the tired stereotypes and prejudices of race? As conservative pundits continually remind us, the dream of Martin Luther King Jr. was to live in a world in which children are judged not by the color of their skin but by the content of their character. Wasn't Obama's victory the ultimate evidence of this dream come true?

To accede to this claim, however, ignores the critical role race played in our president's success. Obama did not win the election because race does not matter; he won because he understood how it still does. Despite calls to the contrary, race has not disappeared quite so readily from American society, nor, as I hope to show, should it. King's dream does not champion colorblindness so much as equality. Similarly, Obama's victory does not simplistically prove that a black man can be president; it proves that this exceptionally intelligent and fortunate one can. Obama will always be celebrated as our first black president, but more important to his rise is the fact that he is our first president to use his own race as a political tool; he is our first signifying president. Like the trickster of African mythology, Obama has proved adept at double-voiced performance, maximizing his racial identity to appeal to radically different demographics.[10] In the space between the lived experience of blackness and the fact of blackness, he exploits the instability of racially loaded signifiers to powerful effect. The declaration, "we are the ones we've been waiting for," simultaneously signals multiracial cooperation and alludes to a poem specifically addressed to black women even as it omits specific mention of race. Consistent with the trickster tactics of the African signifying monkey, racial meaning manifests only through coded references and rhetorical play.

Du Bois's color-line resurfaced in the racial smears that dogged Obama's campaign, but the very boundaries of racial meaning that once signified injustice also helped elect our first black president. Former congresswoman Geraldine Ferraro spoke the truth when she told a California newspaper in March 2008: "If Obama was a white man, he would not be in this position. And if he was a woman of any color, he would not be in this position. He happens to be very lucky to be who he is. And the country is caught up in the concept."[11] It would be naïve to claim that race had nothing to do with Obama's candidacy just as it would be naïve to assume that John McCain's race had nothing to do with his success in capturing the Republican nomination. Although previous candidates and presidents have benefited from their racial identities and even played to racialized fears, Obama is the first to utilize the multiple significations of his own race to his advantage.[12]

Ferraro was critiqued for her comments and forced to resign from Hillary Clinton's campaign staff because she spoke openly about race and in our "post-racial" age, race is best kept silent or at least well-coded even as it remains reassuringly visible. The Ferraro episode like the January 2010 flare-up surrounding Senator Harry Reid's characterization of Obama as electable because he lacked a "Negro dialect, unless he wanted to have one," highlights David Theo Goldberg's observation that in our contemporary moment, "racism is reduced in its supposed singularity to *invoking* race, not to its debilitating structural effects or the legacy of its ongoing unfair impacts" (*The Threat of Race*, 360).[13] Addressing race directly betrays the fantasy of our color-blind meritocracy even as visible diversity is a requirement for any respectable institution. In our "post-racial" age, race must be the mark of transcendence, not the sign of special treatment, Importantly, Obama was never hampered by accusations that he benefited from affirmative action or other race-based policies; instead, he safely confirmed the myth of America's meritocracy. As a nation, we continue to be uncomfortable discussing how race may contribute to either the success or demise of individuals. We want to believe that Obama's presidency makes race irrelevant rather than recognize the ways in which race both influenced his rise and frames the attacks made against him. Like no other previous presidential candidate, Obama exploited the tension arising from America's need to simultaneously showcase and silence race.

This precarious balance between the seen and the heard is at the heart of Obama's political success, allowing him to be perceived as both black and transcendent of blackness. While this strategy led to Obama's astounding victory, it elides crucial concerns about how to express and embrace racial difference. Obama's proclamation that "We are the ones we've been waiting for" signifies unity, a collective embrace of some unspecified but brilliant future. However, in "Poem for South African Women," June Jordan applies the phrase in a far different context, asking "And who will join this standing up." This line is posed without a question mark because the women of the poem stand alone, knowing "we are the ones we've been waiting for." Jordan's poem is not a call for unity; instead, the women she describes are "the ones who stood without sweet company" yet "will sing and sing" (*Passion*, 43). They thrive despite the failure of others to join them; their empowerment does not depend upon the participation of others. Jordan's poem is a praise song to those who stand alone, to the courage of difference. Such courage certainly exists in Obama as well, but it is not something he asks of his fellow Americans. In our president's inspiring call, difference is what we must transcend, not what, in Jordan's words, initiates this "standing up."

Race-Specific, Race-Free Language

Obama's victory represents the culmination of racial rhetoric that signifies without specifying, but he is not the first to explore the possibilities of what Toni Morrison terms "race-specific, race-free language" (9). In "Home," an essay included in Wahneema Lubiano's edited volume *The House That Race Built: Black Americans, U.S. Terrain*, Morrison envisions a world crossed by color-lines but not restricted by them. For Morrison, this "world-in-which-race-does-*not*-matter" (3) is home. She explains that such a home does not aim to banish race and thereby form a color-blind utopia where difference does not exist. Rather, seeking a way to "convert a racist house into a race-specific yet nonracist home" (5), she promotes a kind of racialism, or embrace of racial categorization, that is unmarked by inequality or claims of inferiority.[14] Initially Morrison attempted to transform the "racist house" (5) by rebuilding it as "an open house, grounded, yet generous in its supply of windows and doors" (4). However, this endeavor proves to be problematic as she discovers the wisdom of Audre Lorde's warning, "the master's tools will never dismantle the master's house" (*Sister Outsider*, 110). Even if the house is razed to the ground and recreated with more porous boundaries, it will always remain a house, a specific geographic location bound by physical barriers. To truly transform the architecture of racism, Morrison must move beyond traditional conceptions of how space relates to identity and freedom. The structural requirements of a house—its walls, floors, and ceilings—connote the kind of restrictions that make racism possible. In this way, the house is both shelter and barrier, simultaneously fostering safety and insularity. Like a house, the construction of race establishes borders between what is inside and what is outside, between what is human and what is wilderness. The house, so often a figure of peace and mastery, becomes for Morrison a symbol of the complacency and partition that make racism possible.

   In her quest to capture home as "the concrete thrill of borderlessness— a kind of out of doors safety," Morrison explores the possibilities of "race-specific, race-free language," asking "How to enunciate race while depriving it of its lethal cling?" (5). Morrison's home welcomes difference without hierarchy; it is race without racism. In this world, she explains:

> a sleepless woman could always rise from her bed, wrap a shawl around her shoulders and sit on the steps in the moonlight. And if she felt like it she could walk out the yard and on down the road. No lamp and no fear. A hiss-crackle from the side of the road would never scare her because whatever it was that made the sound, it wasn't something creeping up on her. Nothing for ninety miles around thought she was prey. She could stroll as slowly as she liked, think of food preparations, war, of family things, or lift her eyes to stars and think of nothing at all. Lampless and without fear she could make her way. And if a light shone from a house up a ways and the cry of a colicky baby caught her attention, she might step over to the house and call out softly to the woman inside trying to soothe the baby. The two of them might take turns massaging the infant's stomach, rocking, or trying to get a little soda water down. When the baby quieted they could sit together for a spell, gossiping, chuckling low so as not to wake anybody else. The woman could decide to go back to her own house then, refreshed and ready for sleep, or she might keep her direction and walk further down the road, past other houses, past the three churches, past the feedlot. On out, beyond the limits of the town, because nothing at the edge thought she was prey. (10)

Morrison's conception of home is free of the confines of a house. Its architecture is composed not of walls and doors but of the ambiguous, meandering path of her sleepless woman, who may visit a friend or return to sleep or wander past the edge of town. Her home contains all of these possibilities because here nothing "thought she was prey." The invocation of the possibility that this woman might be considered prey disrupts the lyricism of the passage. It imposes the presence of race by alluding to a time in which this woman was treated as an object to be hunted. Morrison's race-free language is made race-specific by this imbedded reference to history. Her home is one that dwells in the freedoms afforded by the present while understanding the violence of the past. This passage highlights the necessary ambiguities of "race-specific, race-free language" and the generative contradictions that arise in its expression: home is not a place but the freedom to leave a place, identity is anonymous yet intimate, safety lies in darkness, and history marks but does determine the path ahead.

How may we apply Morrison's eloquent description of home to the language we use to articulate race? How may we fashion words to create a world in which, as she writes, "race both matters and is rendered impotent"? Is it possible to express difference without imposing hierarchies of domination and value? Morrison admits that, regarding such matters, her thoughts are "aesthetically and politically unresolved" (5), suggesting that such writing is very much a work in progress. However, it is precisely this lack of certainty that comes to define the home Morrison envisions and the language that can express it. Home is created in the reach toward a place of simultaneous freedom and safety as well as in the failure that inevitably results. She narrates the home of her sleepless woman as a series of possibilities, things she "could" do, not things she actually does. These actions, held in suspense, bespeak a puzzling timidity, reminding us that home is the place we dream of, rarely the place we are.

America is a nation founded on the freedom and protection that Morrison imagines for her sleepless woman, a nation that has borne as many failures as successes in its pursuit of "a more perfect union." In March 2008, Obama reminded the country of this grounding aspiration in his speech on race delivered at Philadelphia's Constitution Center. He observed that the opening line of the Constitution did not abolish slavery or grant equal rights to all citizens of the fledgling United States. Instead, as he explained, "What would be needed were Americans in successive generations who were willing to do their part—through protests and struggle, on the streets and in the courts, through a civil war and civil disobedience and always at great risk—to narrow the gap between the promise of our ideals and the reality of their time" ("A More Perfect Union," 238). The union is ours to perfect, this house of America ours to rid of racism and inequality, this house ours to make a home.

Despite Obama's presidential victory and the promise of racial equality it suggests, we are still far from a perfect union. We do not live in a post-racial utopia as skin color remains a significant obstacle to success, and communities of color continue to suffer from disproportionately high rates of unemployment, poor health care, and dysfunctional schools.[15] Morrison's vision of home suggests that the very notion of post-raciality is misguided, that we should aspire not to a color-blind future but to one that adamantly recognizes difference, including distinctions of race. Consequently, our concern must be with understanding how race operates as a social and political reality, even as that reality is fraught with representational paradoxes. In her essay, Morrison implies that as a language changes so does the landscape of a country, affirming that words have the ability to reframe the world in which we live. And, as evidenced by both the public discourse surrounding Obama and a new trend in American literature, the language that we use to represent race is indeed changing. Though it may seem incongruous to unite analysis of political rhetoric alongside that of literary texts, both arenas demonstrate a profound shift in how race is expressed and conceptualized in contemporary America. "Race-specific, race-free language" reflects the legacy of multiculturalism through its expectation of diversity even as it reveals persistent anxieties about how to confront difference.

In "Discourse in the Novel," Mikhail Bakhtin explains that languages evolve through exchange with other languages, a process he called "hybridization."[16] While Bakhtin notes that within the novel such hybridization is a deliberate construction of the author, he acknowledges that language development can also occur more broadly and without a single or specific motivating agent. "Unintentional, unconscious hybridization is one of the most important modes in the historical life and evolution of all languages. We may even say that language and languages change historically primarily by means of hybridization, by means of a mixing of various 'languages' coexisting within the boundaries of a single dialect, a single national language, a single branch, a single group of different branches or different groups of such branches, in the historical as well as paleontological past of languages—but the crucible for this mixing always remains the utterance" (The Dialogic Imagination, 358–359). Like Morrison, Bakhtin claims that new forms of language allow us to understand and live in the world in important new ways. As he elaborates, "such unconscious hybrids have been at the same time profoundly productive historically: they are pregnant with potential for new world views, with new 'internal forms' for perceiving the world in words" (360). Changes in language reflect the development of innovative paradigms by which to understand who we are and how we relate to others.

Morrison's "race-specific, race-free language" identifies a new hybrid language that American writers and politicians are using to express race. The radical nature of this discourse resonates with Homi Bhabha's characterization of "the possibility of a cultural hybridity that entertains difference without an assumed or imposed hierarchy" (*The Location of Culture*, 4). "Race-specific, race-free language" represents a merger between language that explicitly names racial identity and language that occludes or ignores racial difference. Consequently, such discourse identifies race through signs other than skin color or family origin, emphasizing instead certain linguistic and cultural codes. Despite the liberatory potential of this language, which allows us to move beyond a strict black/white binary concerning matters of race, it can also be employed to both racist and antiracist ends. Although Morrison's most significant exploration of this kind of prose occurs in *Paradise* (1997), her novel *Beloved* (1987) includes a scene in which race is conveyed through action. She describes how Paul D and Sethe, both former slaves, step aside for a group of oncoming women. The reader knows the women are white because of the deference required by Paul D and Sethe. Like the previously cited passage from *Paradise* involving the sleepless woman, racial identity is encoded through a description of the degree of freedom or limitation, as in the case of Paul D and Sethe, experienced by individuals.[17]

Race-specific language would explicitly name the oncoming women as white while race-free language would suggest that race has no bearing on the obvious social inequality apparent in the scene. Because *Beloved* is set during Reconstruction, there can be no pretense that race is not a decisive factor in the lives of Morrison's characters; race-free language is simply not an accurate tool for describing the lives of former slaves. However, as numerous critics and historians suggest, due to the victories of the civil rights movement and sweeping changes in how Americans perceive race and racism, we now live in a time in which race does not always signify in predictable or simplistic ways. Blackness does not equate with bondage or inferiority, and whiteness does not always imply power and privilege. While Morrison could never present characters living in mid-nineteenth-century Ohio in race-free language because race then defined so much of social and legal identity, in twenty-first-century America race-free language may at times present a more viable means of describing our current social landscape. Racial identity does not necessarily circumscribe the life choices and possibilities of individuals even as it remains a slippery form of prejudice.

Despite volumes of academic study exposing the artificiality of race and increasing numbers of people who do not easily fit into prescribed racial categories, race continues to function primarily as a visual mark. Skin color is still the most significant determinant of racial identity. How then does the visuality of race translate into language? In an oral context with a visible speaker, we can still rely upon physical traits to understand how race impacts speech. Obama is black, and thus his speech must reflect that blackness. His success was largely derived from the fact that his rhetorical "we" is not directed exclusively toward African Americans. His "we" is inclusive, open to all races; and thus, he implicitly speaks of multiracial cooperation. The marvel of his rhetoric is that it appears not to be racially exclusive. His language cannot solely be defined as black; as such, it is not threatening or alienating, but welcoming, even familiar.[18]

However, to translate race onto the page is more complicated. Although American literature has historically assumed a white male perspective, the development of new ethnic canons and a greater sensitivity to diverse identities has overturned such a predetermined subject position. The racial identity of literary characters has to be made explicit, or, as evident in some works by Morrison discussed in chapter 1, racial ambiguity is made to serve other textual ends. "Race-specific, race-free language" moves the mark of race away from the visual. It conceptualizes racial difference not as emerging from physical characteristics but as connoting identifications that can be heard or read and therefore as a type of shared meaning not necessarily understood by everyone. Morrison's sleepless woman is black because she was once considered "prey," a critical detail that not all readers may comprehend. The mark of race is not evident by skin color but rather is implicated in an entire history of racial persecution. In this new form of racial textuality, the visual is often ignored, instead making racial meaning the site of intimacy between those literate in racial codes.

This book is dedicated to exploring how racial meaning functions as a type of interpretative understanding and how our language often fosters rather than clarifies this ambiguity. In an era in which direct discussion of race is often taboo even as we live in an increasingly multiracial world, the language referring to race has become a series of contested signs. How we read those signifiers, which increasingly are not neatly color coded, determines how we understand both America's history and its current reality. Analyzing political rhetoric alongside recent literary texts, I argue that contemporary racial textuality, that is, the presence of race in language, depends upon a type of reading practice that relates to Du Bois's characterization of black identity. Importantly, Du Bois did not alone define "the Negro" by skin color or association with a specific cultural heritage. He wrote instead that "the Negro is a sort of seventh son, born with a veil, and gifted with second-sight in this American world,—a world which yields him no true self-consciousness, but only lets him see himself through the revelation of the other world" (2). Du Bois linked racial identity to a type of vision or consciousness; to be black is to see a doubled reality. This double consciousness results in the Negro's struggle "to merge his double self into a better and truer self" so that he can "be both a Negro and an American, without being cursed and spit upon by his fellows" (3).

More than one hundred years after the publication of *The Souls of Black Folk* (1903), we have a president who identifies himself as a black American, a man who demonstrates some end to the conflict that has haunted generations of African Americans. Yet the dilemma of double consciousness abides, encrypted within the very language we use to express race. Du Bois's formulation has crucial resonance for how race is both represented and read in today's discourse. In our fraught contemporary moment, racial signification depends upon the gifts of one's sight or more precisely the gifts of one's reading practices because the multiple, signifying revelations of racial meaning occur not visually but linguistically. Double consciousness provides a critical paradigm for Morrison's "race-specific, race-free language," a way to understand, for example, how Obama, despite his physical appearance, can be conceived as both too black and not black enough. Neither interpretation is necessarily right. The gift of Du Bois's "second sight" implies the recognition that to be either black or American does not represent a more important or a more accurate identity. The gift is to see and experience both. The complexity of our national discourse on race demands the cultivation of such "second sight," the ability to simultaneously read and read beyond the codes of "race-specific, race-free language."

Although Morrison identifies "race-specific, race-free language" as the foundation for a home that is simultaneously liberating and safe, it is not to be understood as a singular good. While such discourse facilitated the remarkable election of our first black president, like any language it is a tool of power directed according to the objectives of its practitioners. The purpose of this book is not only to describe how "race-specific, race-free language" operates in contemporary literary texts and political exchange but also to critique its uses. When too closely coupled to an antiracialist perspective, which, as Goldberg writes, "seeks to wipe out the terms of reference"—that is, all categories of race—we are in danger of "wip[ing] away the very vocabulary necessary to recall and recollect, to make a case, to make a claim" (21). The entirely race-free language promoted by the champions of our newly "post-racial" world threatens to erase the historically constituted categories that still powerfully impact national institutions and social relations. Just as a color-blind approach to the world makes one blind to persistent forms of racial discrimination, entirely race neutral language dispenses with the words necessary to understand our stratified society. Such language leaves Morrison's sleepless woman not only race-less but without the knowledge to understand what her freedom means. The danger of "race-specific, race-free language" is that it will rob us of the still urgent need to speak about how race impacts public life. Yet, at its best, this new form of racial discourse preserves the history of race relations in the United States without imposing hierarchies of difference.

From Our "First Black President" to Our First Black President

"Race-specific, race-free language" represents the culmination of America's uneasy relationship to race. When former President Bill Clinton launched his 1997 race initiative, "One America in the 21st Century," by asking the country to participate in "a candid conversation on the state of race relations today," numerous national leaders and social commentators lauded his efforts.[19] But, as even he came to admit, the initiative was a huge disappointment.[20] Many ascribed this failure to the growing Lewinsky scandal and the increasing likelihood of war in Iraq. The former president of the National Urban League, Hugh Price, called the effort "stillborn" (*Conversations*, 345), but "One America" was plagued by numerous internal difficulties as well. The seven-member presidential advisory board was charged with promoting a national dialogue on race and creating a plan to ease racial tension. However, without precedence for establishing lasting change through advisory board recommendations, there was little expectation from the onset that meaningful reform could occur.[21]

As a result, press coverage and critical discussion of "One America" focused primarily on the often-contentious exchanges among the advisory board panel, which was chaired by esteemed black historian John Hope Franklin. The aging but tireless scholar accepted the position despite the protests of some who felt Franklin should be spared the demands of such a public and inevitably difficult appointment. Moreover, Franklin proved to be a leader of another generation in that he continually framed American race relations as a black/white conflict. Attorney Angela Oh vigorously championed a more inclusive understanding of how difference functions within and between other minority populations. In the first official meeting of the advisory panel, Oh explained her hope for articulating a new vision of American race relations: "The old terms are going to be tossed. We're going to be hearing some new language, because it is time for some new language to be introduced, and we're going to help find that new language. . . . And as we move through this process of dialogue I just want to make sure that we go beyond the black-white paradigm. We need to go beyond that because the world is about much more than that, and this is sort of the next horizon. For us as a nation we need to go beyond that."[22] By contrast, Franklin, continually emphasizing the primacy of black/white relations, argued in direct response to Oh, "This country cut its eye teeth on racism in the black/white sphere. They didn't do it with Native Americans, they did it on black/white relations. . . . And I think that gives us the kind of perspective we need."[23] Although both Oh and Franklin later stated that the press exaggerated their opposing perspectives, their conflict highlighted the struggle of all those involved with "One America" to establish any kind of consensus or meaningful progress on racial matters.

In response to persistent calls that the panel excluded concerns of Asian and Native American communities, the final work of the advisory board erred on the side of treating separate ethnic and racial groups as undifferentiated equals. Patricia A. Sullivan and Steven R. Goldwiz explain, "Clinton equalized difference in his emphasis on pluralism" ("Seven Lessons," 163), resulting in a failure to recognize the unique experiences of separate populations. Despite Franklin's commitment to stressing problems confronting African Americans, the final report did not acknowledge the legacy of forced migration versus voluntary relocation to the United States among other key differences between minority communities. Assessing the outcome of "One America," Mary Frances Berry wrote, "If there is any overriding theme in the report from the Advisory Board to the President's Initiative on Race, it is that African-Americans are just another group of 'colored people' with no special place in the pantheon of those who have suffered from subordination."[24] There was no way to reconcile Oh's concern for a more expansive language by which to conceptualize racial and ethnic difference with the need to preserve the unique history of various minority groups. The options were either strife or ineffectual appeals to find unity in diversity. In his 1997 commencement address at the University of California–San Diego in which he first announced "One America," President Clinton spoke of "the problem of race," not the problem of racism.[25] Like contemporary champions of "post-raciality," Clinton treated difference with skepticism and too often ignored structural inequalities facing minority populations.[26] The work of the advisory panel ultimately sought to reify what Karla Holloway has called Clinton's "race-free public policy" (*Codes of Conduct*, 81) as if race were the key element to be expunged from our utopian "One America."

The race initiative also suffered from its dependence on town hall meetings, which were organized to provide Americans with an opportunity to personally engage in the national conversation about race. Although town hall meetings had been crucial to Clinton's successful campaign strategy, when dedicated entirely to the divisive and often ill-defined issue of race, the meetings proved ineffectual if not outright disastrous. Martin Carcasson and Mitchell F. Rice argue that the failure of "One America" was due in large part to "the heavily fractured nature of the audience" ("The Promise and Failure," 246), which undermined attempts to create a meaningful and focused exchange. Meetings devolved into "serial monologue, an airing of grievances and personal perspectives" that brought little closure to longstanding conflicts.[27] Clinton's unsuccessful initiative reflected America's discomfort and even inability to confront racial issues directly. The town hall meetings he envisioned in which Americans of all racial backgrounds might constructively discuss their prejudices and individual experiences of discrimination were no more than fantasy.

Even as commercial advertisements and popular media featured a multiracial citizenry as never before in the 1990s, Americans simply could not talk about race across racial divides. Leon Wynter calls the outburst of racially diverse images in marketing and popular culture—from the slick Benetton campaign to Disney's casting of pop singer Brandy as Cinderella for its revival of the *Wonderful World of Disney* in 1997—"Transracial America." Wynter describes this pervasive cultural trope as "a vision of the American dream in which we are liberated from the politics of race to openly embrace any style, cultural trope, or image of beauty that attracts us regardless of its origin" (*American Skin*, 135). However, this image of a multiracial utopia depends upon a dubious "liberation" from the politics of race. As suggested in Clinton's UCSD commencement address, this approach assumes that race somehow shackles our ultimate potential, that race is an impediment to our multicultural destiny. However, we will never be liberated from race because, no matter what it signifies, it will always signify something. We may be able to choose whatever "style, cultural trope, or image of beauty" we like, but that choice will have social consequences, will mark difference. Obama may be the president, but, as demonstrated by his forced separation from former mentor the Reverend Jeremiah Wright and other incidents explored at length in chapter 4, he is not always free to mark himself racially. In this way, Obama's election is another iteration of Clinton's failed race initiative. In the twenty-first century, Americans still like their diversity displayed, not discussed.

Ten years before endorsing Obama in his campaign for the presidency, Toni Morrison famously referred to Bill Clinton as "our first black President," writing in *The New Yorker*, "Clinton displays almost every trope of blackness: single-parent household, born poor, working-class, saxophone-playing, McDonald's-and-junk-food-loving boy from Arkansas" ("The Talk of the Town," 152). By contrast, in an open letter addressed to Obama and published on a variety of major news websites in January 2008, Morrison directly mentions race only to discard its significance, writing, "nor do I care much for your race[s]."[28] Although I explore Morrison's twin statements on Clinton and Obama in greater detail later in this book, her shift from race-specific language to prose that elides racial specificity while benefiting from the intimacy of intraracial exchange emblematizes how American racial discourse has changed.

Morrison's pronouncement on Clinton shocked many readers and critics, but by bringing race into the national conversation about privacy, sexuality, and the presidency, she unveiled a critical component of how prejudice operates. As with Clinton's race initiative, she sought to make race visible, a task clearly unnecessary in the case of Obama. Instead, her letter to the junior senator from Illinois exploits the possibilities of "race-specific, race-free language" by making race the context, not the subject of the exchange. Race moves from being the critical invisible ingredient in Clinton's impeachment spectacle to being the unspoken grounds of intimacy with Obama. In her open letter, race has meaning not as a classification with far-reaching social implications; rather, it functions, as I expand upon later, as a coded trope. Like Obama's inclusive "we," Morrison stages an intimate exchange that performs a deliberately constructed version of black speech, thereby making it familiar and affirming for readers of all racial backgrounds.

Importantly, our current president shares only one item on Morrison's list of the "trope(s) of blackness"—"single-parent household." The meaning of race has shifted such that "blackness" does not necessarily mean blackness anymore. This is the result of many wide-ranging demographic changes outlined by Ytasha Womack who has reintroduced the term "post-black" to describe a racial population that has been transformed by a massive influx of African immigrants, the development of new "urban impresarios" who undermine easy associations between blackness and poverty as well as greater tolerance for sexual, religious, and cultural differences.[29] Although the significations attached to blackness are beginning to change, it continues to function as a meaningful category of identity. One main objective of this study is to explore the dynamic relationship between social reality and language construction in order to understand how "race-specific, race-free language" represents fundamental changes in the ways that racial categories evolve and operate.

The Double Consciousness of "Race-Specific, Race-Free Language"

Our national discomfort with frank conversations about race, so apparent in Clinton's failed "One America," elucidates much of Obama's appeal. If "race-specific, race-free language" signifies without specifying, then we might read Obama as the embodiment of such prose. He is race-specific because his racial identity is widely known, but he is race-free in that he routinely ignores racial matters. While campaigning for the Democratic nomination and then the Oval Office, Obama avoided directly addressing racial issues. However, he was keenly aware of how race was pivotal to his popularity and could be used to fulfill his presidential aspirations. Michael Eric Dyson identified the key to Obama's historic presidential campaign as mastering "how to wink at black America while speaking to white America."[30] Dyson's apt description suggests the importance of employing race-neutral language while highlighting an implicit intimacy between himself and the black community. There is a critical divide here between insider and outsider, between those who catch the wink and those who only hear the words. Obama became president by exploiting a kind of linguistic intimacy that moves beyond visual registers of race.

Consistent with Morrison's desire for "race-specific, race-free language," Obama's victory was significantly derived from his ability to evoke race without directly mentioning either color or ethnicity. Early on he understood that he required a broad coalition of supporters because he could not win the presidency by securing only the black vote. Consequently, he needed to craft a language that spoke to the widest possible audience, that fostered trust in both white and black constituents, in communities both wary of racial issues and eager to address them. This impetus for unity defined the speech that first brought Obama to national attention, the keynote address at the 2004 Democratic Convention. In a typical rhetorical flourish that balances human detail with broad vision, Obama told the country: "The pundits like to slice-and-dice our country into Red States and Blue States; Red States for Republicans and Blue States for Democrats. But I've got news for them, too. We worship an awesome God in the Blue States, and we don't like federal agents poking around in our libraries in the Red States. We coach Little League in the Blue States, and yes, we've got some gay friends in the Red States. . . . We are one people, all of us pledging allegiance to the Stars and Stripes, all of us defending the United States of America."

Although Obama briefly mentions the fallacy of "a Black America and White America and Latino America and Asian America" ("Keynote Address," 451), he does not dwell on racial difference. Instead, he focuses on common stereotypes associated with Democrats and Republicans, both nonracialized groups. In his vision, everyone has been maligned by false prejudices, everyone has a greater humanity unrecognized by media pundits and superficial assessments. Richard Thompson Ford understands this appeal as fraught with racial implications. As Ford explains, "When Obama spoke of bridging partisan differences and bringing Democrats and Republicans together for the greater good, it was impossible to miss the subtext: he was also uniquely positioned to bridge racial differences because he had, of necessity, been doing so his entire life" (*The Race Card*, 360). Obama literally embodies the promise of racial unity, although importantly he never made such a lofty claim about his presidential candidacy. To identify himself as "post-racial" would have brought race to the forefront of his campaign, thereby jeopardizing his national appeal. As his victory would come to prove, America craves someone who embodies the visual symbol of racial unity, not someone who constantly speaks of racial unity.

After listening to one of Obama's campaign speeches, Dyson concluded, "if you weren't familiar with black culture, most of what he said and how he said it went right over your head—and beyond your ears." Dyson connects Obama's rhetoric to the tradition of black sermonizing, noting that the president uses anaphora and "the black preacher's dictum: 'Start low, go slow, rise high, strike fire and sit down,'" in much the same style as Martin Luther King Jr. Moreover, when Obama expressed his frustration with media efforts to label him a Muslim, he drew a startling allusion to Malcolm X: "They try to bamboozle you. Hoodwink ya. Try to hoodwink ya. All right, I'm having too much fun here." Dyson understands this invocation of a key speech by Malcolm X as a form of signifying, which he understands as language "in which the speaker hints at ideas or meanings that are veiled to outsiders."[31] In *The Signifying Monkey*, Henry Louis Gates Jr. calls signifyin(g) "the black trope of tropes"; it is "black double-voicedness;

because it always entails formal revision and an intertextual relation" (51). To this end, Obama's reference to Malcolm X presents a clever rhetorical play. He uses the line to denounce attempts to frame him as a Muslim despite the fact that its original speaker is the most famous Black Muslim in American history. By ventriloquizing Malcolm X, Obama appropriates the most powerful aspect of the former's legacy, his fiery rhetoric, while leaving behind the less understood and, in this contemporary moment, more threatening part of his identity—namely, his Muslim faith. However, to listeners unfamiliar with Malcolm X, the line is simply an adamant denial of Obama's otherness; he is not a Muslim, only an unfairly maligned man.

If signifyin(g) is, as Gates contends, "repetition, with a signal difference" (51), then Obama can be understood here as presenting himself as black but with a difference. Obama's specific ancestry—his father was born in Kenya, his white mother in Kansas, and he in Hawaii—makes him distinct from African Americans whose ancestors were forcibly transported to the United States as slaves. This difference elicited concerns that he was "not black enough," despite the fact that he defines himself as a "black American" (xvi) in *Dreams from My Father: A Story of Race and Inheritance*.[32] The debate over Obama's self-defined racial identification and his biracial origins demonstrates the necessity of confronting race in new ways. Even though Obama calls himself a black American, his life history and thoughtful consideration of racial issues, especially evident in his first book, indicate that race is not a simplistic binary of black and white. The label "black American" represents a chosen identity for Obama because given his background he could just as easily describe himself as biracial, white, Kenyan, or Hawaiian. In this way, Obama signifies upon outdated modes of understanding race that emphasize biological or even sociological differences. As someone who is black both by blood and by choice, he exemplifies Hollinger's development of a post-ethnic perspective, which emphasizes "that the identities people assume are acquired largely through affiliation" (7). Post-ethnicity is a useful frame to understand America's greater respect for the multiplicity of identity and the constructed nature of ethno-racial groups that facilitated Obama's rise. However, the ongoing tension that Hollinger observes between prescribed and chosen affiliations requires a mastery of language that bridges conventional social and racial divides. It is here that Obama's rhetorical talents are best displayed.

Writing in *Slate*, Christopher Beam observed that Obama's favorite rhetorical device is the false choice. To cite one example, in his inaugural address, Obama stated, "As for our common defense, we reject as false the choice between our safety and our ideals." For Obama, these values are not mutually exclusive but must work together to function effectively. Beam describes numerous instances in which Obama outlines two apparently polarized positions and then demonstrates how they are in fact united by a common vision. Beam concludes that this "device works well for Obama because he revels in nuance. Rejecting false choices allows him to toss out the paradigm—the 'old battles,' as he likes to call them—and show people a new, third way."[33] We might apply Obama's use of the false choice to racial discourse. If race-free language errs by denying difference and race-specific language threatens to reify essentialist conceptions of identity, "race-specific, race-free language" provides a third way, a way to acknowledge both the truths and fictions of race.

Such ambiguous prose, however, depends on the ability of readers and listeners to decode the subtleties of racial references. Shifting race from obvious visual marks to carefully constructed linguistic references requires an audience attentive to the nuances of racial textuality. Like Dyson, Zadie Smith detects multiple meanings in Obama's rhetoric. She commends him for his ability to speak in tongues: "This new president doesn't just speak for his people. He can speak them." She wonders if all members of his audience understand the complexity of his language and demonstrates her own multilingual sensitivity by carefully reading Obama's line: "We worship an awesome God in the Blue States, and we don't like federal agents poking around our libraries in the Red States."[34] According to Smith, in a single sentence Obama moves from the Midwest to the South, from the church to the kitchen table, and blurs blue and red into a single America; race is in all these places, but its use depends entirely upon the perspective of the listener. Does it matter if not everyone perceived Obama's adept rhetorical appeal or only heard the appeal that rang true for them? "Race-specific, race-free language" allows for multiple interpretations such that race is there if you look, and absent if you do not or even cannot see it. This ambiguity allowed Americans of diverse backgrounds to reflect their own personal experiences onto Obama; white or black, Asian or Latino, male or female, each one of us could fill the space left blank in his rhetoric.

"We are the change we have been waiting for" resonates with distinct but silent peculiarity.

The interpretive range of "race-specific, race-free language" linguistically reframes Du Bois's characterization of double consciousness, which he described as "this sense of always looking at one's self through the eyes of others." Obama's speeches as well as such controversial incidents as Congressman Joe Wilson's outburst of "You lie!" at the president's 2009 address to a joint session of Congress and the arrest of Professor Henry Louis Gates Jr. encode a double consciousness of race: Was Wilson racist? Did Gates overreach? In these and other incidents explored in chapter 4, race is both there and not there, or there only for those who have the gift of Du Bois's "second-sight in this American world" (2). In the absence of specifically racialized language, individuals interpret codes and behaviors in multiple and even contradictory ways. "Race-specific, race-free language" performs a form of double consciousness by making race apparent only to the discerning reader. Even as Smith and Ford read race in Obama's discussion of the false antagonism between Red and Blue States, it can also be understood as no more than a desire for meaningful bipartisanship.

"Race-specific, race-free language" signals an important evolution in our nation's long record of representing race. It demonstrates both a refreshing comfort with racial diversity as well as new anxieties about how to speak about race. Such prose embodies the very paradox of the ways in which race operates in American society. It is both a fiction with no biological basis as well as a fundamental structure of social life. "Race-specific, race-free language" captures the tensions and deceptions of America's aspirations. Through language we tell the story of who we want to be, a country where opportunities are open to all and yet where difference is celebrated. This dream, both noble and seemingly impossible, generates language that is fraught with contradictions as it aspires to lay the foundation of a new racial home.

Overview of Chapters

Obama's rhetoric, which signifies without specifying, has moved coded racial discourse into mainstream venues. However, the double consciousness of race that his speeches perform has been an evolving phenomenon in recent American literature. While this book analyzes much of the rhetoric surrounding Obama's presidency, I am most concerned with how "race-specific, race-free language" operates in literary texts by such authors as Morrison, Colson Whitehead, and Jhumpa Lahiri. Such prose allows for multiple interpretations that simultaneously express and occlude difference. Readings of these texts help us to understand public discourses about race in important ways. Race is now widely accepted to be a social construction, yet it continues to define key aspects of society and human behavior. This paradox has led contemporary writers to explore new paradigms by which to conceptualize what race means. Using injury as a mark of difference, Whitehead's novel *Apex Hides the Hurt* (2006) presents blackness as a trauma that is both chosen and inherited. Lahiri's short stories examine what race signifies in intimate encounters, confronting a conspicuous gap in our literary canon. While previous American texts have largely avoided how long-term family and sexual relationships are affected by interracial contact, Lahiri approaches these issues directly, asking: Does the language of race disappear between lovers and family members of different racial backgrounds? How do we talk or not talk about differences that love should make incidental?

Obama's election demands new ways to conceptualize race relations in the United States. It urges us to discover a language that might embrace a first family that is reflective of the black diaspora and consequently to forge the kinds of interracial intimacy that Lahiri's stories explore. The Obama family makes clear that the problem of Du Bois's color-line is not the problem of today's color-line. The mandated segregation and legal inequality that Du Bois railed against are struggles of the past. However, Obama's presidency and the generations of black women that surround him in the White House present new racial challenges and questions for the future: not *if* America can recognize the humanity of all its citizens, but *how* to recognize and work with the differences that race still inscribe. By considering the ways in which contemporary writers newly confront the effects of race, we may discover the reading practices necessary to contextualize and critique the coded discourse of our president and his successors. Literary fiction, which like political rhetoric depends upon the development of intimacy between speaker and audience, provides critical explorations of how we might transform the racist house of America into a home of racial difference.

Morrison has stated that the second word immigrants to the United States learn is "nigger."[35] To be educated as an American is to become aware of one's place in the nation's racial hierarchy. The three texts by Morrison I discuss in chapter 1 examine how race is a foundational language that Americans must learn. This education is at the forefront of Morrison's most recent novel, *A Mercy* (2008), which describes the history of our nation's racist language as well as the foundation for our contemporary "race-specific, race-free" discourse. Set in the seventeenth century when blackness had not yet become an irrevocable sign of bondage, *A Mercy* explores the origins of America's racist house and charts how its protagonist, Florens, a black slave girl, becomes literate in the emergent codes of racial meaning. By describing a type of pre-racial world, the novel demonstrates how blackness comes to signify evil and inferiority. Yet, even as skin color is used as a convenient sign of degradation for religious zealots and avaricious traders, the interracial cooperation in the Vaark household offers the promise of a "race-specific, race-free" home. The pioneers in Morrison's *Paradise* (1997) who establish Ruby, an all-black town, also long for a home, free of racial prejudice. However, unlike the women of *A Mercy*, their vision of paradise depends upon what Dana Nelson has described as the violence of racialization, tragically apparent in how the Ruby settlers fashion a self-serving mythology. I read the novel's stark opening line, "They shoot the white girl first" (3), as a fiction constructed to fulfill the ideological needs of the town's anxious patriarchs. The myth of Ruby requires a white female victim as well as the destruction of the racially ambiguous harmony of the Convent, a shelter for displaced women that exemplifies the tenuous paradise of a world in which "race both matters and is rendered impotent." The Convent demonstrates the paradoxes of Morrison's metaphor of home to describe language that is "race-specific" yet "race-free." She envisions a home that may seem paradoxical, not a specific place but a "borderlessness" where identity is anonymous yet intimate.

Morrison's only short story, "Recitatif," also features primary female characters who are not identified by race. The interracial friendship between Twyla and Roberta underscores how racial difference need not impede friendship between women, although its specific articulation leads to violence. While most discussions of "Recitatif" focus on the ambiguous racial identity of Twyla and Roberta, I shift attention to how these characters operate as racializing agents—that is, how they racialize others. This analysis again demonstrates how racialization depends upon violence and may be used as a way to avoid internal conflicts. If, as Morrison contends, "race is the least important piece of information we have about another person," then to see race is to willfully occlude one's vision.[36] The Ruby men see and kill a white girl in order to justify their attack. Similarly, Roberta sees a black woman kicked by her friend as a way to distance herself from both. Using Julia Kristeva's notion of the semiotic and symbolic, I argue that the "race-specific, race-free" approach that Twyla and Roberta adopt toward one another provides a way to merge the signifying law of the father with the raceless plentitude of the mother. Obama's own description of his mother in *Dreams from My Father* affirms the radical potential of the maternal bond to act as the foundation for language that paradoxically recognizes commonality in difference.

Beginning with a discussion of Obama's self-selection as African American on the 2010 census, chapter 2 explores how blackness, an ever-evolving site of meaning, operates as a chosen identity. Colson Whitehead's *Apex Hides the Hurt* offers a new mode of inscribing racial difference, that of injury and trauma, which moves beyond simplistic demarcations of skin color. This provocative novel does not offer easy equivalences between blackness and physical damage. Instead, it presents visible injury as a type of chosen mark of identity that manifests unease with social norms and with the failure of what Robyn Weigman calls an "integrationist aesthetic" to confront the legacy of racial wounds. Like Ralph Ellison's Invisible Man, the unnamed protagonist of *Apex Hides the Hurt* discovers the limits of language to express identity as well as the ways in which skin color is an insufficient register of racial difference. Although he is African American, his careful avoidance of racial markers indicates that he is more comfortable not choosing a racial identity at all, instead becoming a skilled chameleon in the corporate world. His experience demonstrates the demands not of invisibility but of what Ellison termed, "hypervisibility," the proliferation of multiracial images that presents new challenges for the recognition of racial difference. Like our hypervisible president, Whitehead's protagonist must maintain a fragile balance between professional performance and authentic alienation.

Influenced by the psychoanalytic insights of Anne Anlin Cheng, I argue that the anonymous protagonist of *Apex Hides the Hurt* injures himself in order to manifest his blackness. As a "nomenclature consultant" for an "identity firm," the protagonist is tasked with naming products. His most significant challenge arises when he is asked to rename the town of Winthrop. Originally settled by former slaves who called it Freedom, the town acquired the name Winthrop after it was incorporated by a white entrepreneur who built a lucrative empire on the production of barbed wire. However, a new corporate magnate, who owns a prosperous software company, wants to change the town's name to New Prospera. The novel focuses on how the protagonist settles the dispute by finally deciding upon the name Struggle, which was originally suggested by one of the founding former slaves. As he recognizes how his success as a nomenclature consultant requires a destructive form of camouflage, Whitehead's protagonist comes to embrace struggle or, as characterized by Obama in his March 2008 reiteration of the Constitution, the hard work necessary "to form a more perfect union." The choice to struggle, to reject the conformist culture of the corporate world and its emphasis on individual achievement, offers a fresh approach to what race signifies. Although Whitehead's protagonist enacts a kind of masochism to preserve his identity, he resists the commodification of racialized representation that manufactures the illusion of multicultural harmony. Whitehead offers some escape from the paradox of racial meaning by inscribing difference upon the body in a way that can never be invisible.

In chapter 3, I examine how the language of race is simultaneously elided and exposed in intimate relationships involving sex and family. To explore the ways in which intimacy impedes the expression of racial difference even as race strongly influences these dynamics I consider three short stories by Jhumpa Lahiri from *The Interpreter of Maladies* (1999) and *Unaccustomed Earth* (2008). Lahiri uses a type of "race-specific, race-free language" that, unlike the work of Morrison and Whitehead, does not revel in racial ambiguity or evasion. Lahiri identifies the race of her characters through cultural cues associated with either India or the United States, offering a model of racial identification that exceeds simplistic visual

marks. In her stories, nationality and geographic origin allow for movement across more permeable boundaries of identity though significantly
difference is always constituted between South Asians and whites. Although
Lahiri's characters never mention race directly, it continues to play a
crucial role in their interactions. The absence of specifically racialized
language produces glaring silences and an inability to speak about difference. Despite having clear racial identities, Lahiri's characters adopt a
form of intimacy that seems to transcend difference. The difficulties
derived from this fragile illusion are especially evident in the sexual fantasies that Lahiri's characters develop when confronted with a racial other.
Their unspoken fantasies demonstrate troubling racial prejudices and
projections. However, like elided discussions of race, the language of
fantasy remains unspeakable, providing an apt corollary to "race-specific,
race-free language." In Lahiri's stories, both race and fantasy remain taboo
topics that frustrate attempts to forge meaningful forms of intimacy.
I conclude this chapter with a reading of Obama's account of his parents'
courtship in *Dreams from My Father* to explore how love can coexist with
fantasies of the racial other. Genuine interracial connection does not necessarily banish the prejudices of race, but instead provides the opportunity
to explore their complex significations.

The final chapter argues that "race-specific, race-free language" has
had its most important consequences in the public sphere as it emblematizes a new way of speaking about race. No longer an obvious mark of
social status or violence, race is instead subject to wide-ranging interpretations. Because the racial identity of politicians and other popular media
figures is already known, coded language about race works on the national
stage by performing intimacy. This approach is evident in Morrison's
endorsement of Obama, a letter directed to him but widely published
online. Morrison's public exposure of a private confidence seemingly
disregards the importance of race yet echoes an essentialist appeal. Her
letter demonstrates an increasingly ubiquitous form of communication
between black intellectuals and politicians, the shared private epistle,
which exploits the political possibilities of "race-specific, race-free language."
Letters by Obama, Alice Walker, Jesse Jackson Jr., and others capitalize on
positioning readers as spectators to a private correspondence. The public
presentation of black private epistles also insures that intimate black speech

is familiar and safe. Obama's use of "race-specific, race-free language" demonstrates how keenly he understands the importance of establishing intimacy between himself and his multiracial constituents. He has become our storyteller-in-chief, telling intimate narratives that stress national rather than racial identification. By both conjuring and obscuring race in his campaign, Obama mastered America's ambivalences concerning the election of its first black president.

I conclude with a discussion of Lee Daniels's 2009 movie, *Precious: Based on the Novel by Sapphire*, which was released approximately one year after Obama's victory. As twin figures, Obama and Precious present sharply opposed images of blackness. While our president embodies the fulfillment of a national dream, Precious is a study in abjection. Both, however, reveal the vital importance of establishing cross-racial intimacy. Obama assumes such intimacy by fostering sufficient ambiguity in his speeches that listeners can project individual desires and interpretations onto him. This wildly successful rhetorical approach effectively renders his audience raceless. By contrast, *Precious* makes clear that the language of its protagonist is singular, even isolated. To understand her story requires more than translation, but the initiative of others to resist the post-racial myth of reductive commonality by announcing their difference. "Race-specific, race-free language" has had powerful effects on the political stage, but the intimacy it both assumes and performs demands an audience that refuses the convenient posture of raceless invisibility.

In *NurtureShock: New Thinking About Children*, Po Bronson and Ashley Merryman cite child development researchers who "argue that children see racial differences as much as they see the difference between pink and blue—but we tell kids what 'pink' means for girls and 'blue' means for boys. 'White' and 'black' are mysteries we leave them to figure out on their own" (52). This research debunks the notion of a color-blind utopia by suggesting that humans simply cannot be color-blind; children, like adults, see difference, and, in the case of race, we are often at a loss to understand and communicate what that difference means. Race is an ever-shifting signifier whose specification is increasingly submerged rather than overt. Obama has fundamentally changed what blackness represents in American society while contemporary writers are exploring new ways to conceptualize and express racial difference. The marks of race abide even as they reflect new realities and possibilities. Because we cannot simplistically tell our children what white and black mean, we must teach them to understand how race signifies in multiple and even contradictory ways, for white and black will always signify differently. To signify without specifying is to master America's racial language. This book offers a primer on how to read such language through awareness of its doubled aims and conscious intimacy.

1

~~~~~~~~~~~~~~~~~~~~~~~~

Violence and Toni Morrison's Racist House

In the fall of 2008 with the presidential election only months away, Toni Morrison published her ninth novel, *A Mercy*. At the very moment when the country was anxiously, incredulously looking toward the future, Morrison directed her readers backward. Moving well past the history of antebellum slavery, *A Mercy* examines a time in which America was not yet America and, more important, a time before blackness became inextricably linked to bondage. Morrison implicitly dismissed discussions of a "post-racial" world by calling attention to the pre-racial colonies of the early seventeenth century. Investigating what it means to "to remove race from slavery," she presents a multiracial cast of characters who experience various degrees of bondage and freedom.[1] In her stark re-vision of historical conditions, race does not alone determine social status. By exploring a world populated by white indentured servants, free blacks, and enslaved Native Americans, Morrison describes how race came to mark a spectrum from human to animal, from good to evil.

If race does not function as a meaningful category of identity in a post-racial world, then Morrison's pre-racial novel offers a glimpse into what it means to rely on other measures to determine human worth. However, the absence of racial meaning does not imply an absence of social hierarchy. Morrison demonstrates that capitalist imperative and religious absolutism demand the institutionalization of inequality. Skin color thus becomes a convenient, visible mark of irrevocable difference, indicating that race is not the root of racism; exploitation is. The fragile race-free world of *A Mercy*, tentatively idealized in the all-female Vaark household, proves unsustainable against the needs of patriarchy. *A Mercy* describes the history of America's racist house, reminding us that race did not always signify as it does now. The novel charts the development of racialized language, moving from race-free prose to language deeply embedded in the specific meanings accorded to skin color.

The novel uses various narrative perspectives but consists primarily of the desperate address of Florens, a black slave girl, to her beloved blacksmith. The opening chapter belongs to Florens who describes a series of puzzling images, "a dog's profile plays in the steam of a kettle . . . a corn-husk doll sitting on a shelf . . . a minha mãe standing hand in hand with her little boy."[2] These images are all given specific contexts later in the novel, but their as yet uncertain meanings underscore the two questions Florens poses on the text's opening page: "One question is who is responsible? Another is can you read?" (3). *A Mercy* is a book fundamentally about reading practices. Its central concern is how individuals interpret the signs of a radically changing world, demonstrating various ways in which meaning is constructed from specific images. Race is a sign that Florens must learn, blackness a loaded symbol just like the dog's profile and the corn-husk doll that each carry devastating meaning for the young girl. In the course of the novel, Florens becomes violently racialized, made aware that her black skin connotes evil and inferiority. *A Mercy* is an account of her education into the strictures of race and her uneasy introduction to America's racist house.

Even as Florens learns to read race, she cannot answer her first question, "Who is responsible?" Who is responsible for the language of racism? Who is responsible for America's racist house? When asked about her writing process, Morrison has often said that each of her books begins as a question and the answer is the novel. *A Mercy* is her only book that states its question so explicitly, but its answer is as complicated as the network of signs Florens confronts. As she observes, "Often there are too many signs, or a bright omen clouds up too fast. I sort them and try to recall, yet I know I am missing much" (4). Orphaned and alone, Florens misses the story of her mother, told in the novel's final chapter, and its defining transformation. Having survived the Middle Passage to arrive in Barbados, Florens's mother states: "It was there I learned how I was not a person from my country, nor from my families. I was negrita. Everything. Language, dress, gods, dance, habits, decoration, song—all of it cooked together in the color of my skin" (165). This insight is denied to Florens who never learns her mother's history and consequently must teach herself the crippling language of race. The ruthless passion for the blacksmith that ultimately consumes Florens results from both her devastating inauguration into the racial symbolic and this foundational fracture between mother and daughter.

Tracing the Origins of the Racist House

The language of *A Mercy* reflects the emerging meaning accorded to race in seventeenth-century America. Throughout the novel there are few direct references to skin color; instead, social status and power are encoded through other means. All the characters, except one, have a definable race, but often this aspect of their identities is not readily provided in order to highlight other, more crucial qualities. When race is mentioned, references address not color, but the freedom such color provides or hinders. Florens is first understood as a slave girl because she describes how she is taught to read secretly, her blackness, at least initially, irrelevant to her bondage. As a child, Florens is not yet aware of what her dark skin means to religious zealots or enterprising traders. In her pre-racial consciousness, the visual is not a stable mark of social identity. Even after she is sold into the Vaark household, she is lovingly raised by Lina, a Native American slave, and together they work alongside their white mistress. Distinctions between free and slave are not readily apparent among the women because color has yet to become the ultimate determinant of social status.

By contrast, Florens's Anglo-Dutch owner Jacob Vaark is more attuned to how race is beginning to establish differing levels of social status. Along his journeys he understands that "even with the relative safety of his skin, solitary traveling required prudence" (11). Aware of the privilege provided by his whiteness, Jacob does not depend upon it entirely to safeguard his passage. An ambitious trader who abhors slavery, he connects the newly emergent category of race to the aftermath of Bacon's Rebellion, an uprising led by wealthy planter Nathaniel Bacon in Virginia in 1676. It marked one of the first instances in which poor blacks and whites were united in common cause. However, the possibility of such cross-racial coalition frightened the ruling class and led to new laws that protected white privilege and linked African ancestry to slave status. Jacob reflects upon the stringent laws enacted to discourage alliances across racial and class divides:

> By eliminating manumission, gatherings, travel and bearing arms for black people only; by granting license to any white to kill any black for any reason; by compensating owners for a slave's maiming or death, they separated and protected all whites from all others forever. Any social ease between gentry and laborers, forged before and during that rebellion, crumbled beneath a hammer wielded in the interests of the gentry's profits. (10)

Bacon's Rebellion illustrates how racial difference became a tool to sever blacks and whites of similar social status from one another. To maximize the power of the upper class legislation defined the racial divide and protected racist practices. By tracing the roots of race beyond the arrival of enslaved Africans, Morrison demonstrates that America's racist house originates in the consolidation of capital.

Although Jacob is disgusted by the traffic of human cargo, he is a slave owner. At the start of the novel, he agrees to accept eight-year-old Florens as payment for an outstanding debt by Jublio D'Ortega, a noxious Portuguese plantation owner. The exchange that occurs at Jacob's visit to D'Ortega is the central event of the text. Jacob initially asks to have the serving woman, Florens's mother, as payment, but while D'Ortega equivocates, the slave woman falls to her knees and begs Jacob to take her daughter in her stead. Both disgusted and moved, Jacob accepts Florens. This act is the mercy referred to in the novel's title, a single human gesture of lasting import. While this incident haunts Florens for the rest of her life and contributes to her desperate love for the blacksmith, the scene is also significant for how it affects Jacob. Though he despises D'Ortega's opulence and arrogance, he envies his fine house and in particular its impressive fence and gate. He imagines a house of his own to rival that of D'Ortega, but one that is "pure, noble even, because it would not be compromised as Jublio was" (27) through its exploitation of slave labor. The construction of this house becomes his primary obsession, as he strives to match D'Ortega's fortune without sacrificing his conscience through the abuse of others. Jacob's quest reflects the development of the United States as a whole and the struggle to create a home built on noble ideals.

Jacob agrees to take Florens in part because he hopes that Rebekka, his wife, still grieving over the death of their only daughter, "would welcome a child around the place" (26). Jacob's ability to conceive of Florens as a type of substitute for his dead child indicates that he does not conceive of race as an ultimate mark of human difference. However, his participation in the slave trade highlights a troubling contradiction in his seemingly benign approach to the world. After resolving to create a house to rival that of D'Ortega, Jacob decides to invest in the rum production and sugar fields of Barbados. He comforts himself with the conclusion: "there was a profound difference between the intimacy of slave bodies at Jublio and a remote labor force in Barbados. Right? Right, he thought, looking at a sky vulgar with stars." Those vulgar stars are as distant to him as the slaves who will generate the money necessary to finance his "grand house of many rooms rising on a hill" (35). Jacob thinks of rooms, not of people, of a "rising" house rather than the fall of human lives that his dream demands. Unable to abide witnessing the worst atrocities of human bondage, he is kind to the multiracial women who inhabit his home. He is not a racist, motivated by a deep-seated fear and hatred of the other, but rather a savvy entrepreneur, seeking the comforts of a still familiar American dream. Raw racism does not drive him even as racism comes to structure his ambition and ultimately poisons his legacy.

Jacob's house is a powerful figure of the racist house Morrison describes in her essay "Home." Just as the founding fathers espoused values of freedom and equality for all but offered these rights only to white male propertied citizens, so too is Jacob marred by latent hypocrisy. He stops to free an entrapped raccoon only to return to a home of enslaved women. When Rebekka questions the need for such a grand house, he replies, "What a man leaves behind is what a man is" (89). His response reveals the influence of patriarchal legacy in his complicity with the slave trade. With no children to inherit his fortune, Jacob undertakes the house's construction with noted glee: "when he decided to kill the trees and replace them with a profane monument to himself, he was cheerful every waking moment" (44). The narcissism of Jacob's project negates the possibility that it will ever become a meaningful home for either him or others. He understands the house as a demonstration of his own power, not as a site of communion, shelter, and care.

Jacob does not live to see the completion of his dream, and ironically an egalitarian utopia is best realized not in the empty house he constructs but in the modest, well-built home he continually leaves to finance his misguided ambition. This home is inhabited by four women: Rebekka, Florens, Lina, and Sorrow, a woman of ambiguous racial origin. Despite differences of race and social status, all four women exist in varying states of bondage, and all are orphans. Born in London, Rebekka was sent by her parents to the New World in response to an advertisement for "a healthy, chaste wife willing to travel abroad" (74). Aware that "her prospects were servant, prostitute, wife" (77–78), Rebekka welcomes the perilous journey and its uncertain outcome even though she is literally bought and sold. At fourteen, Lina is the first woman to join Jacob's household. Although initially adopted by Presbyterians after French soldiers burned her village, Lina is sold when she is discovered beaten by a man who had been her lover. When Lina first encounters Rebekka the two women are wary of one another; however, the birth of Rebekka's first child along with the necessity of working together on the farm turns hostility into real intimacy: "The fraudulent competition was worth nothing on land that demanding. Besides they were company for each other and by and by discovered something much more interesting than status. Rebekka laughed out loud at her own mistakes; was unembarrassed to ask for help. Lina slapped her own forehead when she forgot the berries rotting in the straw. They became friends. . . . Mostly because neither knew precisely what they were doing or how. Together, by trial and error they learned" (53).

Struggle makes prejudice of any kind a liability. Initially suspicious of each other, Rebekka and Lina develop a strong bond through common purpose and their shared alienation as orphans. They simply cannot afford to let their social differences interfere with the cooperation necessary for their survival, suggesting the peculiar luxury of adhering to racial paradigms. Moreover, though Rebekka is free, as a married woman she has no property of her own; legally, she is the property of her husband. Unlike Jacob, neither Rebekka nor Lina can indulge in material dreams. With Jacob often away managing his investments, the women encounter one another largely as equals, united in the struggle to survive. By presenting the female Vaark household as a space free of racial hierarchy, Morrison links the violence of racism to patriarchy and its need to secure a male heir through inheritable property. Jacob invests in slave labor in Barbados to secure a material legacy for his children. Ironically, his grandiose house, the symbol of his fierce ambition, leads to the death of his final child, appropriately named Patrician, who is killed during its construction. By contrast, the four women of his household are less invested in their respective legacies than in their day-to-day survival and the ways they may preserve the fleeting joys of their lives.

Although the home created by the women is free of racial prejudice, it is not equally welcoming to all. Rebekka and Lina's generosity is tested by the arrival of Sorrow, a girl of dubious origins who is discovered half dead on a riverbank. The sawyer who finds her gives her to Jacob, certain that the trader will "do her no harm" (51) unlike his own lecherous sons. Born and raised on a ship captained by her father, Sorrow does not speak of her childhood and appears daft and disturbed to others. Lina deems her "bad luck in the flesh" (53) and irrationally blames her for the death of Rebekka's infant sons. Lina's suspicion is born less of Sorrow's ambiguous racial identity than from the latter's peculiar ways and her inability to complete basic tasks around the house and farm. Mute, she imagines that she has an identical self, which she names Twin. Sorrow's alienation from the other women of the Vaark household reflects not racial prejudice but their utilitarian values. She is "useless" (53) and therefore ostracized from the others. Although the women of *A Mercy* do not live in simplistic harmony, their conflicts are not derived from manufactured prejudice.

The women in Jacob's house are largely untouched by racism though certainly not from discrimination and oppression. Lina isolates Sorrow from the others, and once Jacob dies they are all endangered by their liminal status. Rebekka is marginally protected because she is legally free, but her safety will only be guaranteed once she marries again. The others, as Lina reflects, are far more vulnerable: "alone, belonging to no one, became wild game for anyone" (58). Their fragile race-free utopia is only possible through Jacob's benign oversight. While the women are protected from racial discrimination within the confines of their home, once Florens leaves to find the blacksmith, who offers the only hope of curing Rebekka of the disease that killed Jacob, she discovers a world that has already begun to define itself by race.

Florens's Racial Education

The key scene of Floren's racial education occurs when she arrives, tired and hungry, at the door of the only house lit in a small village. A woman, who introduces herself as Widow Ealing, feeds Florens and warns her that there is danger lurking. Inside the house, Florens meets the widow's daughter Jane, who has skewed eyes and bears bloody wounds on her legs. The wounds are self-inflicted, necessary to prove to religious zealots that the girl bleeds and therefore is not a demon. In the morning, the house is visited by a group of village authorities who inspect Jane's legs, but they are soon distracted by Florens, whom they take to be "the Black Man's minion." Their horror at Florens's dark skin racializes everyone in the room; though unmentioned by Florens, it becomes clear that Widow Ealing and Jane are white. The town authorities dismiss the letter penned by Rebekka attesting to Florens's urgent errand and force her to strip off her clothes. They examine her teeth, limbs, and genitals. Florens silently endures their inspection: "Naked under their examination I watch for what is in their eyes. No hate is there or scare or disgust but they are looking at me my body across distances without recognition. Swine look at me with more connection" (113).

With its emphasis on probing eyes, the scene attests to the visual origin of racial difference though Jane's whiteness underscores how other forms of physical difference also incur hostility and fear. The distant gaze of the town authorities negates Florens's humanity, much as the physical distance negates the humanity of Jacob's slaves in Barbados. Jacob has no visual image of the black bodies he exploits, thus rendering his action less a matter of racism than of sheer avarice. Unlike the religious zealots, he does not participate in the creation of racialized categories; the racial identity of the slaves in Barbados is irrelevant to his decision to invest in the sugar fields. This observation does not absolve Jacob of racialized violence, but rather highlights how oppression does not depend upon racial difference. Jacob is guilty of exploiting a system ripe for justification through the fabrication of essential human differences. The group inspecting Florens establish this rationale by reading her skin as a mark of evil and debasement. The history of America's racialized language begins here.

The scene at the Widow Ealing's represents Florens's initiation into the racist house of the United States, where her body is described as suspicious, possibly animal, possibly demonic, never human. This encounter mirrors the experience of her mother's arrival in Barbados where she is reduced entirely to her skin color. The physical sign of her bondage becomes an inescapable inheritance for her daughter. Florens is thus defined by a single quality; her blackness represents all that she is, a symbol not just of bondage but of evil. Immediately before the town authorities arrive at the Widow Ealing's house, Florens observes a kettle boiling in the fireplace. She watches "its steam forming shapes as it curls against the stone. One shape looks like the head of a dog" (110). Florens's emphasis on the "dog's profile" (3), referenced on the novel's opening page, demonstrates her emerging vocabulary of signs and her eagerness to find meaning in the images around her. However, the shifting shape of the steam is as puzzling as her own blackness, demonstrating the arbitrariness of racial signification. Florens attempts to read an omen in the profile of the dog, but the steam is as disconnected from the town authorities as her skin is from evil.

Florens initially perceives a little girl who accompanies the village authorities as a figure of "myself when my mother sends me away" (111). Florens's ability to project herself onto a person of a different race demonstrates how, prior to this moment, she has yet to recognize race as a meaningful category of identity that posits permanent difference. The town authorities sever such empathetic identification by alienating Florens from everyone around her. She experiences the encounter at Widow Ealing's house as a loss of self, marked by a conflation between her outside darkness of skin and what she identifies as an internal darkness: "I am not the same. . . . Something precious is leaving me. I am a thing apart. With the letter I belong and am lawful. Without it I am a weak calf abandon by the herd, a turtle without shell, a minion with no telltale signs but a darkness I am born with, outside, yes, but inside as well and the inside dark is small, feathered, and toothy. Is this what my mother knows? Why she chooses me to live without?" (115). Florens believes that her mother offered her to Jacob because of some wickedness inside of her, some primal instinct that the town authorities have uncovered by stripping her and probing her body for "a tail, an extra teat, a man's whip between

my legs" (114–115). This inner darkness, "feathered and toothy," is animal in
nature, like the animal characteristics the authorities search out on her
body. Reduced to this dark core, Florens is uncertain if her skin signals
what she believes to be her essential wickedness.

This crisis of meaning is exacerbated by her loss of the letter written
by Rebekka authorizing her trip to the blacksmith. The letter represents
a form of stable signification in which there is a reliable relationship
between signifier and signified. Rebekka's words give Florens purpose
and value, anticipating the authenticating power of whiteness. Thus, to be
without the letter is to be without an identity that will anchor her in the
unknown world through which she journeys. By contrast, the town authorities use not the familiar code of letters to make meaning but rely instead
on the color of her skin. Once Florens is made a sign, not a person, she
becomes vulnerable to dubious reading practices, including her own. She
believes that her blackness separates her from the women she has come to
know and care about in Jacob's house. This realization lends sudden
urgency to her quest to find the blacksmith because he has "the outside
dark as well." Her desire to find him now moves beyond adolescent passion
into a frantic need for racial connection. Addressing him, she reflects,
"The sun's going leaves darkness behind and the dark is me. Is we. Is my
home" (115). Florens here identifies home as racially marked, a darkness
that belongs to both the blacksmith and her. Defined by blackness, it is
exclusive and envisioned as an isolated union of two.

Florens's conception of home proves impossible precisely because it
refuses to welcome others; it is not the "concrete thrill of borderlessness"
Morrison envisions, but a tight enclosure, dangerously racialized. When
she is at last reunited with the blacksmith, she is dismayed to find that
he has adopted a young dark-skinned boy, Malaik, whose father was found
dead on his horse. Florens is immediately wary of the boy who reminds her
of her brother, the child she believes her mother chose over her during the
exchange with Jacob. The blacksmith leaves the two alone together while
he returns to heal the dying Rebekka. Although Florens initially keeps her
distance from Malaik, she is disturbed by a dream she has of her mother,
"a minha mãe," who is "holding Malaik's hand in her own" (138). Like her
brother, Malaik threatens to sever her most important bond. Although
they are both black and anxious for the blacksmith to return, Florens can

see no commonality with the boy: "Again he is standing in the lane holding tight the corn-husk doll and looking toward where you ride away. Sudden looking at him I am remembering the dog's profile rising from Widow Ealing's kettle. Then I cannot read its full meaning. Now I know how. I am guarding. Otherwise I am missing all understanding of how to protect myself" (139). Florens's remembrance of the dog's profile demonstrates her need to make meaning out of the images around her. She decides that the dog's profile is an omen she could not previously decipher, and thus she recalls it now to signal the threat she feels from Malaik. Where once she failed to heed its warning, now she knows to be on guard, to protect herself from the attack she suffered at the hands of the town authorities. Consequently, she attacks first, taking Malaik's doll and putting it on a high shelf because she believes it "must be where his power is" (139). Desperate for meaningful signs, Florens simply fabricates them, much like the town authorities who empower themselves by labeling black skin evil. When Malaik begins crying, Florens pulls his arm, dislocating his shoulder.

As Malaik faints, the blacksmith enters the cabin, calling the boy's name and knocking Florens away. She understands his action as "No question. You choose the boy" (140). Appalled by her attack on Malaik, the blacksmith orders Florens to leave. She is so enamored with him that she can only perceive Malaik as a rival, not a helpless boy. Although she once saw herself reflected in a white girl, Florens is now unable to empathize with a boy of her same race. The encounter at Widow Ealing's house has left her bereft of compassion for others, entirely focused upon the construction of her home—the one she desires to share only with the blacksmith. Like Jacob, Florens seeks a home that is a monument to herself and her needs, not a place of shelter for others.

Reflecting on her final encounter with the blacksmith, Florens concludes that she has at last been transformed into her mother. Writing to him, she states, "You are correct. A minha mãe too. I am become wilderness but I am also Florens" (161). Florens believes that her mother gave her to Jacob to protect her younger brother, and thus she seems to share her mother's ruthlessness, for, as she explains to the blacksmith, she has "No ruth, my love." Florens's rejection of Malaik appears to mimic her own abandonment by her mother. In both cases, a child is sacrificed for a greater love. However, while her mother seemed to heartlessly cast her off, the blacksmith tends to Malaik and tells Florens that she is "nothing but wilderness. No constraint. No mind" (141), a person who will harm a child to fulfill her own desire. Florens accepts this definition of herself; she is "wilderness," but as she writes, she understands how this transformation occurred. She remembers the blacksmith's insight: "That it is the withering inside that enslaves and opens the door for what is wild." She concludes, "I know my withering is born in the Widow's closet" (160). Florens's wilderness begins at the moment in which she became reducible to her skin color, at the moment in which she acquired a racial identity. According to the blacksmith, she is "a slave by choice" (141) because she is willing to disregard the life of another person to obtain what she wants. She allows herself to become mastered by her inner darkness, the animal essence that threatens to destroy even the man that she loves: "I know the claws of the feathered thing did break out on you because I cannot stop them wanting to tear you open the way you tear me" (160). Charging the blacksmith with a hammer after the incident with Malaik, she becomes the demonic creature the town authorities believed her to be.

Even as the blacksmith may lie dead from Florens's attack, the ultimate tragedy of the text is that she wholly misunderstands her mother's intentions. The older woman did not offer Florens to Jacob because she loved her son more but because she feared that D'Ortega's lascivious appetite would fall upon her growing daughter. Florens's mother concludes the novel by providing the same insight given by the blacksmith: "In the dust where my heart will remain each night and every day until you understand what I know and long to tell you: to be given dominion over another is a hard thing; to wrest dominion over another is a wrong thing; to give dominion of yourself to another is a wicked thing. Oh Florens. My love. Hear a tua mãe" (167). As in *Beloved*, the disruption of the mother-daughter bond proves to be the ultimate sin of slavery. Without her mother's history and insight, Florens is vulnerable to the crippling definitions of others. Race is shown to be the province of patriarchy, created to justify the dehumanization of others necessary for material gain and religious power. The only character in *A Mercy* who escapes racial definition is Sorrow, who renames herself Complete after the birth of her daughter. Florens notes that "Sorrow is a mother. Nothing more nothing less" (159). Motherhood seems to offer some escape from racial signification, a way to establish identity apart from the imposed categories of race. However, even as Sorrow defines herself primarily through her new maternity, her anticipated escape from the Vaark estate suggests that she will soon discover the same racial definitions that ultimately cripple Florens.

Banished from the blacksmith's home, Florens returns to her former life. Rebekka's recovery has led her to a newfound piety, and, where the women once lived in relative harmony, they are now isolated according to their socially mandated status. Lina and Rebekka no longer talk and laugh as friends. Though Sorrow shows some improvement in her ability to work on the farm, she focuses primarily on caring for her new child. Florens meanwhile has become savage, severing the deepest bond among the women, that between her and Lina. As the narrator observes, "They once thought they were a kind of family because together they had carved companionship out of isolation. But the family they imagined they had become was false. Whatever each one loved, sought or escaped, their futures were separate and anyone's guess" (155–156). Jacob's death brings a new demand on Rebekka to distinguish herself from the other women. She imposes stringent household rules and becomes disturbingly committed to the church, adopting the same approach to racial meaning as the authorities at the Widow Ealing's house. Florens observes of Rebekka: "Each time she returns from the meetinghouse her eyes are nowhere and have no inside. Like the eyes of the women who examine me behind the closet door, Mistress' eyes only look out and what she is seeing is not to her liking" (159). Florens's description suggests that Rebekka has come to value the visual over all other forms of human distinction. This perspective negates the possibility of empathetic identification, thus irrevocably othering her previous companions. Based in religious strictures, Rebekka's behavior demonstrates a new way of ordering the people in her life, one that accords to racial markers. Like Florens, she too has received an education in racial meaning.

Despite the completion of Jacob's grandiose house, Rebekka forbids anyone from entering. The mansion is rendered irrelevant, given the racist house she has constructed within her household. At night, however, Florens secretly retreats to the empty house, refusing Sorrow's invitation to escape to the North so that she can complete her own project. Willard and Scully, white indentured servants who work the farm, believe that Jacob's ghost haunts the house, unaware that Florens is etching her story onto its walls and floors. She is both Jacob's ghost and his heir, the only one brave enough to claim his extravagant dream and transform it into something of her own. As she writes her story, she directly addresses the blacksmith, although she at last admits that he will never read her words because he is illiterate. This recognition leads her to consider another plan: "Perhaps these words need the air that is out in the world. Need to fly up then fall, fall like ash over acres of primrose and mallow." Florens will burn her work along with Jacob's house in a complete rejection of the racist education forced upon her. By uniting her destruction of the racist house with the release of her words into the world, Florens seeks a language of escape, a language that will not equate her blackness with evil. There is no promise that she will ever forge a new home. Instead she concludes, "Slave. Free. I last" (161). Florens survives even as the building is razed, for her words endure, bearing the mark of America's racist house and the urgent need for shelter.

Creating *Paradise*

Florens's unnarrated escape from Jacob's racist house finds expression in *Paradise*, Morrison's seventh novel. It describes the attempt to create a home free of racism by presenting readers with two different versions of paradise, each a study of a kind of race-free home. Both models explore Morrison's quest to transform America's "racist house" into a "race-specific yet nonracist home." How is race to be reconciled with the foundation of paradise? The town of Ruby, settled in the mid-twentieth century, seemingly obviates the need for racial designation because all of its inhabitants are black. By contrast, the Convent, the home of a motley collection of women is structured without regard to race. As she leaves the race of the outcast women of the Convent ambiguous, Morrison gestures toward the possibility of a home in which race is not the primary determinant of identity.

Perhaps due to the especially ambitious scope of *Paradise*, the novel received the worst reviews of Morrison's career. The first book published after she received the Nobel Prize for Literature in 1993, *Paradise* was called by the *New York Times* critic Michiko Kakutani a "contrived, formulaic book" in which "Morrison is constantly having her characters spell out the meaning of her story."[3] David Gates wrote, "we're asked to swallow too many contrivances," while Brook Allen claimed that the novel's "male-female dichotomy" is a "cliché and Morrison plays it too heavily."[4] Although there were key detractors such as Louis Menand of the *New Yorker*, the most striking disagreement among the critics was not how they rated the novel, but how they variously interpreted its opening line: "They shoot the white girl first" (3). Allen identified the novel's opening victim as Pallas, a "privileged white girl." Menand wrote that it was Seneca, "a white runaway."[5] Most critics neither hazarded a guess concerning the identity of this pivotal figure nor commented on Morrison's refusal to describe the women living at the Convent by race. In a 1998 interview, Morrison explained her decision to withhold the racial identity of many key characters in *Paradise*. She sought to emphasize the importance of knowing "much more than simply a racial marker" when encountering others: "so that the reader knew everything, or almost everything, about the characters, their interior lives, their past, their faults, their strengths, except that one small piece of information which was their race. And to either care about that, like the characters, dislike them, or dismiss the characters based on the important information which was what they were really like. And if I could enforce that response in literature, it was a way of saying that race is the least important piece of information we have about another person. Forcing people to react racially to another person is to miss the whole point of humanity."[6]

Written at the time that Morrison published "Home" and first expressed her attempt to fashion "race-specific, race-free language," *Paradise* represents her most sustained exploration of this kind of prose. The women of the Convent succeed in creating an environment in which race is incidental to their interactions. They are each defined by strong character traits and key experiences. Even when they encounter people outside their home, they attract attention that is not explicitly racial. For example, the townspeople who witness Gigi's arrival in Ruby are stunned by her "screaming tits" (55) and make no mention of her skin color. Similarly, when Sweetie, a resident of Ruby, visits the Convent, she envisions the women as a collection of "birds, hawks . . . Pecking at her, flapping" (129). Racial identification is only made when the men from Ruby arrive at the Convent intent on destroying the women inside. They violently explode the peace and safety of this home as well as the ambiguous racial identities of its inhabitants.

This astounding attack is intimately linked to Morrison's abrupt use of race-specific language in the novel's opening line: "They shoot the white girl first" (3). Dana Nelson's understanding of racial representation in nineteenth-century American literature usefully elucidates Morrison's striking first sentence. Nelson argues that there is "an essential violence embedded in the very concept of 'race.'" She explains: "The ideological figuration of 'race' is structurally violent in its reductiveness, denying the perceptual evidence of multitudes of colorations among 'whites,' 'blacks,' and 'reds' for the continuance of its own cultural agenda. At the same time, the notion of 'race' is necessary for a certain kind of violence, established and promulgated to justify the domination of one group of human beings over another" (*The Word in Black and White*, xii). According to Nelson, the racial identification of another is an inherently violent act because it severs individuals from the infinite possibilities of identity. Racialized subjects are circumscribed by the dictates of prejudice and stereotype. In this way, racial classification encodes hierarchy through the imposition of difference.

Morrison makes the violence of racial representation explicit in the opening of *Paradise*. Two actions occur here, physical attack and racialization, demonstrating that to establish racial difference is to inflict a type of injury. The perpetrators of this violence are the male founders and self-appointed guardians of Ruby, Oklahoma. *Paradise* chronicles the conflicted development of Ruby and the settlers' quest to establish a place of freedom and safety. Importantly, the violence of *Paradise*'s first sentence is not enacted by a white subject upon a black body; instead, Morrison reverses the historical racial hierarchy such that racial violence is perpetuated by blacks upon a white victim. This inversion indicates that the imposition of race, not merely America's specific history of racial oppression, is responsible for such violence. To become a racial subject through what Nelson calls "the oppressive reduction of the apparently infinite diversities among humans to an oppositional binary, always hierarchically figured" (xii) is to experience an act of violence. The "white girl" becomes a symbol of her race and, for the men of Ruby, representative of all they struggled against in the development and protection of their town.

Nelson's understanding of the relationship between race and violence implies that the very creation of Ruby enacts a type of self-injury. The founders and citizens of the town necessarily identify themselves as black in order to live there; consequently, they restrict the possibilities of their own paradise. Most importantly, however, they come to police themselves, encouraging townspeople not to couple with light-skinned strangers who threaten to contaminate their original vision of black self-sufficiency. Throughout the novel, numerous incidents intimate the possibility of violence as a means of controlling the townspeople and thereby securing the original vision of its founders. Town elder Steward Morgan ends an argument over the motto on the Oven, the symbol and physical center of Ruby, by threatening to shoot anyone who dares to ignore or change it. His equally formidable twin, Deacon, is so unnerved by the questioning youth of Ruby that he took to "blowing out the brains of quail to keep his own from exploding" (104). Violence structures the town, drawing the borders of what is deemed acceptable. Forced to "give back or return" a "pretty sandy-haired girl" (195) Menus loses the house he bought for her and becomes a perpetual drunk. However, the most devastating example of this enforcement involves the mother of Patricia Best, a light-skinned woman. She dies in childbirth because none of the men was willing to drive her to a neighboring white town. Both of these cases demonstrate the conflation of racial and sexual power as men protect the purity of blood by keeping out the corrupting influence of women. However, the women of Ruby do little to counter the law of their husbands, ultimately sanctioning the self-injury of the community.

And yet the concept of an all-black town should eliminate race all together. If everyone is black, then there is no need to discriminate on the basis of racial difference. Ruby promises independence, self-sufficiency, and freedom from white intervention, but the initial descriptions of Ruby as an ideal home all hinge upon the threat of violence. In the opening chapter, the Morgan twins recall how Ruby men respond to unwelcome strangers who "might spot three or four colored girls walk-dawdling along the side of the road" (12). This invasion requires the use of race-specific language, the girls are "colored" because violence looms with the presence of the strangers, one of whom "has opened the front of his trousers and hung himself out the window to scare the girls." But the men of Ruby are vigilant and they "come out of the houses, the backyards, off the scaffold of the bank, out of the feed store. . . . Their guns are not pointing at anything, just held slackly against their thighs." The strangers leave, the girls are safe and the men remember this incident as a defining moment in "the one all-black town worth the pain" (5). Thus, even as Ruby can internally function without reference to race because all its inhabitants are black, its survival requires both the use of violence and the imposition of racial identity. For Ruby to be race-free, it must be hypervigilant of racial incursions along its borders.

However, Ruby's borders are not only geographic, and these other edges, which are threatened by the injection of new ideas and new blood, cannot be easily policed by men wielding guns. Ruby suffers from its isolation and the rigid hierarchy of its founding patriarchs. The citizens reinscribe the very prejudice they sought to flee by prizing dark skin, what the informal town historian Patricia Best calls "8-rock," referring to a deep level in coal mines. Pat characterizes the original settlers as "Blue black people, tall and graceful, whose clear, wide eyes gave no sign of what they really felt about those who weren't 8-rock like them" (193). In a key event in the town's history, later named the Disallowing, the first settlers nearly starve before arriving at the all-black town of Fairly, Oklahoma. The travelers are provided with food but must move on due to their dark skin. This defining insult leaves a destructive legacy; light-skinned townspeople like Pat are shunned for manifesting the blood prized by Fairly citizens. Just as dominant white society fears racial mixing so Ruby citizens are vigilant against impurity and the dissolution of 8-rock blood. This threat of color-based corruption breeds an oppressive approach to women who are consigned to strict domestic roles and barred from participating in the governance of the town. Pat notes of the founders, "everything that worries them must come from women" (217). Female sexuality poses the one vulnerability to absolute patriarchal power. As a result, the utopia promised by a town uninfected by white supremacy becomes dangerously insular and authoritarian. As Reverend Misner, a relative newcomer, notes, the town so emphasizes the preservation of certain traditions, including racial continuity, that "rather than children, they wanted duplicates" (161).

The second version of paradise in the novel is the world created by the women of the Convent, a massive old house located seventeen miles from

Ruby. First owned by an embezzler, the mansion was taken over by nuns who used it as a school for Native American girls. Later the Convent becomes a haven for troubled and lost women from Ruby as well as from more distant locations. When Mavis, the first of these women, arrives, the Convent houses only two people, the ancient and bedridden Mother Superior, also known as Mary Magna, and Connie, her caretaker, who always wears sunglasses and lives off the money she makes selling hot peppers, spicy relishes, and other potent concoctions. Born in Brazil, Connie was stolen as an infant from the slums of Rio by the nuns and raised at the Convent. The women of the Convent succeed in creating an environment in which race is incidental as they are each defined by their unique personal backgrounds. Mavis is haunted by the bewildering death of her infant twins, Gigi's seductive facade belies a romantic streak, Seneca's neediness reflects her childhood abandonment, and Pallas is nearly mute with grief after her boyfriend takes up with her mother. These women, united only by their exile from normative society, do not relate to one another in explicitly racial ways. Mavis and Gigi despise one another, but their feud is largely based on Gigi's immodesty and Mavis's anxiety. For Mavis, these spats that sometimes evolve into prolonged physical confrontations are actually affirming, acting as "proof that the old Mavis was dead" (171). In the Convent, violence is not based on the reductive classification of race, but rather reflects the generative if conflicted dynamic of its inhabitants.

This absence of race in the Convent does not suggest that the women are oblivious to racial difference. Instead, they recognize race most often as a way to understand intimate relationships between women. For example, while driving cross-country, Mavis picks up a series of female hitchhikers, noting, "The white ones were the friendliest; the colored girls slow to melt" (33). Similarly, when she observes a meeting between Connie and Soane, she sees "the black woman opened her arms. Connie entered them for a long swaying hug" (43). These moments of racial identification do not adhere to Nelson's formulation that race encodes violence because Mavis does not impose "an oppositional binary, always hierarchically figured." In the first example, Mavis expresses her own recognition of difference between white and colored girls. She does not then select one type of hitchhiker over another; rather, she uses this information as a way to further her connection to all the girls she encounters. Born in Brazil, Connie is the one

Convent woman who is definitively not African American. Thus Mavis's identification of Soane as black registers the significance of their interracial friendship. Unlike the men of Ruby who define race through violence, Mavis perceives race as a forerunner to intimacy. In both encounters, race is necessarily defined by an encounter with difference. However, while the Ruby men assume a position of aggression and ultimately destruction, Mavis and the other Convent women approach race as the foundation for further interaction.

Who Is the White Girl?

Kathryn Nicol argues that the first sentence of *Paradise* "sets the reader on a racial investigation, looking for the textual or bodily 'tell' which will disclose which of the Convent women is in fact white." Despite the numerous reviewers and critics who have specifically identified the white girl, Morrison's stated intention regarding *Paradise* as well as her vague references to racial differences among the Convent women frustrate any definitive claim we might make. Because the novel forecloses specific racial identification within the Convent, Nicol notes, "The question that should be asked is not the question of the identity of the white girl, but the question of who identifies her as white, and why" ("Visible Differences," 222). Why then do the "New Fathers of Ruby, Oklahoma" (18) set out not only to kill the Convent women but also to identify one of them as white? The answer to this question demonstrates the violent origins of Ruby's racist house. It is not racial difference that threatens the creation of paradise but the need to racialize that exposes the lie of Ruby's false home.

As the men begin their attack on the Convent, hunting their victims in the massive house, they remember Ruby's forerunner, the town of Haven, once "a dreamtown in Oklahoma Territory" that had turned into "a ghost-town in Oklahoma State." They recall, "Freedmen who stood tall in 1889 dropped to their knees in 1934 and were stomach-crawling by 1948. That is why they are here in this Convent. To make sure it never happens again" (5). The "it" of this last sentence is difficult to define. Haven was the first all-black town founded by the forefathers of the Ruby settlers. Led by nine patriarchs, this collection of former slaves from Louisiana and Mississippi ventured west to settle the Oklahoma territory. After the outrage of the

Disallowing, they established the town of Haven, which thrives for a few decades. However, during the 1930s many young people begin leaving in large part due to World War II. When the prominent Morgan twins, Deacon and Steward, return from the war, they are infuriated by Haven's state of neglect. They decide to pack up the remnants of the town and search for a place to begin again. Along with fourteen other families, they settle in an isolated area ninety miles from the nearest town. The townspeople name their new home Ruby, after the Morgan sister who died during the journey. The New Fathers of Ruby arrive in the Convent vowing to protect their town from the kind of destruction that befell Haven, but Haven's demise was induced by its own citizens. The townspeople were neither threatened nor pushed out; instead, they abandoned their home in search of something better. They chose to give up on Haven. The men of Ruby fixate on the importance of not repeating history even though history reveals the complicity of Haven's citizens in its destruction. This contradiction structures how Ruby's fate is overdetermined by the legacy of Haven and elucidates the many historical discrepancies in the text.

Descriptions of the origin myths of Haven and Ruby boldly contradict one another; at one point the settlers initially heading west to Oklahoma number "one hundred and fifty-eight freedmen," but in another account they are described as "all seventy-nine," exactly half the number first given (13, 95). No logical answer explains this difference, but the discrepancy points to Morrison's overarching concern with the mutability of historical narratives. The stories of a nation or a community become mythologized through deliberate omissions and exaggerations. This carefully constructed master narrative enshrines a certain identity for its citizens. The mythic history of Haven, best represented by the Disallowing, involves a story of racial oppression and fierce will that impelled a people to create a home in opposition to discriminatory forces. Any narrative that threatens this story must be eradicated even though historically Ruby has no Disallowing of its own. While they laud the heroic efforts of the Haven settlers, the Ruby fathers experience these feats as anxious uncertainty concerning their own capabilities. Pat Best observes that during the annual Christmas pageant there are fewer families represented than the original nine. The children of Ruby reenact the Nativity story, searching for shelter, but rather than a single Mary and Joseph, the pageant includes representatives of the

first families to settle Haven. The story of Christ's birth has been reconfigured to reflect the more important history of the town. Pat recognizes that
her own family, the Catos, have been eliminated from the pageant because
her father married a light-skinned woman. The Ruby myth is malleable,
but it shifts only to codify its values more rigidly and to consolidate power
in the righteous few.

Reverend Misner notes how the townspeople, neglecting the immedi-
acy and uniqueness of their own lives, continually tell stories of their
forefathers: "Over and over and with the least provocation, they pulled
from their stock of stories tales about the old folks, their grands and
great-grands; their fathers and mothers. Dangerous confrontations, clever
maneuvers. Testimonies to endurance, wit, skill, strength. Tales of luck
and outrage. But why were there no stories to tell of themselves? About
their own lives they shut up. Had nothing to say, pass on. As though past
heroism was enough of a future to live by" (161). Misner's reflections suggest that the Deacon twins proposed leaving Haven and starting anew as a
way to replicate the experience of their forefathers. When faced with the
challenge of endurance, of keeping Haven prosperous and populated, the
only solution they were able to imagine is the one enacted by the original
settlers. Ignoring the obvious differences between the dreams of former
slaves and their own postwar disillusion, the twins set out to reenact the
narrative of righteous migration, a story that as Nicol notes moves "from
tale to memory to rememory" (224). The mythical past determines the
action of the present. When Dovey and Soane learn that their husbands
have left to attack the Convent, Soane, knowing the women are easy
targets, states, "They're different is all." Dovey agrees, adding, "I know, but
that's been enough before" (288). This subtle reference to a prior attack
upon a group labeled "other" reaffirms how the Ruby men set out to
reinscribe a preestablished narrative. They repeat history rather than
acknowledge the unique contexts of their lives that demand new forms of
action. Similarly, they adhere to divisive notions of race, inherited from
their forefathers, instead of finding new ways to account for the nearby
Convent women.

As mentioned before, the primary narrative in the history of Ruby
is the story of the Disallowing, which, as Andrew Read notes, is not only
humiliating for the early settlers but produces traumatic effects that are

"transgenerational" (529). In gathering her informal history of the town, Pat Best observes, "Everything anybody wanted to know about the citizens of Haven or Ruby lay in the ramifications of that one rebuff out of many" (189). Read argues that the New Fathers repeat the original trauma of the first Disallowing: "Subsequent contacts with the outside world only reinforce these men's traumatized need to Disallow anyone inside or outside of their community who transgresses their values and threatens to bring (further) shame upon them" (532). The men of Ruby attack the Convent because they believe that the women who reside there threaten the values and integrity of their town. Assessing the "outrages that had been accumulating," the men conclude, "the one thing that connected all these catastrophes was in the Convent. And in the Convent were those women." The "evidence" includes: "A mother was knocked down the stairs by her cold-eyed daughter. Four damaged infants were born in one family. Daughters refused to get out of bed. Brides disappeared on their honeymoons. Two brothers shot each other on New Year's Day. Trips to Demby for VD shots common" (11).

None of these events can be traced to the Convent women, but logic is not a necessary component to fulfilling the ultimate objective of the Ruby men. Like the town authorities who racialize Florens, the men read evil omens to suit their own political needs. The New Fathers need to blame someone, to identify a specific threat that they can then bravely annihilate. The Convent women with their unorthodox ways are easy scapegoats as they conveniently reify strict binaries of good and evil, male and female, purity and corruption. All of the "catastrophes" observed by the men demonstrate threatening aspects of female agency—women who disrupt traditional gender roles and flaunt their sexuality. Moreover, the first example of a mother "knocked down the stairs by her cold-eyed daughter" is not even factually true; Pat explains that it was she who chased her daughter Billie Delia "up the stairs with a 1950s GE electric iron ... clutched in her fingers to slam against her daughter's head" (203). In order to direct their rage at the women of the Convent the men of Ruby ignore both truth and logic.

Consequently, these "bodacious black Eves unredeemed by Mary" (18) must be destroyed though their identification as "black" is peculiar. This description either suggests that all of the Convent women are actually black or that the Ruby men have so absorbed the conventional connotations of "blackness" that they use it to signify evil. To find a "white girl" among these "black Eves" is violent indeed. By identifying and shooting the "white girl," the men of Ruby link their attack on the Convent with the founding narrative of their town. Just as the original settlers sought a place free of white intervention, so they destroy the white girl who threatens to contaminate their town. Emphasizing the importance of national mythologies in the development of political action, Marni Gauthier argues, "the Disallowing has created a totalizing master narrative that engenders the chronic disallowings that plague the integrity of the Ruby-nation" ("The Other Side of Paradise," 408). The mythic history of Ruby structures how the men respond to the women of the Convent. They create a narrative of righteous racial vengeance to justify their attack.

Read goes so far as to claim that in the opening scene of Ruby "the men form a conventional *white* lynch mob" and argues that "Morrison's ultimate indictment of Ruby's patriarchy is that it reproduces ideologies and practices of racist white men" ("'As if word magic,'" 538). Read's interpretation depends upon an understanding of racial difference that is reducible solely to hierarchies of power; the Ruby men are white because they attack the women based upon a misguided belief in their moral righteousness. From this perspective, racial identity is a function of material and ideological power. Read's provocative claim makes whiteness the agent of violence rather than the entire system of racial classification. To read the Ruby men as "racist white men" is to deny the specific contours of their racist behavior. The very object of their violence, a group of women, demonstrates the stark contrast between them and a "conventional *white* lynch mob," which most often attacked black men. We can no more conflate racial differences between black and white as we can easily gloss over the sexual difference between the victims of these two mobs.

To consolidate both their racial and gendered power, the men of Ruby need a white girl to shoot. Her identity and even her existence are secondary to the demands of their predetermined trajectory. Consequently, there may in fact be no white girl at all. The men of Ruby need to tell a story of race and violence that grants them the courage and fortitude of their forefathers who risked their lives to create and protect their new home. Morrison further implies that the white girl is no more than a necessary fantasy of the Ruby men by embedding a blatant factual error in the novel's second paragraph. Paralleling the text's first sentence, it reads, "They are nine, over twice the number of the women they are obliged to stampede or kill" (3). Simple math indicates that if there are nine men, then the women should number at least four. But five women are living at the Convent when the men arrive: Connie, Mavis, Gigi, Seneca, and Pallas. What accounts for this error?[7] Is Connie not included in the women they are "obliged to stampede or kill" because of her previous history with the people of Ruby? There is no mention of such an exceptional status in the text. And when Pat recounts the attack she concludes, "nine 8-rocks murdered five harmless women" (297).

This error demands that we read the entire attack on the Convent not as factual history, but as mythology. The novel's opening provides an account not of what happened but of what the men needed to happen, the story they needed to tell to safeguard and perpetuate the myth of Ruby. Once again the men have protected the people of Ruby by eradicating the threat of miscegenation and white intervention. The men conjure race to justify their misguided narrative, blaming a racial and gendered other to avoid an examination of their own culpability in Ruby's deterioration. Moreover, just as we must question the very existence of the white girl, we must also be skeptical about the massacre that reputedly occurred. When Roger returns with his hearse to pick up the bodies, there are none: "No bodies. Nothing. Even the Cadillac was gone" (292). What abides in Ruby is not the death of the women, but the story of their death.

When Reverend Misner and Anna visit the Convent, they see an abandoned home—"there was nothing recently lived-in about the place" (303). Similarly, in the basement, Anna does not see "the terribleness K.D. reported . . . it wasn't the pornography he had seen, nor was it Satan's scrawl. She saw instead the turbulence of females trying to bridle, without being trampled, the monsters that slavered them" (303). The basement pictures refer to the outlines the Convent women drew of themselves as a way of confronting and combating the demons of their past. These "monsters" are not the men of Ruby but the traumas they have endured. Where K.D. sees evidence to justify his attack on the women, Anna sees an entirely different narrative. Which is true? Perhaps Anna only sees a reflection of her own struggles, monsters she recognizes as her own. The inherent bias of individual perspective is inescapable, although, unlike K.D., Anna is invested in possibility, not violence. As she and Reverend Misner prepare to leave the Convent, they sense something new: "It was when he returned, as they stood near the chair, her hands balancing brown eggs and white cloth, his fingers looking doubled with long pepper pods—green, red and plum black—that they saw it. Or sensed it, rather, for there was nothing to see. A door, she said later. 'No, a window,' he said, laughing. 'That's the difference between us. You see a door; I see a window.'"

For Anna and Reverend Misner, the difference between them is not antagonizing but generative: "What did a door mean? what a window?" Although both images suggest the possibilities of a new home, the transparency of Anna's window is especially critical to how Morrison represents race in the novel. Unlike Misner's door that, when closed, can occlude vision, the window implies the absence of borders, a way to both live in a home and see beyond it. However, by "focusing on the sign rather than the event," Anna and Misner avoid "reliving the shiver or saying out loud what they were wondering. Whether through a door needing to be opened or a beckoning window already raised, what would happen if you entered? What would be on the other side? What on earth would it be? What on earth?" (305). Anna and Reverend Misner distract themselves with "the sign" because the event, though more thrilling, is also more dangerous.

This emphasis on the sign rather than the event provides a parallel to the question of who is the white girl. For the marauding men of Ruby, the sign they create is whiteness; the event is violence. Whiteness is their justification to attack, and, while scholars may continue to debate the identity of the white girl, it is the violence that signifies, the violence that makes Ruby a racist house. By contrast, what Anna and Reverend Misner glimpse is another vision of home, one unencumbered by the violent need to racialize another.

The final pages of *Paradise* describe each of the Convent women reconciling with some aspect of their painful individual histories. Gigi skinny dips with a companion; Pallas returns to her mother's home to retrieve a pair of shoes; Mavis meets her daughter Sal who tells her mother that she always loved her; and Seneca finds herself the object of her mother's search rather than the reverse. Most critics read these encounters as evidence of how the women, as Channette Romero claims, "escape into 'another realm.' A spiritual door/window in the sky" ("Creating the Beloved Community," 416). Shirley A. Stave argues that the "text makes clear that the women do die" ("The Master's Tools," 227) while Justine Tally suggests that the women are "revenants" or spirits of those "who have been violently killed . . . and [return] to visit the living" (*Paradise Reconsidered*, 46). However, if the identification of a white girl was simply a justifying ploy on the part of the Ruby men, then perhaps the massacre of the women is also a necessary fiction for the protection of Ruby's mythology. Perhaps Anna and Reverend Misner find no bodies because there are no bodies to find. Any definitive understanding of the fate of the Convent women requires some degree of interpretive subterfuge. If they are in fact dead, then what has happened to their bodies? If they have escaped to another spiritual world, then how is that to be reconciled with the novel's final injunction to begin "the endless work they were created to do down here in paradise" (318)? And if they are alive, then how are we to account for Connie's death which Soane, Dovey, and Lone witness? In claiming that the women do not die, I argue that the massacre is not history but myth, and beyond the myth are infinite narrative possibilities of escape, reconciliation, and survival.

To that end, it is instructive to note that *Paradise* was in part inspired by a research trip Morrison took to Brazil where she learned about a convent of black nuns. The nuns, who cared for abandoned children, practiced Catholicism on the first floor and a form of voodoo in the basement. According to legend, a group of local men attacked the convent and killed the nuns. However, the story has since been proved false. Despite being no more than a fabrication, this encounter became the basis for Morrison's study of how communities construct narratives for political and social purposes. The fiction yields other truths, and in the case of *Paradise* all truth claims are subject to the bias of its tellers.

Race, Violence, and *Paradise*

Prior to the violent intrusion of the Ruby men, the Convent is not a place devoid of race. Its inhabitants do not simplistically transcend distinctions of color, class, and culture. They live not in a raceless world but in a home that uncouples Nelson's union of race and violence. Mavis and Gigi draw blood when they fight; Seneca continues to cut herself in secret places on her body; Connie often drinks herself into a stupor and internally rages at the needy women occupying her home. Is this paradise? Just as there is no white girl, there is also no paradise, at least not in the sense of an ideal social space. Instead, the novel closes with a promise for the future, not paradise, but the materials to make paradise. Piedade sings to a younger woman at the ocean shore strewn with "sea trash." She looks up to see "another ship, perhaps, but different, heading to port, crew and passengers, lost and saved, atremble, for they have been disconsolate for some time. Now they will rest before shouldering the endless work they were created to do down here in paradise" (318). Although the ship recalls the transportation of African slaves across the Middle Passage, it is "different." The crew and passengers will not repeat past histories but will engage in new work, in the creation of a paradise that, though formed through "endless work," is already here. There is no utopia because there is no stasis, only the repeated reach toward home.

This vexed, unsettled approach to the meaning and development of paradise is further demonstrated by returning to the passage Morrison cites in "Home" concerning the sleepless woman and quoted in this book's introduction. This description is included in *Paradise,* but its placement in the text is striking—directly following the ruminations of one of the men who arrives at the Convent ready to kill the resident women. He first observes, "No criminals had ever come from his town. ... Certainly there wasn't a slack or sloven woman anywhere in town and the reasons, he thought, were clear. From the beginning its people were free and protected" (8). This description of "his town" suggests that the following vision of the sleepless woman is his own. Not only is the lyrical image of an ideal home derived from a male perspective, but it also comes from a man already intent on violence. He dreams of an expansive home for the sleepless woman yet guards her freedom by attacking the Convent. This conception of home echoes the passage in which Ruby is portrayed as a safe haven for "four colored girls" because men with guns are vigilant of unwelcome strangers.

While Morrison extolled the home of the sleepless woman in her essay, here it becomes a safety premised upon violence and specifically an act of racial violence. Is the freedom of the sleepless woman only guaranteed because guns are at the ready nearby? Cyrus Patell argues that this notion of home demonstrates "a patriarch's view of women's freedom"

(*Negative Liberties*, 183). Similarly, John N. Duvall, finding fault with the freedom of the sleepless woman, notes: "The women of Ruby may walk without fear but they also do so without a lamp, and they are, by and large, unenlightened about anything but their domesticity. They walk but do not drive and there is really nowhere to go since the nearest town is ninety miles away. It is a safety based on isolation that approximates the carceral" (*The Identifying Fictions of Toni Morrison*, 143).

Although there is little in the passage from *Paradise* to suggest that the sleepless woman is seriously constrained by domestic responsibilities, Duvall's concern demonstrates the difficulty of extrapolating broad conclusions from a single, largely decontextualized example. When dealing with the hard work of creating both paradise and home, it is imperative to shift discussion to a specific context. Midway through the novel, Morrison provides an example of an actual woman roaming the streets of Ruby. While on his way to work one morning, Deacon spots Sweetie Fleetwood: "He was braking in front of the bank when he noticed a solitary figure ahead. He recognized her right away but watched her carefully because first of all she had no coat, and because second, he had not seen her out of the house in six years. . . . What could the sweetest girl, named for her nature, be doing coatless on a chilly October morning that far from the home she had not stepped out of since 1967?"

Despite recognizing how strange it is for Sweetie to be out alone, Deacon does not stop to speak with her, even though he knows that his first meeting of the day will be delayed since he can see Aaron Poole's truck still off in the distance. Instead, he concludes, "There should be no occasion when the bank of a good and serious town did not open on time" (114). Sweetie certainly has the freedom and safety to walk where she likes, but there is no home along the road. Deacon's decision to ignore her rather than inquire about her well-being indicates the fundamental failure of Ruby's vision of home. It is not enough that no one considers Sweetie to be "prey" when she is not considered important enough to impede the town's morning routine. A community is not built on isolation both of and between its citizens.

Rather than speak to Sweetie, Deacon insists on adhering to the punctuality demanded of "a good and serious town." For him, the town's reputation is far more critical than its inhabitants. Later Anna rebukes this choice, but Steward cuts her with a stare, reminding her that his brother "was opening up the bank, girl." Her careful reply, "Somebody better speak to Jeff" (124) demonstrates her own acquiescence to the town's patriarchal ethos. Sweetie is not to be directly approached, and Anna is too cowed by Steward to specify who should speak to Sweetie's husband. Ironically, at the end of the novel, Deacon undergoes his own lonely walk through Ruby. Disturbed by his participation in the attack on the Convent, Deacon sheds his shoes to walk barefoot to Reverend Misner's house. Deacon's walk demonstrates his own displacement from the false paradise of Ruby. He arrives at Reverend Misner's door ready to "translate into speech the raw matter" of himself that he has long kept unexpressed. Deacon's walk culminates in the beginning of a new language—words "like ingots pulled from the fire by an apprentice blacksmith—hot, misshapen, resembling themselves only in their glow" (301). These words will require ever more refinement and care, words that will help make sense of Deacon's responsibility in the events at the Convent and provide comfort for the difficult journey ahead. As he tells Misner, "I got a long way to go, Reverend." To which, Misner replies, "You'll make it. . . . No doubt about it" (303). Unlike Sweetie, Deacon's walk ends with the possibility of speech, with the hope that words will give meaning to the work he has done and will yet do. This new language, forged in the fire of history, offers the promise of settling the wasted divisions of race.

The Ruby that depends on violence is no home, no place of solace; it is not, as Morrison wrote in "Home," "a place already made for me, both snug and wide open" (9). Sweetie pushes onward to the Convent where she will find welcoming women, women who must be murdered to safeguard her lonely walk. Significantly, the first person to respond kindly to Sweetie is Seneca, who leaps from the back of a truck to follow Sweetie out to the Convent. For Seneca, this act represents "the first pointedly uninstructed thing she had ever done" (138). Here freedom is construed as offering care to another. Rather than experiencing freedom as merely the absence of predators, Seneca embraces it as movement toward unification with others, as the beginning of a home.

"Recitatif": From Race-Free to Race-Specific

Both *A Mercy* and *Paradise* present all female spaces in which racial difference is recognized but racism does not exist. It is easy to assume from

Morrison's description of the Vaark household and the Convent that racist language thus derives from patriarchy. Seemingly only in the absence of men are women able to operate apart from the violent categories of race. Although these novels suggest that the need to subjugate others in order to guarantee a patriarchal legacy is key to the development of racism, Morrison's only short story, "Recitatif," demonstrates that racial inscription is not solely the province of men. Like *Paradise*, this enigmatic piece explores the possibilities of race-free language made race-specific through the violent imposition of others. In *Paradise*, racial identification is made to preserve the mythology of Ruby and the misguided dream of a static, insular town. Morrison exposes how race is necessary to police the borders of a community too frightened to define itself by anything other than a crippling historical narrative.

"Recitatif" moves the discussion of racial signification away from the broad sweep of *A Mercy* and *Paradise* to focus on the friendship between two girls, one white and one black. However, the text does not specify which is which. Readers of "Recitatif" primarily focus on the racial identity of childhood friends Twyla and Roberta. By contrast, my analysis emphasizes the ways in which these characters racialize other people, demonstrating how racial language develops apart from the mother-child bond in a manner that parallels Julia Kristeva's conceptualization of the difference between the semiotic and symbolic. Just as Kristeva theorizes the relationship between these two realms as a dialectic exchange, the story's "race-specific, race-free language" offers a way to transform race from a site of violence to one of transgressive identification.

Although the two primary characters in "Recitatif" refer to racial difference, their various prejudices and descriptions of the other's race can be applied to both blacks and whites. Upon meeting Roberta, her new roommate, Twyla, the narrator, is outraged to be placed "with a girl from a whole other race." She recalls that her mother warned her "that they never washed their hair and they smelled funny" (445). Despite her initial skepticism, Twyla and Roberta soon become friends, united by the fact that they have both been abandoned by their mothers. Roberta does not ask Twyla for details about why her mother has also left her at St. Bonny's, a state-run shelter for children. This tacit understanding leads Twyla to conceive of herself in parallel with Roberta despite their racial difference: "I liked the way she understood things so fast. So for the moment it didn't matter that we looked like salt and pepper standing there and that's what the other kids called us sometimes. We were eight years old and got F's all the time" (446). Consistent with Morrison's reflections about her intention with *Paradise*, "Recitatif" demonstrates how race is not an essential determinant of identity. Twyla and Roberta are young enough to move beyond the prejudices of their mothers to encounter one another independent of delimiting stereotypes. Twyla explains in the first sentence of the story that she and Roberta are thrown together because "my mother danced all night and Roberta's was sick" (445). Both "dumped" (446) in St. Bonny's, they cling to one another, united against the threatening older girls and curious about Maggie, a mute kitchen worker. As in *A Mercy*, the struggle to survive is more important than racial difference.

While racial clues are largely elided in *Paradise*, "Recitatif" is rife with perplexing tells that can ultimately be read both ways. Though Twyla and Roberta are able to put aside stereotypes when encountering one another, this move away from the centrality of race is more difficult for readers who attempt to track the ambiguous clues of the text. Which racial group does not wash their hair? Which smells funny? To assign either Twyla or Roberta a racial identity is to concede to stereotype. One may conclude that Twyla is black because she waitresses for a living while Roberta marries a rich widower. Or is Twyla white because, of the two friends, she arrives in the shelter able to read while Roberta is illiterate? Either interpretation depends upon stereotypes about race and the intersection of racial identity with certain class characteristics. Is attendance at a Jimi Hendrix concert more likely for a young white woman or a young black woman? Which girl has the Bible-thumping mother? To read race into the text is ultimately to enact a type of racism. Morrison makes the signs of race so ambiguous that no objective reading practice can distinguish Twyla and Roberta by race. Instead the very notion of a racially inflected reading practice is exposed as racist. By frustrating attempts to make the story's language race-specific, Morrison questions the need to racially identify characters. Why must we know who is black and who is white?

The comments of Twyla on the nature of her childhood friendship with Roberta are especially instructive in understanding how best to approach the racial ambiguity of the two friends: "Two little girls who knew what nobody else in the world knew—how not to ask questions. How to believe what had to be believed. There was politeness in that reluctance and generosity as well. Is your mother sick too? No, she dances all night. Oh—and an understanding nod" (455). Just as the two girls do not press one another for details about their mothers, their racial identifications remain undisclosed to readers. The girls bond over their abandonment and tacitly understand that their race does not prevent the hurt caused by failed mothers. Racial specificity does nothing to elucidate that far greater component of their respective identities. Morrison thus challenges her readers to "believe what had to be believed"—that is, race does not pose insurmountable barriers to intimacy.

By not defining Twyla and Roberta racially the text does not offer a simplistic model of the irrelevance of race; rather, the tension of the story rests on how the two friends respond to the racially ambiguous Maggie. Just as the opening of *Paradise* demands that we consider why the identification of whiteness is necessary to the men of Ruby, "Recitatif" compels readers to critique how the friends perceive and racialize Maggie. Maggie is initially described as "old and sandy-colored" (447). Mute and wearing a child's hat, she is an easy target of ridicule for all the orphaned girls. In Twyla's first memory of St. Bonny's, she and Roberta watch Maggie fall down while the older girls laugh at her. Although Twyla admits, "We should have helped her up," they are too scared to do anything. Later they call her names to see if she can hear or not. Maggie does not respond, and Twyla recalls that "it shames me even now to think there was somebody in there after all who heard us call her those names and couldn't tell on us" (447–448).

In their second meeting as adults, Twyla runs into Roberta, now married to a rich widower, at an upscale grocery store. The first memory Twyla mentions from their time at St. Bonny's involves Maggie's fall in the orchard, but Roberta corrects her: "No, Twyla. They knocked her down and tore her clothes" (456). Twyla is troubled by Roberta's version of events and her insistence that they both witnessed the abuse. When they meet again, Twyla spots Roberta among a group picketing the mandatory bussing of school children to different neighborhoods. They argue over the plan, and soon Twyla's car is surrounded by women who start rocking it back and forth. Although Twyla reaches her arm out for help from Roberta, the mob is only dispersed when the police arrive. Roberta then levies a damning accusation at Twyla:

> "Maybe I am different now, Twyla. But you're not. You're the same little state kid who kicked a poor old black lady when she was down on the ground. You kicked a black lady and you have the nerve to call me a bigot."
>
> The coupons were everywhere and the guts of my purse were bunched under the dashboard. What was she saying? Black? Maggie wasn't black.
>
> "She wasn't black," I said.
>
> "Like hell she wasn't, and you kicked her. We both did. You kicked a black lady who couldn't even scream."
>
> "Liar!" (460)

Roberta assigns Maggie a racial identity at the moment in which violence is inflicted upon the mute kitchen worker, thereby affirming Nelson's contention that racial classification is a violent act. Within the context of the story to be black is to be the victim of physical abuse. Whether Twyla is black or white, if she kicked Maggie, she assumes the position of the dominant race. However, this is the one aspect of Roberta's narrative that Twyla absolutely refuses ("I know I didn't do that, I couldn't do that" [462]). Instead she is confused by the issue of Maggie's race: "When I thought about it I actually couldn't be certain. She wasn't pitch-black, I knew, or I would have remembered that. What I remember was the kiddie hat, and the semicircle legs." Prior to Roberta's outburst, it would seem that Twyla had not assigned Maggie a racial identity. This indeterminacy mirrors her insistence that she was only a witness, not a participant, in the violence.

Twyla concludes that Maggie's race is irrelevant to the desire she shared with Roberta to kick her. Even if she did not participate in the violence, she wanted to, and by not calling for help she abetted the abuse. Seeming to elide the issue of race, Twyla refocuses the incident on what Maggie meant to her, confessing, "Maggie was my dancing mother," a woman who was also "Deaf, I thought, and dumb. Nobody inside. Nobody who would hear you if you cried at night" (462). In Maggie, Twyla sees her mother, not a woman defined by race. Like *A Mercy*'s Sorrow who "is a mother. Nothing more. Nothing less" (159), Maggie is simply a mother for Twyla. This representation of a type of race neutral mother suggests that maternal figures are somehow beyond the symbolics of race.

If race is a language or a series of codes that we must all learn, then the exchange between mother and child represents a language prior to the imposition of social paradigms. Hence we might conceive of the mother-child bond as the one relationship free of racial ascription, at least until race intrudes upon the child's consciousness. This formulation coincides with Kristeva's notion of the semiotic in which the subject exists in harmonious fusion with the maternal body, such that there is no distinction between self and other. The semiotic is inevitably destroyed by entrance into the patriarchal symbolic, a world governed by language and defined by positions of judgment.[8] Here the symbolic correlates with racial signification while the semiotic or the maternal bond offers the one exception to racial meaning because difference of any kind is not yet recognizable. Both Maggie and Sorrow, as racially ambiguous maternal figures, operate as powerful representations of the semiotic. However, it is important to note that these characters are largely mute. Consistent with the preverbal qualities of the semiotic, neither woman is able to communicate effectively with others. Their shared muteness underscores the need to merge the semiotic with the symbolic into a liberating discourse, for as Domna Stanton notes, "only the eruption of the semiotic into the symbolic can give rein to heterogenous meaning, to difference, and thus subvert the existing systems of signification" ("Language and Revolution," 74). Such language might name the race of the mother without violence, might become race-specific without becoming racist.

Roberta's insistence that Maggie is black racializes an encounter that for Twyla operates beyond, or more precisely, prior to categories of racial identification. Where Twyla sees her mother, Roberta sees race. This difference in perception emerges as the most critical one between them. Their opposing reading practices, not their racial difference, is what most separates them. While Twyla approaches Maggie through the semiotic, Roberta does so through the symbolic, identifying the abused woman as black. However, it is also important to note that when Roberta first tells Twyla that Maggie is black, Twyla immediately replies, "She wasn't black" (460). This denial might be read as Twyla's need to conceptualize Maggie in a semiotic, pre-racial state, but it may also suggest her own affirmation that she is not black in the way that Maggie is black—that is, a woman defined by powerlessness. In her final encounter with Twyla, Roberta faces this same dilemma; she admits that Maggie also shared similarities with her mother: "I really did think she was black. . . . But now I can't be sure. I just remember her as old, so old. And because she couldn't talk—well, you know, I thought she was crazy. She'd been brought up in an institution like my mother was and like I thought I would be too. And you were right. We didn't kick her. . . . But, well, I wanted to. I really wanted them to hurt her" (463–464). As with Twyla, Roberta cannot merge Maggie's possible blackness with her maternal figuration. Maggie cannot be both black and her mother. The fact that both friends confront this same barrier suggests that their hesitation is not racially marked; even the black woman of this duo does not want to identify Maggie as her mother.

Twyla's and Roberta's shared reluctance to identify Maggie as their mother reflects a desire not to be Maggie, not to be mute, powerless, and victimized. For both women, Maggie's blackness bears this excessive symbolic import. By fixating on Maggie's racial identity, they are guilty of the very reading practices that Morrison exposes as false through the deliberate ambiguity she applies to Twyla and Roberta. To read Maggie as black is to reify blackness as a trope of abjection. The bolder choice is to see Maggie not as white or black, but as their mother, a category that originates as raceless. By making Maggie race-specific, they participate in the symbolic work of racism that associates blackness with silence and impotence. Morrison's short story is thus an invitation not to make the same errors as its characters, to create a new language that does not simplistically link blackness to abjection but that combines elements of the semiotic and the symbolic. This unspoken language of Maggie is the emergent language of Sorrow, the language Florens needed to hear from her mother and the language that allows Twyla and Roberta to be race-free and race-specific, if only to one another. Their exceptional friendship demonstrates the intimacy possible through such an approach as well as the persistent habit to slip into the convenient figurations of race.

Is it possible to understand this radical form of discourse as more than just a literary conceit? Morrison's texts demonstrate that race is embedded into the very language of the United States; it structures the education and development of any American, whether born in *A Mercy*'s pre-racial world or in today's "post-racial" society. Obama's first book, *Dreams from My Father*, chronicles his journey to racial consciousness, culminating in his self-identification as a "black American." To that end, the book is largely a meditation on his absent father and the vexed legacy of his blackness. It is, in short, an account of Obama's racial education. And yet, writing in 2004, almost a decade after its initial publication and a year before he became a U.S. senator, Obama expresses in the preface the regret he felt in focusing his memoir so insistently on his father. Following the sudden death of his mother, Ann Dunham, he reflects, "I think sometimes that had I known she would not survive her illness, I might have written a different book— less a meditation on the absent parent, more a celebration of the one who was the single constant in my life."

Obama's regret suggests a desire for a language separate from the divisions and demands of race. His search for his father and for an understanding of his own blackness was a necessary component of his maturation. But the image of his mother promises yet another vision, something akin to the semiotic language of Morrison's racially ambiguous maternal figures. Obama explains, "In my daughters I see her every day, her joy, her capacity for wonder. I won't try to describe how deeply I mourn her passing still. I know that she was the kindest, most generous spirit I have ever known, and that what is best in me I owe to her" (xii). While Obama set off in search of his patrimony, his mother offers another kind of racial meaning—not one defined by whiteness, just as it would be a mistake to define Obama's father and his legacy solely by blackness; instead, Dunham offers a kind of racial meaning that unites difference and commonality. Obama has neglected his mother's story, that of a woman in search not of racial identity but of a home for her multiracial children, perhaps because this story resists all the violent lessons of race we have necessarily learned—the rigidity of color codes and patriarchal inscriptions, the hierarchy of difference that structures our American language. But even as Dunham's story remains untold, she has bequeathed to her son another kind of reading practice, a liberating racial education: the ability to see a white woman reflected in the faces of two black girls.

2

Hiding the Invisible Hurt of Race

Metaphors of race in African American literature have generally been characterized through visual terms—the invisibility of Ralph Ellison's protagonist, the veil that prevents the young W.E.B. Du Bois from joining his white classmates, the yearning of Pecola Breedlove for blue eyes and the liberating vision they promise. Even when marks of racial difference are not visible on the skin, as explored in many passing narratives such as Nella Larsen's *Passing* (1929) or James Weldon Johnson's *The Autobiography of an Ex-Colored Man* (1912), there is always the threat that the color of a child may betray its mother or more subtle marks like hair texture or fingernails may give away one's true racial identity. At the end of the twentieth century Robyn Wiegman argued that "the 'logic' of race in U.S. culture anchors whiteness in the visible epistemology of black skin" (*American Anatomies*, 21). However, in the twenty-first century color is neither a stable measure of difference nor a simplistic barrier to social achievement. Even if we do not live in a post-racial utopia, black skin did not prevent Obama from winning the presidency. His victory complicates previous ways in which race has been conceived primarily through visual registers. Though Obama possesses black skin and in the 2010 census defined himself as "Black, African American, or Negro," throughout his campaign he was dogged by criticisms that he was not "black enough." He possesses almost none of the characteristics that led Toni Morrison to label Bill Clinton our "first black president"; instead, Obama radiates the tastes and privileges of the elite.

Writing in *The Nation*, Melissa Harris-Lacewell argued of Obama: "the real threat he poses to the American racial order is that he disrupts whiteness, because whiteness has been the identity that defines citizenship, access to privilege and the power to define national history" ("Black by Choice"). Obama's victory challenges conventional notions of both white and black identity. What is the domain of whiteness when it no longer includes the Oval Office?[1] What happens to black identity when it is more mainstream than marginalized? The rampant proliferation of what Wiegman terms an "integrationist aesthetic" on college campuses, in media campaigns as well as among governing bodies suggests that we can no longer depend upon visual markers of race to signify abiding forms of inequality. Rather, Obama's presidency, like the superficial diversification of many political and corporate institutions, occludes meaningful engagement with structures of power that continue to support oppressive racial hierarchies.

In the aftermath of Obama's presidential victory, Toni Morrison said that "if Ralph Ellison was alive he would [change the title of] his masterpiece, *Invisible Man*, to 'The Visible Man.' "[2] While Morrison has long stated that invisibility is not the best metaphor by which to understand black subjectivity because it depends upon a white gaze, her comment emphasizes the need to rethink how race operates upon visual registers in our contemporary moment.[3] In his 1981 introduction to *Invisible Man* (1952), Ellison warned that "despite the bland assertions of sociologists, 'high visibility' actually rendered one *un*-visible" (xv). He may very well have countered Morrison's assertion about the title of his book by arguing that Obama's win only inaugurates a new form of failed visibility; the excessive visibility of our president does not indicate that he is seen or known in meaningful ways. Ellison's observation suggests that invisibility and visibility do not function as neat opposites; instead, the visual is an always vexed register of identity.

The term "un-visible" characterizes the impossibility of perceiving subjectivity solely through the visual. Obama does not necessarily become visible simply because his image is now ubiquitous in American and international media. Instead his hypervisibility, like the wide-ranging reach of Wiegman's "integrationist aesthetic," poses new challenges to recognizing how race operates beyond the enthusiastic embrace of color. These issues drive Colson Whitehead's 2006 *Apex Hides the Hurt*, which offers a new model of conceptualizing racial difference, that of injury and trauma. His novel avoids a simplistic conflation between blackness and physical damage by describing bodily injury as a type of chosen demarcation of identity that marks difference from others. *Apex Hides the Hurt* signifies upon many of the tropes and ideas introduced in Ellison's *Invisible Man*. Both novels center on anonymous loners who climb the ranks of white-dominated institutions. However, while Ellison's narrator explains "I am invisible, understand, simply because people refuse to see me" (3), Whitehead's protagonist is invisible because he refuses to allow others to see him. He conforms to the expectations of others, passively allowing his race to fuel the color-blind fantasies of others, if not his own. *Apex Hides the Hurt* explores the inadequacies of visual and even linguistic marks to convey racial difference, instead linking blackness to a chosen form of struggle.

The Ineffability of Blackness

The notion of racial difference presented by Whitehead in *Apex Hides the Hurt* resonates with Morrison's formulation of race as a matter of individual initiative. She explained in a 1987 interview: "Now people choose their identities. Now people choose to be Black. They used to be born Black. That's not true anymore. You can be Black genetically and choose not to be. You just change your mind or your eyes, change anything. It's just a mind-set."[4] Morrison's description of blackness as a mindset counters essentialist approaches to race by locating identity firmly within the individual. Morrison, however, leaves unexplored how one can "change your mind or your eyes" to inhabit a different racial identity. At the end of *The Bluest Eye* (1970), Pecola Breedlove believes that she has acquired blue eyes. Does this belief, this choice, make her white? Or is such a radical shift in racial identity only possible because of her madness? Morrison's comments ascribe power to the seen, not to the one who sees and parallels her initial response to reading Ellison's *Invisible Man*: "invisible to whom? Not me," she declared.[5] While Ellison constitutes his protagonist's identity through a white gaze, Morrison has continually stressed the importance of active self-creation and the role of a supportive black community in the development of individual subjectivity.

To understand Morrison's conception of blackness as a chosen identity, it is necessary to consider how she defines blackness. In

"Rootedness: The Ancestor as Foundation," she explores the characteristics that define black literature: "I don't regard Black literature as simply books written *by* Black people, or simply literature written *about* Black people, or simply as literature that uses a certain mode of language in which you just sort of drop g's. There is something very special and very identifiable about it and it is my struggle to *find* that elusive but identifiable style in the books. My joy is when I think that I have approached it; my misery is when I think I can't get there" (*The Norton Anthology*, 2288). Morrison's observations suggest the provocative conclusion that she may not always write black literature since she admits that she sometimes struggles to achieve that "very special and very identifiable" quality. Importantly, Morrison frames blackness as a destination to which she does not actually arrive; it is a place she only "approache(s)." However, while she leaves her arrival in suspension, she figures her writing difficulties as no more than a supposition. She only "think(s)" she "can't get there," presumably because her arrival is inevitable. Blackness here becomes a location that is never reached yet always guaranteed. This conception strongly resonates with Morrison's vision of home and paradise. The work of creating both is arduous and necessary, and though the exact contours of this destination remain uncertain, its promise is realized in the journey toward it.

Morrison's comments on the demands and joys of black literature reflect her general approach to the limitations of language. As she explained in her Nobel Lecture: "language can never live up to life once and for all. Nor should it. Language can never 'pin down' slavery, genocide, war. Nor should it yearn for the arrogance to be able to do so. Its force, its felicity is in its reach towards the ineffable" (*What Moves at the Margin*, 203). Just as the beauty of language resides in its attempt to express reality, so blackness functions as a type of ideal that both inhabits African American texts and exceeds precise capture. For Morrison, both language work and the expression of blackness are products of deliberate endeavor. She must labor to craft prose that may be labeled "Black literature," implying that her ability to write black literature is not a foregone conclusion. Morrison's novels are not black literature simply because she has written them. They are black literature because she has chosen to capture the dynamic reality and history that constitutes blackness. Consequently, to be a black writer is not a matter of visual pigmentation but involves an open embrace of this struggle to express in words the contours of black life.

If every novel charts a journey of discovery, then the destination of *Apex Finds the Hurt* is both literally and figuratively struggle. "Struggle" is the name that Whitehead's protagonist, a "nomenclature consultant," bestows upon Winthrop, a town in an unspecified region of the American West whose city council cannot decide what name it should have. Originally settled by free blacks, the town was later incorporated by the Winthrop family who became wealthy through the production of barbed wire. Because of the financial and industrial development offered by the Winthrop family, the city council agreed to change the town's original name of Freedom to Winthrop. However, a new corporate magnate, Lucky Aberdeen, has established himself in Winthrop through his prosperous software company. Hoping to change the image of the town from a largely unknown backwater to an exciting destination for new talent, Lucky convinces the city council to hire the protagonist's former firm to rename the town. However, their proposed name, New Prospera, does not sit well with the other members of the city council: Mayor Regina Goode, who is descended from the original settlers, and Albie Winthrop, heir to his family's fortune. While Albie wants the town to remain Winthrop, Regina hopes to return it to its original name, Freedom.

Because of this impasse, the unnamed protagonist is called in to settle the matter. Following a vaguely referenced "misfortune" (6) in which he fainted at an awards ceremony and had to have his toe amputated, the protagonist quit his job. At the beginning of the novel, he is living in almost complete seclusion from others. However, he agrees to accept the Winthrop job, provided that the city council concedes to one condition: whatever name he chooses must be adopted for a year. Afterward the town can change its name, but for a year his decision will stand. This condition, which forecloses the possibility of total failure, highlights the protagonist's skittish relationship to others. Having once been the most successful nomenclature consultant in his firm, he has since retreated from public life, effectively going underground to nurse a very private wound, one that is both physical and psychological.

There are rich comparisons between Whitehead's protagonist and Ellison's Invisible Man, but perhaps the most striking contrast is that while the latter only promises to end his prolonged "hibernation," the former returns to society through his work with the Winthrop city council. As Whitehead's protagonist confronts the limits of language to express identity as well as the ways in which color proves an inadequate sign of racial difference, he ultimately embraces struggle. The choice to struggle, to reject the false pleasures of material comfort and uncritical conformity, demonstrates a new way of thinking about race. Although Whitehead's protagonist engages in a kind of masochism to ensure his sense of self, he resists the rampant commodification of racialized representation that defines his corporate world. In this way, he marks difference upon the body in a way that moves beyond visual registers of race.

Whitehead's Invisible Man

The protagonist of *Apex Hides the Hurt* is African American, but his conspicuous evasion of racial markers suggests that he prefers not to have a racial identity at all. He seems to aspire to a kind of transcendent, postracial self that implies his blackness has had no bearing on his success. For most of the novel, the protagonist seems to be a man who deliberately avoids struggle, and, because race imposes the challenge of negotiating difference, he smoothly elides the topic. Although not entirely detached from the world around him, he tends to react to others rather than taking any initiative of his own. This passivity allows him to become defined by others, a consequence that is both a relief and a convenience. Opportunities appear before him, and he casually accepts them, as if no commitment is truly binding nor truly indicative of who he may be. If race is a choice to embrace the challenges of identity as Morrison contends, then Whitehead's protagonist is a passive chameleon who allows others to determine his racial identity.

At the start of the novel, he accepts a new job in his former capacity as a "nomenclature consultant," a fancy way of saying that he is in the business of naming things. However, due to a mysterious "misfortune" that later proves indicative of latent tensions, he has taken an extended sabbatical or an early retirement; he is too apathetic to decide which it is. Despite his almost complete seclusion from the outside world, he accepts the new job: "He was into names so they called him. He was available so he went" (8). Detached but obedient, the protagonist's default mode is to conform to the expectations of others. In this way, he has much in common with Ellison's Invisible Man; both nameless men sequester themselves from others and have only a vague connection to family and community. They are social climbers who excel at making others comfortable.

However, while the Invisible Man struggles to attain the trappings of white achievement—material gain, influence over others, and the approval of powerful, specifically white men—Whitehead's protagonist easily enters and succeeds in white-dominated institutions. This difference highlights the success of multicultural reforms of the late twentieth century, but, as the novel repeatedly insists, these changes do not herald a new age of equality. The protagonist of *Apex Hides the Hurt* attends Quincy, a prestigious university whose graduates "formed the steel core of many a powerful elite, in politics, business, wherever there were dark back rooms" (69) because their admissions department "reached out to him in his last year of high school." The protagonist does not choose Quincy; it chooses him. Despite this deliberate targeting, he claims, "What clinched it" was the fact that while at a weekend for prospective freshmen he had sex for the first time. Consequently, "the Quincy name now meant manhood" (70). The promise of manhood provides an important gender orientation to the school's mission and to the protagonist's own dream of himself. He can quietly avoid the role race has played in his selection of Quincy and instead believe that the achievement of a raceless manhood has determined his future. In this neat conflation of meaning, the protagonist forces a kind of color-blind perspective on himself such that his race becomes an invisible element in his life. If even he cannot see the effect of his blackness, then it must not exist at all.

Consistent with the triumph of multicultural liberalism, Quincy "believed in diversity" (70). Though it welcomes students from various backgrounds, Quincy does not itself change. Instead it produces students in its own rarefied image: "The sons and daughters of the working class attended and became prows to pulverize the swells of new middle-class oceans. The presidents of foreign countries sent their sons to be educated at Quincy and they returned double agents, articulating American and Quincian directives in their native tongues" (69). This emphasis on a shift in language again highlights how visual racial difference is far less important than the linguistic codes absorbed by "double agents." Quincy recruits students from a broad range of life experiences, before forming them into promoters of the school's righteous elitism, even as this transformation requires students to betray their origins. Like the school that the Invisible Man briefly attends, Quincy is dedicated to maintaining the status quo. For Dr. Bledsoe's warped college, this involves the perpetuation of white supremacy and black subservience. Quincy opposes such obvious racism, but it is only one of many models of racial integration in the novel that demonstrates the hypocrisy of superficial diversity efforts. The university illustrates what John Michael terms "liberalism's dream of universality" (12) in which universality is coded as elite, white, and male. The school flaunts its multicolored student body but remains an imperialist institution. The shift in the kind of racism evident in Quincy and the Invisible Man's college underscores how overt representation can mask abiding inequalities. Racial diversity appears to thrive at Quincy, but the "double agents" it produces reveal that any meaningful conception of racial difference has not simply become invisible but has been wholly erased.

The ease with which the protagonist is accepted into Quincy highlights his characteristic passivity and demonstrates how his race largely functions apart from his own agency. Although he is black, the description of his recruitment by Quincy, which occurs well into the novel, is the first definitive indication of the protagonist's racial identity. Prior to this passage, one of the only other hints regarding his race is provided in a scene in which he reflects upon his coworkers. Starting out as a nomenclature consultant, he assumes that he will not stay long at the job because he feels that he does not belong among the people around him: "He wasn't cut out for corporate life. He believed himself to be of a different caliber than those men. Jocky white guys. He didn't need the same things. The cheap posturing. The signature colognes. The obscure wafting. They scrambled and wanted to be heard by the men who wrote performance reviews and determined bonuses. They wore suspenders" (34).

The protagonist's characterization of his colleagues as "Jocky white guys" implies his own racial difference, but the ensuing description indicates that more than color is at work here. It is possible that he too is white and he simply does not share the preening ambition that characterizes his coworkers; they wear suspenders and distinctive colognes while he does not. Though the protagonist is black, this alone does not distinguish him from the others. Instead, he is separated by the fact that he "didn't need the same things," yet what he needs remains as unexpressed as his own race. His difference exists apart from simple distinctions of color. Its very inexpressibility almost seems to justify his avoidance of the topic altogether. While he elides race, he also does not mention other standard markers of identity—where he grew up, details about his family, childhood community, or significant influences in his life. This absence of self suggests that he may be even more invisible than the Invisible Man because he seems to be invisible to himself.

Such disturbing self-invisibility is accompanied by an advantage that largely eluded Ellison's protagonist. Unlike the Invisible Man, Whitehead's nomenclature consultant effortlessly fits in among affluent and ambitious white men. His quick ascendance through the ranks of his "identity firm" demonstrates his talent for naming, but more important is his ability to put others at ease, to repress difference and contribute to the conformist fraternity of his coworkers. Almost magically gifted at naming, the protagonist initially lets others take credit for his ideas. He knows that his rise through the firm will happen more smoothly if he does not quibble with others along the way. While the Invisible Man was always haunted by the puzzling advice of his grandfather, Whitehead's protagonist seems totally unencumbered by his past.

Although we might read the protagonist's anonymity as establishing a key parallel to Ellison's Invisible Man, it also reflects his own frustration with the ineffectual, often misleading nature of names. As a nomenclature consultant, he is keenly aware of how words fail to convey meaning and may even purposely deceive. During an awards ceremony to honor his lucrative achievements, he envisions a world in which we bear our true names. Gazing at his dinner companions: "He imagined that all of them had their true names written on their name tags. That would be something. That would be honest, he whispered to himself. LIAR. BED WETTER. . . . If everyone could see everyone's true name, we could cut out all this subterfuge and camouflage. . . . Of course it began at birth—by giving their children names, parents did their offspring the favor of teaching them how to lie with their very first breath. Because what we go by is rarely what makes us go" (170).

From this perspective, the protagonist's actual name is meaningless since it is not his "true name," only a lie given to him by his family. This belief in the existence of "true names" structures much of the protagonist's approach to the world. And yet, the labels he produces for others—"LIAR," "BED WETTER"—are crudely reductive, hardly capable of capturing any individual. These names conflate individual character flaws with truth, as if we are all best defined by our sins and weaknesses because they represent "what makes us go." This troubling formulation reflects the protagonist's own anxieties and the centrality of his latent guilt. His simplistic labels for others disprove the very notion of a "true name." Nonetheless, the text provides one of these labels for its protagonist: "FUGITIVE" (171). This is a name easily understood in the specific context that it is bestowed; just as he hears his name calling him to the front of the room to receive a prestigious award, he slips out the door and ultimately out of the profession that has brought him such success. He begins the novel as a fugitive from the business world, general society, his absent family, and even from himself.

However, we might also understand the protagonist as a fugitive from racial identity or at least from the language conventionally used to describe race. In this way, he emblematizes the fulfillment of a post-racial society; he is a man who has vacated race and consequently any means of identifying himself outside his professional associations since ties of family or community would necessarily bear a racial mark. However, in a calculated bit of pedantry, the protagonist frames his lack of racial identification as a linguistic problem, not one of presumably vexed personal relationships. He reflects upon the limitations of words to describe a concept as fluid and unsettled as racial identity. While reading the local librarian's history of Winthrop, he notes the antiquated references to race: "Colored, Negro, Afro-American, African American. She was a few iterations behind the times. Not that you could keep up, anyway. Every couple of years someone came up with something that got us an inch closer to the truth. Bit by bit we crept along. As if that thing we believed to be approaching actually existed" (192). This passage resonates strongly with Morrison's characterization of black literature as a destination that she approaches and eventually will attain. However, unlike Morrison, Whitehead implies that this final resting point of racial authenticity is no more than a fantasy.

Although each new word provides a more accurate description, ultimately no word can capture the nature of black identity. Tracking backward rather than forward into the more progressive "African American," the protagonist considers: "Before colored, slave. Before slave, free. And always somewhere, nigger."

The only stable signifier of black identity is its most pernicious iteration—"nigger," a word used less to define a racial group than to define the very boundaries of permissibility and otherness. Despite its lasting import, "nigger" is hardly the foundation of a new racial terminology. As the protagonists observes, this is a vocabulary yet to be discovered: "What was next? In the great procession. Because things never remain still for long. What will we call ourselves next, he wondered. If he knew what was next, he'd know who he would be" (192). Given the protagonist's marked isolation from others, it is striking that he invokes a collective pronoun here— "What will we call ourselves next." The next sentence shifts back to the singular as he anticipates the possibility of knowing "who he would be." The existence of a new term to define race offers the possibility of community for the protagonist, as if words might counter his puzzling alienation from others. The group's name will confer identity upon him as an individual, suggesting that the protagonist is nameless because his community lacks a proper name. Afro-American, African American, black—all of these labels are insufficient to allow him to know "who he would be." We may read this statement as a gesture toward a community that somehow operates beyond racial distinctions; all of these names are inadequate because they draw upon antiquated categories of color or ethnicity. However, we might also understand this observation as an indication that any group is too mutable to be contained by a label. The phrase, "Because things never remain still for long" can be interpreted as a commentary both on how words evolve and on how groups change. Either way, the phrase neglects the persistence of history; even as things in the present do not remain still, the past abides. This disregard of history is consistent with the protagonist's ambiguous origins and absent family. By focusing on what might come next, he erases the very progression that might lead him there. Regardless of how we read this passage, ultimately it underscores the fact that words will always fail to capture the complexity of who we are. Although Whitehead offers no answer to his provocative question, his novel shifts attention from words to other forms of communication and alternative ways of signifying difference.

Hiding the Hurt

Just as the protagonist easily enters Quincy, so he smoothly rises to success as a nomenclature consultant. He is initially hired at the unnamed identity firm in part because his interviewer is also a Quincy man "and it turned out the firm had been founded by Quincy men" (28–29). During his interview he is made to understand the importance of his alma mater, "The name meant something. He fit right in" (29). The protagonist certainly does "fit right in" at his new job, ascending quickly to the top of his field even as he develops a reputation for generosity among his coworkers. This suitability, however, is more a matter of masquerade than of genuine belonging. He knows how to adapt to his environment in such a way that his racial difference becomes irrelevant and thus hardly requires mention.

Though his clients believe him to have the power to create the signifier, a nearly mystical ability that he even likens to divine power, he is better understood as a master of camouflage. And for Whitehead's protagonist, camouflage is not a professional skill but a personal necessity. The observation that nomenclature consultants "try to give you a glimpse of your unattainable selves" (99) because advertising thrives on deceiving consumers is equally resonate in matters of social advancement. As a black man in white-dominated institutions, the protagonist has learned to present a self that others want and expect of him and to hide the rest. To clients and colleagues, he promises the opportunity to work with an innovative, highly successful leader in his field. Sheer skill trumps any regard to racial sensitivity. Much like Obama, the protagonist seems to ensure the promise of a color-blind meritocracy, a world in which racial difference does not matter.

However, following his "misfortune," his extraordinary talent has begun to erode. When he enters the bar where he will have his first meeting with members of the Winthrop town council, he "lost his balance" due to his amputated toe. Although no one sees his near stumble, when in conversation with Regina and Lucky, he struggles to project his familiar veneer of casual control: "He wondered, are they seeing the man I want them to see? That devil-may-care consultant of yore? His hand was a fist on the table. He imagined a wooden stick in his fist, and attached to the end of the stick was a mask of his face. He held the mask an inch in front of his face, and the expressions did not match" (18). This passage describes an important distinction that the protagonist observes between the "true" and the "right," a dichotomy he applies to the nature of names. The mask represents the "right" image to convey to his new clients—competent, composed, attentive—while his actual face reveals his "true" condition— desperate and unsettled, a fugitive who cannot escape. This difference reveals the fundamental task of a nomenclature consultant: to determine the right, not the true, name of an object: "A name that got to the heart of the thing—that would be miraculous. But he never got to the heart of the thing, he just slapped a bandage on it to keep the pus in. What is the word, he asked himself, for that elusive thing? It was on the tip of his tongue. What is the name for that which is always beyond our grasp? What do you call *that which escapes?*" (183).

As a nomenclature consultant, the protagonist is responsible for find- ing the "right name" for commercial products—a sleeping pill, a brand of toys, a new detergent, or style of diapers. He recognizes, however, that, although he has an exceptional talent to find the "right name," the "true name" (182) of things continues to elude him. The "right name" is that which will sell the most products, which will make material profit of words. This distinction between the demands of the market and the essence of objects and people makes his entire profession a sham. He is charged not with the job of naming things, but of misnaming them, of finding the label that will most resonate with the needs, real or manufactured, of con- sumers. The names he develops do not reflect upon the objects themselves but reveal the deliberate manipulation of the people who will buy and use them. As a result, he disrupts the conventionally understood relationship between signifier and signified. His names do not seek to represent objects in and of themselves, but aim to strategically position the products within the marketplace of consumer goods. His objective is not to name, but to sell. Lauren Berlant, elaborating on the purpose of advertising, highlights in particular the ways in which commodities are linked to the creation of national mythologies: "Advertising makes explicit the routes by which persons might individually and collectively give a name to their desire.

It does not tell the truth about desires that already exist, although it does not merely invent desires for people. But advertising helps bring to consciousness a will to happiness that transcends any particular advertisement or commodity, but which becomes authorized by them" (1997, 11).

The "will to happiness" at the heart of *Apex Hides the Hurt* involves a multiracial utopia that is represented by the protagonist's crowning success as a nomenclature consultant, the name "Apex," which he bestowed upon a type of adhesive bandage. Apex's winning innovation is to offer its product in a range of skin tones that match the diversity of its clientele. The slogan, "Apex Hides the Hurt," refers to the essential function of the product, but also resonates in the broader landscape of racialized America: "In the advertising, multicultural children skinned knees, revealing the blood beneath, the commonality of wound, they were all brothers now, and the multicultural bandages were affixed to red boo-boos. United in polychromatic harmony, in injury, with our individual differences respected, eventually all healed beneath Apex. Apex Hides the Hurt" (109). The Apex advertisements feature three nearly identical scenes in which a mother, standing in a "middle-class suburban kitchen," holds a dishrag. A small boy enters and announces, "I hurt." In the first scene the mother and son are white, in the next they are black, and in the final one they are Asian. The commercial concludes with "shots of the mothers holding their children's smiling heads to their aprons as the tagline manifested itself on screen and wafted through the speakers: Apex Hides the Hurt" (108).

The Apex ad campaign capitalizes on commonality while also appearing to accommodate difference. As in Quincy, diversity is showcased superficially, and integration means conforming to preexisting values. In the commercial, the specifically middle-class setting is home to all races, as if suburbia is the "apex" of human progress. The protagonist reflects, "Didn't history rise to a point? Couldn't they look down from today and survey all that had come before, all that little stuff we squinted at that was not special and so far away, and pronounce ourselves Apex?" (100). Despite this manufactured homogenization, the product rests upon its recognition of visual difference—human skin is not a pasty pink but instead a rainbow of hues. Unlike its competitors, Apex appreciates how people are not the same. And yet there is a dangerous implication to Apex's vision of the world that is apparent in its clever slogan. Apex promises to "hide" the hurt, not heal it. Adhesive bandages will do little to alleviate the hurt of the three boys, and yet their concluding smiles seem to erase the original wound. Like the commercial, the product works through camouflage and the deflection away from injury and its complications. It represses rather than recognizes trauma. There is a strong parallel here to how the protagonist deals with his own identity as he elides race in order to avoid the struggle of confronting difference. Although he did not actually create the product, the protagonist embodies its fundamental ideal.

The Apex commercial also demonstrates a key ideological approach to racial difference through its assumption that all little boys get hurt in the same way, and they all run home to the same housebound mother. We might understand this suburban utopia as another iteration of Morrison's renovated racist house. Though Apex appears to have dismantled oppressive hierarchies, racism determines the very architecture of this home. Here all families are structured identically despite their racial differences. They all prize male subjectivity, enjoy the same middle-class luxuries and are nurtured by the same caring matriarch. With its absent father, this vision offers an Oedipal dream as the son enjoys unobstructed access to his attentive mother. Most importantly, however, the commercial presents a kind of color-blind utopia that is clever enough not to be color-blind. Race is reduced to the variety of colors on an adhesive bandage, a difference neatly contained in a crayon box of skin tones. The repetition of the three scenes compartmentalizes racial difference as if intermingling between black, white, and Asian is, if not impossible, at least undesirable.

While the commercial appears to offer an egalitarian model of racial difference, only one version of family and community is offered. This suburban fantasy recalls the Dick and Jane story that begins Morrison's *The Bluest Eye* (1970): "Here is the house. It is green and white. It has a red door. It is very pretty. Here is the family. Mother, Father, Dick, and Jane live in the green-and-white house. They are very happy. . . . See Mother. Mother is very nice. Mother, will you play with Jane? Mother laughs. Laugh, Mother, laugh" (3). There is no need for Morrison to identify the racial identity of Jane and her family. It is a perfect example of "race-specific, race-free language." The familiar portrait she presents, derived in part from the popular 1940 stories by William Elson and William Gray, is obviously white. However, while Morrison explores in *The Bluest Eye* how applying this idealized version of American childhood destroys black families, in Whitehead's text this fantasy is seemingly available to members of all races—or at least to the sons who will inherit this noble world and the mothers who tend to them. The promise of a racial home is seemingly fulfilled by a neatly segregated vision of bourgeois mainstream America.

Nearly forty years of dramatic racial progress separate the publication of *The Bluest Eye* and *Apex Hides the Hurt*, but the marks of social success remain the same. In both novels, suburban plenty promises to protect the innocent, both the young and the willfully ignorant, as well as to vanish the nuisances of race. Miscegenation or interracial contact of any kind is too unsettling, too unpredictable to broach. The black and white families described in *The Bluest Eye* do not interact with one another, just as the Apex commercial draws firm boundaries between its racialized subjects. Significantly, Apex only offers different colored bandages in the same box for school nurses who are responsible for administering care in well-integrated schools, not for individual families. Those school nurses must tend to a diverse student body under the court mandate of *Brown v. The Board of Education*, implying that intrusive government intervention is to blame for the disruption of the commercial's tidy "separate but equal" vision.

The protagonist believes that the genius of the Apex product is its recognition that not only do "We come in colors," but "we want to see ourselves when we look down at ourselves, our arms and legs" (88). He reflects upon this novel approach to identity: "The great rainbow of our skins. It was a terrain so far uncharted. Pith helmets necessary. The fashioners of clear adhesive strips almost recognized this but didn't take the idea far enough. The world of the clear strip was raceless; it did not take into account that we sought ourselves, like sought like . . . The deep psychic wounds of history and the more recent gashes ripped by the present, all of these could be covered by this wonderful, unnamed multicultural adhesive bandage. It erased. Huzzah" (89–90). Although this vision promises a utopia for all, the reference to pith helmets, the favored headgear of European colonists, betrays its markedly Western bias. This undiscovered country requires a proper colonizing force to bring order to such expansive difference and the wounds incurred by inevitably violent contact. Multicolored Band-aids promise to cover up past injuries while still maintaining the integrity of racial difference, assuming of course that racial difference is only visual. These wounds are caused by "history," a vague evasion of the actual forces at work. But Apex is not interested in investigating causes or even healing the resultant wounds; the conflicted past must be made invisible. While the Invisible Man endured the chaos of inhabiting a surfeit of social projections, consumers of Apex are to adopt a single identity, one defined by unblemished skin and the complete absence of historical conflict. The Invisible Man suffered from the repression of his individual history, but the more insidious objective of Apex is to banish all "wounds of history." Because Apex directs its efforts at people of all races, it applies a type of invisibility upon everyone. It operates on the belief that "we sought ourselves," assuming that "ourselves" reside solely in skin color and not in the traumas that bandages cover. By conflating identity solely with pigmentation and erasing the marks of injury that profoundly shape who we are, Apex reduces race to our smooth external surfaces. As difference is made visible, it is also rendered meaningless. Apex deracinates its users precisely through the recognition of various skin tones.

The superficial success offered by Apex's vision of a multicultural utopia highlights what Wiegman terms "the integrationist aesthetic" prevalent in American discourse and advertising of the late twentieth century. She explains how this approach to diversity commodifies racial difference: "By securing the visible, epidermal iconography of difference to the commodity tableau of contemporary technologies, the integrationist aesthetic works by apprehending political equality as coterminous with representational presence, thereby undermining political analyses that pivot on the exclusion, silence or invisibility of various groups and their histories" (117). In its celebration of racial inclusion, Apex displaces historical wounds with the fetishization of our rainbow skin. The image of the three boys and their mothers all enjoying the bounty of suburban America suggests an equality that makes radical political and social change irrelevant. In Apex's world, all are free and happy. The "integrationist aesthetic" works to unite the national body not only into multiracial harmony but also into a mass of dependable consumers. Although the protagonist believes that Apex reveals our "commonality of wound," it ultimately exploits our commonality to buy.

Wiegman traces "the integrationist aesthetic" to America's long history of using skin color as a key feature of bodily commodification.

The marketplace success of Apex similarly capitalizes upon this obsession with visual difference. Wiegman explains: "Such a commodity status is not without irony in the broad historical scope of race in this country, where the literal commodification of the body under enslavement is now simulated in representational circuits that produce and exchange subjectivities through the visible presence of multicultural skin" (117). Once used as the indelible sign of bondage or freedom, skin color is coopted by Apex as the mark of egalitarian inclusion in the marketplace, thus occluding the far more pernicious opposition between producers and consumers. If, as Walter Benn Michaels argues, America's obsession with race distracts from more destructive and persistent inequalities of class, then Apex may be understood as flaunting diversity in order to exploit a larger consumer base.[6]

The vision of multiracial unity offered by Apex is ultimately a frightening dystopia because, as John Michael explains, "identity seems less like a sign of harmonious belonging than a site of contestation and of potential conflict" (*Identity and the Failure of America*, 12). This approach to identity as inherently unstable and evolving generates both dynamic exchange and possibly hostile opposition. It also underscores Morrison's celebration of language whose "force" and "felicity" lie "in its reach towards the ineffable." Identity like language thrives in shifting possibilities, in contradictions and unresolved tensions. The neat representation of middle-class contentment proffered by the Apex commercials occludes abiding histories and contemporary instances of oppression and inequality. Michael persuasively argues that recognition of identity must include more than the superficial appreciation of difference:

> In a discursive space deformed by discriminatory prejudices like racism, sexism, and class privilege, doing justice entails not ignoring the other's identity but recognizing what that identity demands in contexts where injustice and identity have been firmly linked. Identity, in these cases, represents both the possible fulfillment and the present failure of liberalism's dream of universality, the dangerous and necessary essence of America's national self-identity. . . . In the final analysis, these problems of justice and identity in the United States are neither abstract nor theoretical but concrete and practical, the residuum of a specific history of bigotry and exploitation.

The "dream of universality" so poignantly represented in the Apex ad campaign does gesture toward an important type of equality. In this way,
it presents a necessary fulfillment of America's most fundamental ideals,
but, as Michael observes, this vision is also "dangerous" because it threatens to erase difference and history, the twin foundations of existing social
dynamics. According to Michael, "The failure of America has been the failure to do justice to identities and the failure to adequately attend to the
demands those prescribed identities represent" (13). There is no justice in
Apex's "integrationist aesthetic." Instead what is required is the recognition of identity as more than skin-deep, an acknowledgment of difference
that while moored to human universality remains rich with contestation
and contradiction.

The Reach toward Apex

Despite the disturbing consequences of the Apex brand, the protagonist,
"like many citizens, found it near impossible to contradict the reasoning
of the multicultural bandage, which so efficiently permitted the illusion
of a time before the fall" (130). Apex suggests an Edenic paradise in which
everything is its own true name. Here race has no name but Apex because
all of humanity are the same, all are beloved and chosen by God. Apex as
product and ideal fulfills the vision of a true multicolored utopia. The protagonist links this fantasy to the innocence of childhood: "Isn't it great
when you're a kid and the whole world is full of anonymous things? . . .
Everything is bright and mysterious until you know what it is called and
then all the light goes out of it. All those flying gliding things are just *birds*.
And etc. Once we knew the name of it, how could we ever come to love it?
He told himself: What he had given to all those things had been the right
name, but never the true name. For things had true natures, and they hid
behind false names, beneath the skin we gave them" (182).

Race can be understood as among the "false names" because it is only
skin hiding the truth of our commonality; it is no more than an arbitrary
social signifier, unnecessary to understand the original condition of nature.
However, we can extrapolate from the protagonist's reflections further
conclusions about the very nature of language. Names disappoint him
because they corrupt the true essence of objects. By contrast, anonymity

secures mystery and possibility while names only limit and deceive. These observations betray a fundamental pessimism about the very ability of language to preserve the integrity of objects. In this formulation, every name—not only those used for commercial purposes—is false because every name is a gesture of containment rather than of liberation. We can understand this dilemma as well through the challenge of articulating difference, that is, the difficulty of allowing a single object or person to have several names. Wiegman expresses this crucial struggle as finding a way to allow "the possibility of difference to maintain its autonomy, the possibility for a *mutuality of difference* to stand as the fundamentally ethical relationship, a moment of kinship, if you will, that does not settle back into the body of the same" (*American Anatomies*, 131).

Morrison uses another story about paradise to highlight both the value and the challenge of articulating difference. In her Nobel Lecture she reconceives the story of the Tower of Babel as anticipating rather than foreclosing the creation of heaven.

> The conventional wisdom of the Tower of Babel story is that the collapse was a misfortune. That it was the distraction, or the weight of many languages that precipitated the tower's failed architecture. That one monolithic language would have expedited the building and heaven would have been reached. Whose heaven, she wonders? And what kind? Perhaps the achievement of Paradise was prema- ture, a little hasty if no one could take the time to understand other languages, other views, other narratives period. Had they, the heaven they imagined might have been found at their feet. Compli- cated, demanding, yes, but a view of heaven as life; not heaven as post-life. (202)

For Morrison, paradise must accommodate difference, must speak differ- ence. While Whitehead's protagonist imagines paradise as a place that is essentially devoid of language, Morrison understands such a place as static, a garden that, though it may teem with life, is dead of human inven- tion. She perceives language as essentially "generative" because "it makes meaning that secures our difference, our human difference—the way in which we are like no other life." Whitehead's protagonist by contrast under- stands language as always a deception, always a failed representation.

More important, Morrison's position does not inherently rebut this conclusion. By characterizing word work as a "reach," not a capture, she implies that there will always be a gap between the signifier and the signified. Rather than lament this "failure" she recognizes that words function best when they "signal deference to the uncapturability of [the] life" (203). Morrison and Whitehead's protagonist both acknowledge that the word "Blackness" does not capture blackness; while the former takes this break as a challenge, the latter accepts defeated silence on matters of race.

However, the tragedy of Whitehead's protagonist is ultimately not his pessimism about the possibilities of language. Instead, his tragedy lies in the fact that whether remembering his childhood adoration of when "the whole world is full of anonymous things" (182) or dutifully attending meetings at his identity firm or culling impressions of Winthrop along its streets, this is a man who is always alone. Morrison's conception of language assumes the presence of others, of people whose words make language the site of inscribed difference. She writes amid the failed architects of the Tower of Babel, none of whom speak her language. As Bakhtin observed, language is always a social construct, dependent upon the interaction between self and other.[7] But Whitehead's protagonist functions in such stark isolation from others that the only language he prizes is his own. He fundamentally believes that there is a "deep-down place where true names reside" (158). The notion that "true names" exist highlights the protagonist's conception of language as based upon singularity; there is only one signifier for each signified. Although he recognizes the attempts of others to produce such names, he is quick to disparage those he does not generate himself. Regarding the possible names for Winthrop, he admits that the name Freedom embarrasses him: "Freedom. My people, my people. Regina's forebears were the laziest namers he'd ever come across" (95). He determines that New Prospera while not "that bad a name" was certainly "no masterpiece" and signals less the "true name" of Winthrop than the fact that his former firm "still needed him" (52). Bound to the misguided belief that every object, every person has only one true name, he dooms himself to anonymity and isolation.

However, a key contextual difference separates the work of Whitehead's protagonist and that of Morrison. She states in her Nobel Lecture: "we do language. That may be the measure of our lives" (203). By contrast, the work of a nomenclature consultant is not to "do language" but to advertise commodities. As the protagonist reflects upon the man who invented multicolored adhesive bandages, he recognizes this conflation between object and market-oriented task: "When the consultant looked down at his arm, what did he see? Was the man his color, something else, was he flesh-colored? When the man looked down at his arm, did he observe business opportunities, an unexploited niche, an overlooked market, or something else? The man saw the same thing he saw. The job" (90).

Just as the inventor of the Apex bandage sees himself and sees the job, so the protagonist identifies himself as a commodity. For him, there is no distinction between objects and products or even between people and products. In a rare moment of empathetic connection, though significantly it is with the imagined figure of the Apex inventor, the protagonist establishes the barest measure of community through the identification of himself as a commodity. As Roger, his former boss, tells him in a bracingly honest exchange, "Wise up—you *are* the product" (146). If the protagonist truly is the product, then we might interpret the absence of his own name as his refusal to enter himself into the marketplace. This nominal form of resistance, however, reveals a greater lack—the protagonist's failure to develop relationships in which he is not the product. Roger and the Winthrop city council certainly have cause to view him primarily as a bought-and-sold commodity, but the protagonist maintains a wary distance from everyone he encounters. His isolation encourages him to prize only his language, a language steeped in the value of commodity exchange.

When the protagonist encounters someone in the novel who does not depend upon his professional services, he responds with scorn and detachment. The African American bartender at the Hotel Winthrop is the only other major character in the novel who remains nameless, although our nomenclature consultant cleverly nicknames him "Muttonchops" because of his impressive sideburns. Descended from the original town settlers, Muttonchops serves as a key counterpoint to the protagonist and stubbornly refuses to frame their relationship as an exchange of commodities. He always offers drinks on the house, even ignoring the tips the protagonist leaves on the bar. Muttonchops scoffs at the younger man's airy description of his job and maintains that regardless of what the city council decides, "This is Winthrop. Always will be Winthrop. Shit here never changes. You can change the name but you can't change the place. It stays the same" (26). This conviction in stability sharply contradicts the protagonist's privately held views that the limitations of names derive in part from the instability of their objects, but the protagonist, true to his mode of calm camouflage, does not challenge Muttonchops.

Muttonchops can be productively read as what Morrison identifies as an ancestral figure. In "Rootedness: The Ancestor as Foundation," she discusses a key quality of black literature: "There is always an elder there. And these ancestors are not just parents, they are sort of timeless people whose relationships to the characters are benevolent, instructive, and protective, and they provide a certain kind of wisdom." Morrison further observes: "the presence or absence of that figure determined the success or happiness of the character. It was the absence of an ancestor that was frightening, that was threatening, and it caused huge destruction and disarray in the work itself" (2289). Pilate from *Song of Solomon* (1977) is the most readily identifiable ancestor in Morrison's work. The ways in which various characters interact with Pilate provide key insight into how they understand their own blackness. Morrison explains that Hagar's depression and ultimate suicide stem from "how far removed she is from the experience of her ancestor" (2289). Although it is possible to be estranged from the ancestor and still be black, Morrison suggests that self-fulfillment is only possible through reconciliation with this central figure.

We may read the protagonist's testy relationship with Muttonchops as a sign of his own racial anxiety. Just as the Invisible Man struggles to understand his grandfather's advice, the protagonist cannot easily respond to Muttonchop's overtures. Uncomfortable with any interaction that is not based upon the familiar exchange of the marketplace, the protagonist is disarmed by Muttonchop's frank opinions and gruff demeanor. His rejection of an ancestral presence is also evident in his response to Regina Goode, the African American mayor of Winthrop. Over an intimate dinner, Regina explains her desire to rename the town Freedom as a way to honor its original settlers. She explicitly describes how an ancestral presence affects her everyday life:

Sometimes when I have a hard day and I'm too tired to leave the office and I just want to put my head on my desk, I think about how they got here. In their wagons, all that way from the plantations that had been their homes. Think about that: those places were their homes. Places of degradation and death. So I get my ass out of my office because I have a house that is my own and that's what they fought for, why they came all this way. They didn't know where they were headed when they started or that they'd end up here, all they knew was what they had: Freedom. Which was a kind of home that they carried inside them, if you think about it. When they finally arrived here and looked around, what was the word that came to their lips? What was the only thing they can think of when they see this place they have chosen? The word on their lips? (116–117)

The protagonist cannot bring himself to answer Regina's question. He is simply unable to engage in dialogue with someone who has such a powerful connection to community and racial identity. Regina is profoundly moved by the legacy of her ancestors; she understands how they determine both who she is and what she strives for in her daily life. By contrast, the protagonist has no corresponding source of support and identity. Instead, he listens to her as if to a stranger, entirely detached from what her words might mean for him. Prior to Regina's explanation for wanting to name the town Freedom, she describes her own difficult position in the town: "People look at me and they see what they want to see. Black people see me as family, because my name goes way back. The white people know what the Goode name means in this community—tradition, like Winthrop means tradition. And the new people know that I agree with a lot of what Lucky is trying to do" (114). Regina confronts the same battle against invisibility that haunted Ellison's narrator and now stymies Whitehead's protagonist. Here again is an opportunity to forge connection and community, to empathize in a common struggle and recognize himself as part of a shared racial group, but the protagonist remains silent, tending to his own private wounds.

Race as Wound

When Apex bandages are actually utilized in the novel, they fail spectacularly. At the height of his success as a nomenclature consultant, the protagonist stubs his toe. He dutifully applies a series of Apex bandages to his wound, noting that "had Apex been a little more poorly manufactured, it would have slipped off in the shower or in a sock and he would have been aware of the horrible transformation going on under there" (150). The deceptive quality of the product actually aggravates the wound, which, for unstated reasons, must be hidden from view. The fact that the use of Apex fosters its continued necessity demonstrates the product's market-driven logic. Healing wounds will not sell more adhesive bandages; rather, the consumer must always be left in a state of perpetual injury. We may also link this dynamic to the way in which racism thrives not by healing wounds but by exacerbating them. The imposition of a single identity, be it national or market driven, and the concealment of injury do little to heal the wounds of racial conflict. However, it is important to note that Apex bandages are applied to consumers of all races, and thus white subjects are also denied a vital means of recognition and reconciliation. Apex exploits everyone who uses it, demonstrating how racism negatively affects all people while advancing capitalist power.

Assuming that his toe is an unwelcome intrusion at work, the protagonist lets the wound fester rather than risk offending others: "His colleagues were out in the hall, or else he would have cleaned out the wound right then." Instead, "He put a new Apex on the injury. It looked good as new" (150). This veneer of health is, of course, a manufactured conceit, but in hiding the wound the bandage also forecloses discussion of why it must be hidden. What does exposure threaten? Will the wound horrify others? Will it mar the protagonist's reputation for cool control, revealing him as clumsy and inept? Regardless of the nature of his specific fear, exposure of the wound will manifest difference. It threatens to disrupt the protagonist's image of effortless belonging by bringing to light a very human vulnerability and marking him as traumatized.

The wounded toe is especially notable because it is both self-inflicted and seemingly beyond the protagonist's conscious control: "In the days following his accident he learned an astounding fact. Apparently the toe had been strangely magnetized by injury so that whenever there was something in the vicinity with stubbing polarity, his toe was immediately drawn to it. His toe found stub in all the wrong places, tables and chairs of course, but also against curbs, stools, against imperfections in the sidewalk that made him trip but left no visual evidence when he looked back, as passersby chortled" (139). The protagonist's toe is both moved by an invisible force and wounded by invisible obstacles. This emphasis on that which cannot be seen resonates with the dilemma confronted by Ellison's Invisible Man. However, unlike the Invisible Man, Whitehead's protagonist does not perceive himself to be invisible. He flourishes at work, enjoying the challenges posed by new unnamed products and the perks provided by his wealthy firm. Yet his renegade toe and its compulsion for trauma reveals unconscious realities, suggesting that in his twenty-first-century world racial difference has gone underground.

Both Ellison's and Whitehead's protagonists are made invisible by their blackness, but in significantly different ways. The former becomes the projected site of various racial fantasies that cause him to question his very existence.[8] By contrast, Whitehead's protagonist operates in the false utopia defined by the Apex brand where difference is rendered meaningless through its superficial recognition. He is black, but in his multiracial utopia of manufactured equality it makes no difference. His toe's willful search for invisible obstacles, however, suggests a latent desire for recognition of that which is not being perceived—namely, the consequences of his blackness. Ellison's protagonist retreats underground when he at last recognizes himself as invisible, but this epiphany is accompanied by the realization that though he "was through . . . [he] was whole" (571). This conclusion immediately precedes the epilogue, indicating that the Invisible Man's wholeness is the basis for his honest exploration of the past. His reflections ultimately lead him to recognize that he is partly responsible for his own invisibility.

The wounded toe of Whitehead's protagonist demonstrates that he is fundamentally not whole.[9] His far more guarded introspection indicates that unlike the Invisible Man, he has yet to understand how he contributes to his invisibility. Rather than label himself invisible, he first projects invisibility onto the obstacles that injure his toe and then directly onto the wound itself, demonstrating a striking dissociation from his own body: "When he stubbed his toe while stepping into the shower, a thin ribbon of blood snaked from beneath the Apex bandage for a few seconds and then disappeared into the drain. It was blood from an invisible wound" (139). Presumably, as he enters the shower, the protagonist is naked, save for the Apex bandage on his toe. He has progressed to the point that even he cannot bear to see the wound he once hid from his coworkers, a striking parallel to how he ignores his own racial identity. He is wrong to describe his wound as "invisible" because in fact he willfully refuses to see it. Despite his best efforts, he cannot shield himself from the blood that leaks from the bandage, a physical representation of the self he is losing by hiding behind Apex. While Ellison's protagonist confessed that in fostering aspects of his own invisibility he had also "discovered the advantages of being invisible" (5)—that is, the freedom of an unmoored, fluid self best exemplified by the figure of Rineheart—it is more difficult to understand the reasons that Whitehead's protagonist cultivates his "invisible wound." Although the Invisible Man's invisibility is ultimately destructive to his sense of self, it does not involve a self-inflicted physical injury. To understand the masochism involved with the protagonist's self-deception, we must investigate the critical relationship between trauma and race.

In *The Melancholy of Race*, Anne Anlin Cheng presents a conception of racial identity that is based upon constitutive loss. We may usefully consider the protagonist's wound as a sign of race that metaphorically demonstrates what Cheng calls "racial melancholia." She understands "racial identity as a melancholic formation" (24) that is based upon America's long history of exclusion and oppression of minority populations. Applying a psychoanalytic model of how grief functions, she explains: "Racialization in America may be said to operate through the institutional process of producing a dominant, standard, white national ideal, which is sustained by the exclusion-yet-retention of racialized others. The national topography of centrality and marginality legitimizes itself by retroactively positing the racial other as always Other and lost to the heart of the nation" (10). According to Cheng, race in America functions through Freud's conception of melancholia in which the lost object becomes pathologically incorporated into the ego. Racial identities are formulated through a process of loss and compensation in which the racial other is both rejected and retained, both mourned and resented. This creates a dynamic in which the excluded other operates as both a melancholic object for the hegemonic subject and a melancholic subject through the internalization of an impossible whiteness.

Cheng's analysis provides a critical means of understanding how racial identity functions for Whitehead's protagonist. She notes that racial melancholia "has always existed for raced subjects as a *sign* of rejection and as a psychic *strategy* in response to that rejection" (20). From this perspective, his wounded toe can be interpreted as an embodiment of his exclusion from white society as well as a desire to manifest his difference. The protagonist's wound is in part a consequence of his own masochism, but Cheng cautions us not to read his agency as a simplistic form of self-hatred, explaining the need to rethink "the term 'agency' in relation to forms of racial grief, to broaden the term beyond the assumption of a pure sovereign subject to other manifestations, forms, tonalities, and gradations of governance" (15). She elaborates upon this notion by observing that racial melancholia has dual components; it involves "the internalization of discipline and rejection—*and* the installation of a scripted context of perception" (17). The toe injury manifests the continual wounding of raced subjectivity as well as the impossibility for the protagonist to ever achieve psychic wholeness because of his othered racial identity. The protagonist hurts himself as a way to mark his difference, to manifest the wounded nature of his subjectivity.

The protagonist experiences his injured toe as an entity apart from his conscious self: "He decided his toe had developed an abuse pathology, and kept returning to the hurt as if one day it would place the pain in context, explain it. Give it a name" (139). This passage suggests that the reason for the toe's continued wounding lies in its own demand for recognition, for a name by which to identify it. Would such a name negate the pain? Or would the name be the pain, the trauma of his racial identity? Either way, the protagonist is wholly unequipped to name his pain. It is not a marketable commodity, nor a part of "the integrationist aesthetic" of the Apex utopia. Instead, to return to the protagonist's earlier reflections on "true names," his pain represents "*that which escapes*" (183). In the space between signifier and signified lies this unrelenting hurt. It represents the trauma of history and the divisions of race that the protagonist has assiduously repressed. This pain is the pain of his difference, of blackness that is neither contained by the word "blackness" nor recognized by the false utopia of Apex.

Due as much to the protagonist's own carelessness as to the ineffectual use of Apex bandages, his toe becomes infected and must ultimately be amputated. He literally loses a part of himself because of his delusions.

Horrified by the "Advanced State of Necrosis" that develops in his toe, the protagonist sheepishly explains to his doctor: "He hadn't even known anything was amiss down there, apart from the pain of the constant stubbing, which, truth be told, he had accepted as his lot and gotten used to after awhile. The doctor simply said, 'Apex,' shaking his head in morose recognition. 'There's a lot of that going around'" (200). The lesson is clear: a stick-on bandage will not fix anything. Hiding wounds actually creates a false sense of security while it obscures the development of damage. The doctor's final pronouncement likens the use of Apex to a type of disease, a flu that is "going around." Apex is no cure for even the most basic wounds, but, most important, its promise of middle-class harmony is no panacea for racial trauma.

Even after the toe with its inexpressible pain is removed from his body, it continues to leave a mark. The protagonist develops a limp despite the fact that, as his doctor explains, there is no medical reason for it. His limp acts as a compensatory balance to the objective of Apex bandages; while they hide the hurt, he performs pain and embodies lack. Although there is no referent to his hurt, it becomes the lasting mark of his identity. At the end of the novel, the protagonist recognizes the impossibility of finding a cure for his limp. He frees himself from the fantasy that "if he did something, took action, the hex might come off. The badness come undone. He thought, plainly speaking, that he'd lose the limp." Instead, he accepts the truth: "actually, his foot hurt more than ever" (212). If the text offers racial identity as a type of wound that is eventually covered up by assimilation into the American marketplace, then the protagonist's limp presents a type of racial difference that cannot be masked. It structures his very movement, resisting the invisibility that plagued Ellison's protagonist and forcing him into the high visibility against which Ellison warned. We may thus understand Whitehead's protagonist as the impossibly invisible man because his limp safeguards his difference from others.

Struggle

At the conclusion of *Apex Hides the Hurt*, the protagonist submits his decision to the city council and leaves the newly christened town of Struggle. His acceptance of the pain in his foot highlights his own communion with the notion of struggle. More important, however, his decision regarding the town's name signals the only interpersonal intimacy in the text: the protagonist's identification with Field, one of the original settler of Freedom. Through his study of Winthrop's history, the protagonist learns that the town was founded by two freed slaves, Abraham Goode and William Field. They were known as the Light and the Dark because as Regina explains, "Goode was the sunny-disposition guy and Field was the grumpy one" (95). When the town's name was changed from Freedom to Winthrop, Field was ill, unable to attend the deciding council vote. Unlike Goode who had a large family, Field arrived in Freedom alone, after losing all of his relatives to the hardships of slavery. This difference helps explain the original disagreement between the founders concerning the town's first name. While Goode recommended the name Freedom, Field offered Struggle. The townspeople voted with Goode. The protagonist reflects upon the difference between these two names: "Freedom was what they sought. Struggle was what they had lived through" (210). The two proposals for the town reflect the difference between the names of their originators: "Goode" and "Field." While one promises absolute righteousness, the other is open and ambivalent. "Field" suggests the expansive space of Morrison's sleepless woman while "Goode" echoes with the self-importance of Ruby's founders. Similarly, "Struggle" as both verb and noun captures the uneven development of home, recognizing the limits of what any word can signify.

The protagonist feels a deep kinship with Field's name for the town. He recognizes that Field sought not the "right name" but the "true name": "Field's area of expertise wasn't human nature, but the human condition. He understood the rules of the game, had learned them through the barb on the whip, and was not afraid to name them. Let lesser men try to tame the world by giving it a name that might cover the wound, or camouflage it. Hide the badness from view" (211). As a name, Struggle does the opposite of what Apex attempts. Rather than cover up the hardships and challenges that the settlers faced, it embraces them. It banishes the naïve construction of Eden or utopia by recognizing that even as a better place is made through the establishment of the town, this new community will not thrive by banishing history. Instead, Struggle emphasizes the necessity of both vigilance and diligence to create a meaningful home.

As the protagonist reflects upon Field's choice, he understands the fallacy of the Apex name. While once he might have voted for Apex as the town's name, he comes to recognize that the word presents a false image of human progress: "Apex was splendid, as far as it went. Human aspiration, the march of civilization, our hardscrabble striving. Brought it all under one big tent, gathered up all that great glorious stuff inside it. But he had to admit that Struggle got to the point with more finesse and wit. Was Struggle the highest point of human achievement? No. But it was the point past which we could not progress, and a summit in that way. Exactly the anti-apex, that peak we could never conquer, that defeated our ambitions despite the best routes, the heartiest guides, the right equipment" (210–211). Struggle is the name of the town, perhaps the true name of any town because it captures the essence of the human condition: "I was born in Struggle. I live in Struggle and come from Struggle. I work in Struggle. . . . I will die in Struggle" (211). The protagonist's decision to rename Winthrop Struggle indicates his deep affinity with Field. Although he leaves the Hotel Winthrop by flipping off Muttonchops, the protagonist has found in the town's original founder some semblance of an ancestor. Field reminds the protagonist that the very idea of an apex is a myth, that life does not reach a single point but limps onward, aware of pain and all its markings.

Whitehead names the racial house Morrison envisions "Struggle." It is defined not by the apex of a racial utopia but by the hard work necessary to achieve it. Obama offered a similar vision of the United States in his most famous speech, "A More Perfect Union," delivered in March 2008 as a direct rejoinder to the scandal surrounding his former pastor, the Reverend Jeremiah Wright. Beginning with the opening line of the Constitution, "We the people, in order to form a more perfect Union," Obama acknowledges the failures of our nation's founding document:

> Of course, the answer to the slavery question was already embedded within our Constitution—a Constitution that had at is very core the ideal of equal citizenship under the law; a Constitution that promised its people liberty, and justice, and a union that could be and should be perfected over time. And yet words on a parchment would not be enough to deliver slaves from bondage, or provide men and women of every color and creed their full rights and

> obligations as citizens of the United States. . . . I chose to run for the
> presidency at this moment in history because I believe deeply that
> we cannot solve the challenges of our time unless we solve them
> together—unless we perfect our union by understanding that we
> may have different stories, but we hold common hopes; that we may
> not look the same and we may not have come from the same place,
> but we all want to move in the same direction—towards a better
> future for of children and our grandchildren.

Obama's approach to the United States echoes with the same impassioned
reach of Morrison's language and Field's demand to honor the struggle of
creating a better home.[10] It identifies the essence of the nation not in its
founding ideals but in the work necessary to complete its promise. Like the
always failed names of Whitehead's nomenclature consultant, the "words
on a parchment" invoked by Obama are signifiers awaiting fulfillment, and
thus it is our responsibility to give them meaning. But whereas the protagonist of *Apex Hides the Hurt* laments the inherent deception of words,
Obama uses the promise of the Constitution as a guide toward a better
future. Our president seems to understand the necessity and beauty of
living in Struggle.

3

The Unspeakable Language of Race and Fantasy in the Stories of Jhumpa Lahiri

Part I of Obama's *Dreams from My Father* is largely dedicated to chronicling the difficulties of growing up black in Hawaii. With his mother in Indonesia conducting fieldwork for her dissertation, the adolescent Obama lived with his maternal grandparents. Though his grandfather introduced him to a number of older black men, including an insightful poet named Frank, our future president found himself alone in navigating the tensions and ambiguities of his racial identity.[1] Joining the long legacy of African Americans who, as Karla Holloway observes, "make their marks with a list of the books they have read" (*BookMarks*, 6), Obama turned to literature for guidance and wisdom:

> I gathered up books from the library—Baldwin, Ellison, Hughes, Wright, DuBois. At night I would close the door to my room, telling my grandparents I had homework to do, and there I would wrestle with words, locked in suddenly desperate argument, trying to reconcile the world as I'd found it with the terms of my birth. But there was no escape to be had. In every page of every book, in Bigger Thomas and invisible men, I kept finding the same anguish, the same doubt; a self-contempt that neither irony nor intellect seemed able to deflect. Even DuBois's learning and Baldwin's love and Langston's humor eventually succumbed to its corrosive force, each man finally forced to doubt art's redemptive power, each man finally forced to withdraw, one to Africa, one to Europe, one deeper

into the bowels of Harlem, but all of them in the same weary flight, all of them exhausted, bitter men, the devil at their heels. (85–86)

Obama seeks a reflection of his story and vision in works by some of the most important African American writers of the twentieth century. However, where Du Bois, Baldwin, and Hughes retreat into pessimism, fleeing from an ever-broken America, Obama longs for something more. Only the autobiography of Malcolm X offers some hope, for as Obama notes of the remarkably self-disciplined and charismatic Black Muslim, "His repeated acts of self-creation spoke to me." Although the future president admires Malcolm X's bold program for self-reform and social change, he remains troubled:

Even as I imagined myself following Malcolm's call, one line in the book stayed with me. He spoke of a wish he'd once had, the wish that the white blood that ran through him, there by an act of violence, might somehow be expunged. I knew that, for Malcolm, that wish would never be incidental. I knew as well that traveling down the road to self-respect my own white blood would never recede into mere abstraction. I was left to wonder what else I would be severing if and when I left my mother and my grandparents at some uncharted border. (86)

Malcolm X's wish to expunge his white blood is inconceivable for Obama who finds his greatest source of support in his mother and maternal grandparents. Their love for him as well as the limits of that love, most evident in their awkward but well-intentioned approach to racial issues, has no corollary in the books that he carefully studied.[2] Baldwin, Ellison, and Wright, like so many other pillars of the African American literary canon, delve deep into the nuances of black subjectivity but not into the complexities of biracial identity or the love of a black son for his white mother. Just as Obama does not relate to the pessimism of Hughes and Du Bois, he also does not find his particular struggles reflected in the writings of these masters. Biraciality figures in African American letters largely through variations on the theme of the tragic mulatta, the beautiful but forever-doomed archetype, or through "passing" narratives that implicitly deny the celebration of interracial intimacies.

Although the United States has long been figured as a "melting pot" of racial identities and various cultures, American literature has largely ignored the complexities of sexual and familial relationships that exist across racial lines. Depictions of interracial sex are certainly not absent from American texts, but few novels or even short stories explore the challenges of maintaining such committed intimate relationships. Fears of miscegenation haunt much of nineteenth- and twentieth-century American literature from Faulkner's alienated Joe Christmas to the Invisible Man's uneasy fascination with white women. In these and countless other narratives, interracial sex is the site of taboo desire and most often a metaphor for national anxieties about purity and independence. American writers comfortably portray intricate domestic dramas—the rich politics of the Dead family in Toni Morrison's *Song of Solomon* or the consequences of Rabbit Angstrom's selfishness upon his family in John Updike's series of novels—but rarely in such a way that brings individuals of different racial backgrounds in actual communion with one another.

Consistent with this trend, both Morrison and Whitehead approach close interracial relationships guardedly, even as they gesture toward the necessity of language that can broach racial divisions. They use "race-specific, race-free language" to create a degree of racial ambiguity in their works that frustrates any significant exploration of how sustained interracial intimacies operate. Morrison does not divulge the racial identity of key characters in *Paradise* and "Recitatif" while Whitehead's protagonist in *Apex Hides the Hurt* functions as a chameleon in most of his social interactions. These writers demonstrate how "race-specific, race-free language" encodes a type of intimacy that seems to make race not only irrelevant but also dangerously unspeakable. While Morrison avoids specifying race, Whitehead's protagonist avoids intimacy altogether. This strategy poses important questions about what race both signifies and fails to signify, but leaves unexplored what happens to the language of race in intimate encounters. How do lovers and family members of various racial backgrounds speak about difference? What does race mean in these circumstances? Can love simply transcend racial barriers? How does intimacy influence the language we use to represent race? These are only some of the questions Obama found unanswered in his study of African American writers.

Even as the depiction of interracial families and couples remains a neglected subject in African American literature, it is a subject sensitively depicted by South Asian American writer Jhumpa Lahiri. Unlike Morrison and Whitehead, Lahiri does not use "race-specific, race-free language" to encourage racial ambiguity. Instead, she codes race most often through cultural cues that are linked to identification with either India or the United States. To move beyond black/white relations and into identifications based on national and geographic origin suggests more permeable boundaries of identity that emphasize other kind of racial markers than strictly visual ones. It may seem incongruous to analyze texts by a South Asian American writer in a study largely concerned with African American works, but this shift is derived from two considerations. First, as previously mentioned, African American texts that examine familial and sexual relations across racial lines are glaringly absent. But more important, Lahiri's work demonstrates how race operates, according to Angela Oh's characterization, "beyond the black-white paradigm" (in Wu, *Yellow*, 34). Lahiri participates in the "new language" that Oh anticipates, a "race-specific, race-free language" that recognizes race not in binary terms of color but as an amalgamation of multiple social influences.

In Lahiri's stories "America" assumes a certain cultural orientation that is associated with values of individualism, freedom, and independence. Race continues to play a significant role in the constitution of identity, but its demarcations come to have specific cultural referents. Her stories focus on issues surrounding immigration, assimilation, and changing generational values. Even as specifically racialized language can be elided, this gap produces noticeable silences and, much like the case of Twyla and Roberta, an inability to speak about difference. Lahiri's "race-specific, race-free language" implies that race need not divide individuals, yet the characters in her stories are often devoid of the vocabulary necessary to express their differences from one another. Although Lahiri's characters have clear ethnic identities (many are specifically identified as Bengali), they rarely speak about race; instead, they assume an intimacy that seems to transcend difference. However, their unstated racial identities and the racialized associations they impose upon others fundamentally structure how they relate to one another. Kumiko Nemoto observes, "Power dynamics in relationships can be generated by projection and exchanges of racialized images, even though such acts can be mutual" (*Racing Romance*, 4). These complications are especially evident in Lahiri's exploration of the intersection between fantasy and actual sexual encounters with a racial other. Sex is among the most intimate acts of human connection, and yet Lahiri's characters repeatedly fail to find a language that expresses how race influences and in some cases even determines these dynamics.

Lahiri's three works of fiction do not focus primarily upon the particular difficulties and personal insights produced by interracial sexual relationships. They are notable, however, for confronting such dynamics in all their complexity rather than merely thematizing interracial attraction as a form of escape or self-hatred. Lahiri does not rehearse simplistic binaries between mysterious Indians and colonizing Europeans or make interracial encounters the site of national allegories. Rather, she examines the very foundations of erotic infatuation and how differences in culture and race become projections of other needs and desires. While race may seem almost incidental to many of Lahiri's characters, it takes on special resonance in her depiction of interracial sexual relationships. The once invisible influence of race becomes paramount as these characters construct one another through sexual fantasies dependent on racial constructions.

Fantasy acts as the most obvious representation of otherwise submerged racial dynamics in Lahiri's stories. However, she often represents sexual fantasies, like specifically racialized language, as taboo, unspeakable to others. Both are somehow too crude, too obviously determined by external constructions. Fantasy provides a striking corollary to "race-specific, race-free language" by insisting on the coded nature of sexual seduction and revealing desire through indirection. Moreover, both require partners with attentive reading practices. In *The Namesake* (2003), Gogol's relationship with white, upper-class Maxine fails not because they cannot name their racial difference but because they cannot express the small foibles that accumulate into lasting barriers. The persistent silences surrounding both race and fantasy in Lahiri's stories significantly impair the possibility of meaningful exchange between individuals of different backgrounds. Nemoto reminds us that interrogating these silences may lead to more meaningful forms of intimacy: "Examining racialized desires and the outcomes of these desires may not lead to the instant correction of racial inequality, but it may lead to an awareness of the ways in which racial ideologies interact, along with gender, class, and nation, with one's psyche and emotions, and thus are deeply tied to one's conformity to structural inequality" (*Racing Romance*, 7–8).

In the three short stories I discuss here, "Sexy," "Hell-Heaven," and "A Choice of Accommodations," Lahiri demonstrates how personal crises concerning identity and community are mapped onto interracial sexual dynamics. It is important to note that all the encounters described in these stories involve a South Asian man and a white woman. This particular pairing catalyzes specific sexual fantasies—the unattainable white woman and the mysterious South Asian man—that Lahiri explores in various contexts from a torrid affair to a committed marriage. Despite the limitations of this single dynamic, the stories include the perspective of both white and South Asian Americans, suggesting that fantasies of the sexually alluring other animate the imagination of both racial groups. "Sexy," "Hell-Heaven," and "A Choice of Accommodations" are united not only by their focus on interracial relationships but also by how they link such encounters with sexual taboos including adultery, female dominance, and homosexuality. These taboos reflect the malleability of the sexualized racial other as it becomes a body open to transgressions of all kinds. Addressing these projections is paramount to develop a language that might reconcile race and intimacy. To transform sexual fantasies from a site of unspeakable desires into a shared reality requires forms of expression that both occlude and elucidate the play of pleasure. Like "race-specific, race-free language," this is a language of paradox, uniting deliberate obfuscation and stark intimacy.

Silent "Sexy" Fantasies

In "Sexy," a story from Lahiri's first book *The Interpreter of Maladies* (1999), Miranda, a twenty-two-year-old white woman has an affair with Dev, a South Asian man. The cultural identity of the latter is made explicit when Miranda notes that Dev is Bengali, and initially she "thought it was a religion." Miranda's ignorance establishes the basic dynamic of their relationship. Although Dev shows her where Bengal is located on a map of India, when she asks for details, he taps her on the head and tells her it is "nothing you'll ever need to worry about" (84); their relationship is to take place in a world of fantasy, not in real locations. Dev discards the map when he leaves her apartment, but Miranda later retrieves it from the trash and stares at the borders of Bengal, "thinking the whole while about Dev, about how only fifteen minutes ago he'd propped her feet on top of his shoulders, and pressed her knees to her chest, and told her that he couldn't get enough of her" (85). Miranda's inability to merge the physicality of her relationship with Dev with the geography of India highlights the absence of language that might bridge the gap between their bodies and their social identities. Their relationship, conducted with little dialogue, develops instead as a series of starkly physical encounters. Although Miranda is not the narrator, the story is mediated through her perspective, and the significant absence of verbal language between Dev and her highlights a dynamic free not of race but of intimate recognition. Their relationship in fact depends upon silence because silence encourages fantasies of all kinds.

Following the passage involving Miranda's mistaken understanding of Dev's identity, she is described as having "skin pale as paper" (87), explicitly defining her as white. In general, there is little to distinguish Miranda; she seems to have no defining experiences or relationships and exhibits little passion for work or activities of any kind. However, as with Dev, Lahiri emphasizes Miranda's relationship to her place of origin as the most salient aspect of her identity. This focus on place contextualizes the racial difference between them while also emphasizing their shared sense of geographic exile. Miranda has moved to Boston specifically because she knew no one in the city, and this detail about her willingness to leave her midwestern home strongly impresses Dev. Although "Miranda told him it was nothing to admire . . . he shook his head" and replied, "I know what it's like to be lonely" (89). Dev's comment suggests that he interprets her choice to move to Boston as an act with tragic consequences. Although her move might also be understood as a remarkable demonstration of personal initiative and courage, Dev projects his own experience of solitude onto Miranda's life, ignoring her distinct circumstances: while Miranda chose to leave her family, Dev was sent to college in New York by his parents during the Indian Emergency of 1975. Instead of listening to her story by asking about the reasons behind her decision or learning about her relationship with her family, Dev hears his own story, one defined by loneliness. This type of narcissistic inversion is typical of the exchanges between Miranda and Dev. They encounter one another not as specific individuals but as a series of projections that reflect their own selves as well as their personal cultural prejudices.

Despite Dev's subjective understanding of her move to Boston, Miranda derives great comfort from his comment: "at that moment Miranda felt that he understood her—understood how she felt some nights on the T, after seeing a movie on her own, or going to a bookstore to read magazines, or having drinks with Laxmi, who always had to meet her husband at Alewife station in an hour or two" (89). Significantly, Miranda does not express to Dev any of these feelings of loneliness or the scenes in her life that have generated them. Her assumption that Dev understands her is a fabrication, a fantasy built upon her own need for companionship. While Ava Tettenborn argues that their "relationship is tainted from the very beginning" because "Miranda perceives Dev only within the realm of a colonial fantasy and frames his identity in terms of racist stereotypes" ("Jhumpa Lihiri's *Interpreter of Maladies*," 11), the passage quoted above suggests that Miranda's image of Dev fundamentally depends upon her desire to be understood through a common experience of solitude. By believing that he understands her loneliness, Miranda identifies herself apart from whiteness; she assumes a kind of post-racial affinity with Dev that is both imaginary and inexpressible. The unspeakable nature of her fantasy of intimacy parallels her inability to speak about the racial difference between them.

Dev's comment, "I know what it's like to be lonely," indicates his own hope to share his experience of loneliness. Tettenborn is correct to argue that the allure of the racial other plays a significant role in this relationship. However, that sexual dynamic is established upon an original experience of alienation and the seemingly remarkable discovery that loneliness is a cross-cultural experience. Dev and Miranda understand themselves as outsiders within their own families and communities. Miranda is geographically isolated from her family, and her only close friend, Laxmi, a South Asian coworker who regales her with stories about her extended family, is notably not white. Although Lahiri provides little detail about Dev's personal life, his aggressive approach in initiating the affair with Miranda suggests that he is not especially close to his wife. Both Miranda and Dev may be understood as exiles from their families and immediate social environments. However, they do not share their specific experiences of alienation and solitude with one another. The only commonality that might provide their relationship with significant personal connection and meaning is left unexplored.

This failure of communication is underscored by Dev's and Miranda's inability to name the differences between them. In one of their few dialogues, Dev tells Miranda: "'You're the first,' he told her, admiring her from the bed. 'The first woman I've known with legs this long'" (89). Dev's repetition of "you're the first" implies a degree of hesitation about his next comment, as if he were about to disclose a more substantial confession. More likely, he was at the cusp of admitting that Miranda is the first white woman he has had sex with, but instead he opts for a more trivial observation, emphasizing the length of her legs. This physical attribute elides the racial difference between them just as Dev's sly reference to "woman I've known" masks the sexual nature of their relationship. At no point do Miranda and Dev openly confront their vast cultural differences and the prejudices they engender. As bell hooks observes of interracial sexual relationships: "Mutual recognition of racism, its impact both on those who are dominated and those who dominate, is the only standpoint that makes possible an encounter between races that is not based on denial and fantasy" ("'Eating the Other,'" 429). Miranda's and Dev's affair becomes structured precisely through these twin and at times paradoxical elements: denial of their cultural differences and the fantasies these differences encode. In their case, "mutual recognition of racism" would require an examination of how their past experiences with the racial other have influenced their current perceptions as well as how prevailing stereotypes impact their understanding of one another.

Significantly, Miranda does not tell Dev about her first encounter with an Indian family, the Dixits who lived near her childhood home. The Dixits are tolerated in the neighborhood, but their unconventional behavior, such as Mr. Dixit's evening jog in his everyday clothes and their failure to follow the lawn practices of others, elicits both mockery and scorn. Miranda remembers attending a birthday party for the Dixit girl where she was too terrified by a picture of the goddess Kali to eat her cake: "It was a painting of a naked woman with a red face shaped like a knight's shield. She had enormous white eyes that tilted toward her temples, and mere dots for pupils. Two circles, with the same dots at their centers, indicated her breasts. In one hand she brandished a dagger. With one foot she crushed a struggling man on the ground. Around her body was a necklace composed of bleeding heads, strung together like a popcorn chain. She stuck her tongue out at Miranda" (96). Miranda's sense that Kali is sticking her tongue out specifically at her indicates how she immediately inserts herself into an alien image, ignoring even the possibility of a social context outside her own reference. Moreover, she presumes that this cultural other is hostile and rejecting. Like Dev listening to her describe her move to Boston and assuming contiguity between their experiences, Miranda believes that Kali responds directly to her, despite having no foundation to understand what she sees. This approach assumes the centrality of her Western experience and makes Kali's bold stance all the more terrifying to Miranda. What does an image of such obvious female sexual dominance mean to the young girl? Will she be one of Kali's victims or a rival to the goddess's power? Paralyzed and, more important, rendered speechless by the picture, Miranda is unable to reconcile its implications with the birthday cake she is served; Kali makes even the familiar repugnant.

While the memory "shamed her now" as an adult, Miranda compensates for her guilt not by admitting that shame but by replacing the frightening picture of Kali with more appealing though equally clichéd images of Indian culture: "Now, when she and Dev made love, Miranda closed her eyes and saw deserts and elephants, and marble pavilions floating on lakes beneath a full moon" (96). The disturbing image of Kali and her rejection of the Dixits are effectively banished by more appealing sexual fantasies that she fully embraces. In this way, Miranda transforms her perception of South Asian culture; no longer the site of troubling gender roles, it becomes a reassuring background to her affair with Dev. She adopts a largely passive sexual role with Dev that in its rejection of the threatening image of Kali reifies standard conceptions of white femininity. In this safe fantasy, she can even imagine visiting the Taj Mahal with Dev, thus maintaining a semblance of cultural inclusion even as she remains woefully ignorant of the irony of this dream; the Taj Mahal is an icon of marital devotion. Nonetheless, the specter of transgressive sexuality, embodied by Kali, remains.

The taboo of female sexual dominance is sublimated by the lesser crime of heterosexual adultery.

Miranda's relationship with Dev can be understood as a response to her early trauma of encountering the image of Kali. We may even interpret this formative memory as a type of primal scene that establishes Miranda's sexual development. The primal scene is most often understood as the moment in which a child witnesses sex between his or her parents, inducing the process of ego differentiation and recognition of sexual difference. Miranda, who within the confines of the story has no parents just as she has no firm personal identity, first experiences herself as a sexual being when Kali appears to stick out her tongue at her. Miranda is profoundly shaken by what she perceives to be a threatening and hostile image. The scene combines sexual aggression with a menacing racial other and leaves Miranda uncertain as to the nature of her own sexual and racial identity. Her relationship with Dev effectively banishes this experience by replacing it with familiar if ultimately destructive romantic fantasies. Notably, the experience with Kali, like her hackneyed fantasies of visiting India with Dev, remains unexpressed. All these experiences, both real and imagined, with South Asian culture operate as invisible but potent forces in her relationship to Dev, making racial difference unspeakable and intimacy impossible.

As Tettenborn argues, Miranda certainly is guilty of imposing a specifically "colonial fantasy" upon her relationship with Dev. However, I want to stress that the silence between the two lovers fosters her fanciful projections and prevents her from understanding South Asian culture as anything more than a series of polarizing sexual images. Dev does little to help Miranda understand his cultural background and, rather than encouraging her curiosity, he bars her from any meaningful engagement with his Bengali identity. This is not to suggest that he is solely at fault for Miranda's skewed understanding of South Asian culture; instead, they are each responsible for misguided conceptions of one another. Their relationship does not encourage the type of intimate exchange much less hooks's "mutual recognition of racism" that would lead Miranda to share her childhood encounter with the picture of Kali or even her dreams of elephants and pavilions. The language of fantasy, in tandem with the language of race, remains unexpressed even as fantasy and racial difference largely motivate their affair. The story does not provide any description of how Dev imagines Miranda, but his obsessive phone calls, including a daily message he leaves on her home phone at 5:30 P.M. so that "she could hear his voice as soon as she walked through the door" (88) and other extravagant gestures suggest that he is living out a private fantasy of his own. Silence is imperative to preserve the racially marked images they have each developed of one another. This seeming race neutrality ensures that they will remain mutual exiles, homeless in individual temporary fantasies.

Although Miranda's interest in South Asian culture is genuine and perhaps the only means by which she might be dispelled of her Orientalist fantasies, it also points to an emptiness in her own life, underscored by her conspicuous lack of family and community. Consequently, she looks to Dev to provide her with a unique and defining identity. Their first encounter highlights Dev's allure for Miranda. They eye one another at a department store makeup counter where Dev is buying beauty supplies for his wife and Miranda is trying out a new face cream. While Miranda seeks to change her image cosmetically, Dev is clearly anchored to a stable social network, though, importantly, this community will always remain invisible to his soon to be lover. As Miranda walks away, Dev matches his step with hers and tells her, "Part of your name is Indian" (87). He explains that he has an aunt named Mira, but nothing about Miranda is Indian. She is an otherwise nondescript woman who quickly latches on to Dev's overtures. His comment about her name suggests that by finding some secret Indian part of her self, Miranda may escape her unremarkable personal history and find in Dev a defining adult persona. hooks elaborates on the dangers of understanding interracial sex as a gateway to personal transformation: "sexual agency expressed within the context of racialized sexual encounter is a conversion experience that alters one's place and participation in contemporary cultural politics. The seductive promise of this encounter is that it will counter the terrorizing force of the *status quo* that makes identity fixed, static, a condition of containment and death" ("'Eating the Other,'" 425).

hooks's comments allow us to understand Miranda's numerous attempts to learn about South Asian culture as a quest to discover a new, more interesting self, perhaps even an escape from whiteness and the absence associated with her origins. In a bookstore, she studies the Bengali alphabet, and "once she went so far as to try to transcribe the Indian part of her name, 'Mira,' into her Filofax." She struggles to copy the letters correctly and ultimately is not even sure "if she'd written Mira or Mara" (97). Miranda's attempt to identify her name in Bengali, a botched translation of both signifier and signified, demonstrates her utter disorientation in this new field of meaning. She lacks the reading practices necessary to make sense of Dev's racial identity and its impact on their relationship. Moreover, by shortening her name to "Mira," Miranda loses a part of her name, yet she ignores this loss entirely. Perhaps due to her sparse personal history, she does not realize that to adopt a Bengali persona is to sacrifice some essential part of herself. However, her efforts prove largely ineffectual. She is unable to remember the Bengali phrases printed at the bottom of the menu of an Indian restaurant and when she eyes bags of Hot Mix at an Indian grocery she is told by the storeowner that such snacks are "too spicy for you" (99). Like Dev, the male storeowner objectifies Miranda, ogling her body as she wanders through the store. Here and even in intimate moments with Dev, Miranda is prevented from accessing South Asian culture in any meaningful way. Miranda's affair with Dev is not an encounter with Bengali life, but instead underscores her complete alienation from it. Miranda does not even tell Laxmi about the relationship, assuming an objective position while Laxmi describes the ongoing drama about her cousin's adulterous husband. Miranda here has an opportunity to relate fully to Laxmi's family dilemma, but she remains silent as if there is no language to bridge the divide between her reality and the lives of the South Asians around her.

While Miranda may be unable to find the part of herself that is Indian, her relationship with Dev does provide her with another kind of identity. At the Mapparium, Dev whispers that she is "sexy" (91), and this attention to her sexual allure comes to define their relationship. Shaped like the inside of a globe, the Mapparium might help the couple recognize the geographical differences that separate them, but instead they revel in the sensation that "they were standing in the center of the world" (90). Dev's comment seems to give Miranda definition, even a sense of geography, as she becomes rooted not by a place but by his sexual attention. Dev is the first person to call out her name when they have intercourse and to dote upon the peculiarities of her body; he notices, for example, that her legs are longer than her torso. Significantly, the only questions he asks about her personal life concern her sexual history—how many lovers she has had and when she first had sex. Despite these objectifying questions, Miranda revels in his attention. Dev's focus on her sexuality implies that she represents for him another kind of "colonial fantasy"—the untouchable white woman he now fully possesses. Miranda's complete lack of awareness of how such cultural constructions influence his interaction with her indicate that like her child-self looking at the picture of Kali, Miranda believes she alone generates Dev's response. Just as she had no context by which to understand Kali's imposing posture, she, as well as readers, is unable to decode the social history at work in Dev's visceral passion for her. Lahiri's decision not to provide such details about Dev underscores the imbalance of how he and Miranda relate to one another and the impossibility of establishing real intimacy between them.

While readers cannot discern the full nature of Dev's fantasies because the story is framed from Miranda's perspective, she creates an alternative persona for herself based on their relationship. She responds to the return of Dev's wife from India by going on a shopping spree in the basement of Filene's where she buys "herself things she thought a mistress should have" (92). This is the same department store in which Miranda first met Dev, but now she has been literally relegated underground to continue their affair. Among the items that Miranda buys are a pair of black high heels, a satin slip with a knee-length silk robe, sheer stockings with a seam, and a cocktail dress made of slinky silvery material. Dev does not notice the robe when he next sees Miranda as he rushes into her apartment dressed in running clothes and has sex with her immediately and wordlessly. This rough encounter exemplifies the true dynamic of their relationship: sex without intimacy, physicality shorn even of language. This is adultery without the glamour of transgression. Miranda buries the lingerie in her dresser while the dress remains on the floor of her closet, too fragile to stay on its metal hanger. As Dev's mistress, she is certainly a sex object, but he deprives her of any allure associated with this role. Dev is interested in her sex, but not in her sexual identity or any personal identity Miranda may possess. Her self-imposed fantasy as the sexy, sophisticated mistress collapses, exposing the grim physical reality of their affair. For Dev, Miranda is no more than a naked body. Although loneliness may have been the only genuine point of connection between them, it remains the final legacy Dev bequeaths to his mistress.

Miranda's affair with Dev is paralleled by the news she receives from her coworker Laxmi, a married woman whose cousin recently learned that her husband has fallen in love with an English woman. Laxmi's updates on her cousin emphasize the illegitimacy of interracial relationships though it is important to note that consistent with its seemingly unspeakable nature race is never stated as a contributing factor to the affair. Both Miranda's relationship with Dev and that between the English woman and Laxmi's cousin's husband affirm interracial sexual union as adulterous and destabilizing to South Asian families. This simplistic conclusion, however, forces comparison between two relationships that are remarkably different. While Miranda and Dev relish one another physically, Laxmi reports that the affair of her cousin's husband began on an airplane when "he'd had a conversation that had changed his life, and . . . he needed time to figure things out" (83). This unvoiced and unexplored conversation offers the promise that an interracial language of intimacy may exist. However, Lahiri's failure to describe this crucial exchange occludes how such language reconciles fantasies of sex and race. Such genuine interracial connection remains unspeakable.

This unreported conversation has significant consequences as Laxmi later states that her cousin's husband left his family in Montreal to live with the English woman in London. Such commitment is unimaginable for Dev who refuses to spend the whole night at Miranda's apartment so that he can return home for his wife's daily phone call from India. These differences emphasize the complexity at work in any relationship, interracial or otherwise, and warn against generalizing about the ways in which individuals both construct and experience intimacy. The juxtaposition of the affair involving the husband of Laxmi's cousin and Miranda's relationship with Dev underscores the absence of meaningful language to speak about the intersection of race, culture, and intimacy. Lahiri poses these two related affairs as possible stand-ins for one another, but the dynamics of each indicate that they are not interchangeable reflections.

In the final encounter of the story, Miranda babysits Rohin, Laxmi's nephew, while Laxmi takes her cousin out for a relaxing day of spa treatments. Rohin, who is described as "something of a genius" (84), speaks four languages and is training himself to memorize the capitals of all of the countries in the world. The boy's geographical and linguistic knowledge contrasts sharply with Miranda's ignorance of the world and her limited travel experience. Again racial difference is represented not as physical difference but as involving contrasting fields of geographic expertise. Rohin has all the knowledge that Miranda craves, a discrepancy emphasizing just how alien she is from Dev and his worldly lifestyle. Despite this key difference, the two also have significant similarities. Rohin is just as desperate for attention and validation as Miranda, suggesting the immaturity of the latter's need for an externally imposed identity. Rohin demands that Miranda serve him a cup of coffee when he sees her mug, and he follows her throughout the apartment, even joining her in the bathroom. Like Miranda, Rohin seeks an other to supply him with new activities and consequently a firmer sense of self. He mimics Miranda's attempt to forge a stable identity through her relationship with Dev. Both are also fundamentally displaced by the interracial liaisons in their lives; while Rohin is physically separated from his parents due to his father's affair, Miranda ultimately discovers that she will never penetrate Dev's identity. Miranda bonds with Rohin in a way that mirrors her relationship to Dev. In both cases, connection is formed through mutual alienation, that is, through an awareness of their shared sense of exile.

Rohin asks Miranda to draw the things in her living room so that he can memorize them. When she asks why he wants to remember everything, he replies, "Because we're never going to see each other, ever again" (104). While this comment makes Miranda feel slightly depressed, Rohin appears unmoved by his conclusion. He understands that their interaction is transient; they are from separate worlds, separate races, and there is no hope for a long-term exchange between them. Miranda has yet to recognize this simple truth, unaware that Rohin's ties to family and culture, much like those of Dev, require the boy as well as her lover to live apart from women such as Miranda. Perhaps due to this new epiphany Miranda agrees to wear the silver cocktail dress when Rohin finds it in her closet and asks that she put it on. Because Dev never saw it, this is Miranda's first opportunity to wear the dress in front of someone else. Her dream of acting as a glamorous mistress is at last fulfilled, but, with only Rohin as her audience, Miranda's fantasy is exposed as no more than a childish dress-up game.

Upon seeing her outfitted with the stockings and high heels, Rohin proclaims, "You're sexy" (107). This is the very phrase that Dev uttered to Miranda across the Mapparium, a moment she understood as intimate and defining. Now she must recognize that this description is generic and obvious, the comment of a child she hardly knows, not the studied, caring observation of a lover. Language that should be intimate instead proves to be trite and childish. Miranda's fleeting relationship with Rohin mimics that with Dev, although only the boy was frank enough to recognize that their encounter would not last beyond the afternoon. She demands that Rohin explain what "sexy" means and he sheepishly states, "It means loving someone you don't know" (107). Rohin here articulates the damning truth of Dev and Miranda's "race-specific, race-free language" by highlighting the impossibility of knowing someone who is defined only by sex. "Sexy" refers to the one who is not known, and it was this absence of intimacy that acted as the foundation of Miranda's relationship with Dev. Their union was always premised upon the fantasy of the erotic other, a fantasy dependent upon alienation and silence.

However, Rohin's understanding of the word "sexy" implies that he has real affection for Miranda; despite not knowing her, he loves her. Though we may understand this love simply through the attractive image she presents in her cocktail dress, Rohin's comment emphasizes a type of love that might emerge from a basis of mystery, an encounter premised upon an original experience of difference and alienation. While Miranda and Dev both fantasize that they understand their mutual experiences of loneliness, they fail to acknowledge how their cultural and racial differences necessarily impose barriers between them. Rohin's comment suggests that these barriers do not preclude love, but they do require recognition. By never expressing how this alienation operated, Miranda and Dev indulge in fantasies far removed from the person they were actually encountering.

The Fantasy of American Freedom: "Hell-Heaven"

The interracial relationship in "Hell-Heaven" also operates from an adulterous premise, although in this story there is no actual sexual betrayal. The narrator, Usha, describes her mother Aparna's unstated love for family friend Pranab who eventually marries Deborah, a white woman from a wealthy family. Both Pranab and Usha are guilty of betraying their loyalty to Aparna as they become enamored with Deborah's privileged and carefree American lifestyle. Their dual infatuations with Deborah demonstrate how the racial other can act as the site of cultural fantasies about assimilation, revealing more about the personal conflicts of the lover than the beloved. Because the story is narrated by Usha, her attraction to Deborah is given more explication, but we may infer from the parallel established between Pranab and her that he also conceives of Deborah as an escape from South Asian social customs. Moreover, both Usha and Pranab have vexed relationships with Aparna; Usha longs to be free of her mother's traditional ways while Pranab is unable to act upon the love he feels for his married friend.

As in "Sexy," Lahiri again elides specifically racialized language, instead focusing on marks of national origin. Deborah is introduced as "an American" (67) and though later Usha admires her "brass-colored hair" (68), "American" clearly codes as white. The absence of race-specific language in "Hell-Heaven" highlights the permeability of difference. Though Usha cannot become white, from her mother's perspective, she is certainly in danger of becoming American, a type of intermediary identity that emphasizes behavioral practices and linguistic codes over visual marks of difference. Usha is continually warned not to marry an American. Her ultimate betrayal lies not in her homoerotic infatuation with Deborah but in her adoption of an American identity defined by her willingness to engage in interracial sexual relationships. However, Aparna's adulterous love for Pranab provides a point of empathy for the heartache of Usha's later affairs with Americans. Although all of the interracial relationships of "Hell-Heaven" fail, the intimacy Usha at last achieves with her mother demonstrates a meaningful cross-cultural exchange rooted in storytelling. While "Sexy" exposes the fantasies that breed in the absence of shared life histories, "Hell-Heaven" suggests that only by knowing the stories of others can race and social differences be confronted. By shifting focus away from interracial sexual relationships to the conflict between a South Asian woman and her daughter, Lahiri implies that the foundation for meaningful interracial intimacies begins with open communication within individual families.

Usha admits that she "fell in love with Deborah, the way young girls often fall in love with women who are not their mothers," finding in Deborah a beauty and freedom that is antithetical to her mother's cloistered and rigid lifestyle. While Aparna dresses Usha in long dresses and insists that she clips her hair back in a barrette, Deborah wears wrap skirts and lets her long hair loose. Deborah comes to represent the promise of a new American life. She and Usha speak "freely in English" which the latter notes was "a language in which . . . I expressed myself more easily than Bengali, which I was required to speak at home" (69). This new fluency threatens Usha's association with her family's Bengali cultural practices, for as her language changes so also does her racial identification change. She comes to recognize her own displacement in Deborah's uneasy interaction with the South Asian community. Referring to Deborah, Usha explains, "I felt protective of her, aware that she was unwanted, that she was resented, aware of the nasty things people said" (70). Usha never mentions how she is treated due to her own racial difference, but her sensitivity to the hostility surrounding Deborah implies a history of quiet alienation, presumably from both her Bengali and American worlds. Like Dev and Miranda in "Sexy," Usha does not have the language to speak about her difference, but instead she projects her loneliness upon a racial other. This manufactured intimacy flourishes in Usha's silent admiration of Deborah.

While Usha remains the obedient daughter of Aparna, Pranab is able to act upon his infatuation with Deborah. Usha, observing a freedom between the couple that parallels the basis of her own love for Deborah, comments, "Their open affection for each other, their easily expressed happiness, was a new and romantic thing to me" (70). Pranab begins dating Deborah after spending his first months in Boston primarily in the company of Aparna and Usha. Noting the special intimacy between Pranab and her mother, Usha observes, "he was totally dependent on her, needing her for those months in a way my father never did in the whole history of their marriage" (67). However, Aparna's married status makes union between them impossible—no more than a fantasy. Always accompanied by Usha, Pranab and Aparna discover that "they had in common all the things she and my father did not: a love of music, film, leftist politics, poetry" (64). Usha characterizes their relationship in terms of shared interests, a striking contrast to the physical contact she admires between Pranab and Deborah. This difference suggests that the open affection of the interracial couple presents no more than a facade of intimacy particularly because Pranab seems not to discuss Deborah with anyone. He has neither language nor trusted confidante with whom to speak of this new relationship.

When Pranab begins dating Deborah, Usha immediately understands her as a replacement for Aparna, and the two women become opposing figures for Usha who quickly prefers the attractive American: "the more my mother began to resent Deborah's visits, the more I began to anticipate them" (69). Aparna and Deborah represent opposite cultural practices— the strict, tradition-bound Bengali mother versus the carefree American. But there is also a striking homoerotic undertone to Usha's feelings toward Deborah: "Countless photographs were taken of me and Deborah, of me sitting on Deborah's lap, holding her hand, kissing on the cheek. We exchanged what I believed were secret smiles, and in those moments I felt that she understood me better than anyone else in the world" (70). Usha's sense of deep intimacy between Deborah and her parallels Miranda's initial feeling that more than anyone Dev understood the depth of her loneliness. Both these moments are fantasies, however, internally produced intimacies without actual relation to the other person involved. Just as Miranda makes Dev into what she most desires, Usha constructs Deborah as her secret soulmate.

Usha's affection for Deborah also parallels Miranda's attraction to Dev in that it too emerges from a fundamental crisis of identity and an absence of empathetic peers. Miranda and Usha are attracted to Dev and Deborah respectively because their own families and communities do not provide the support and understanding they need. They recognize themselves as outsiders and thus seek validation and intimate contact with someone apart from their cultural upbringing. For Usha, this fascination with Deborah is fundamentally linked to her desire to assimilate into American culture and her growing irritation with her mother. She believes Deborah understands her better than Aparna because Usha does not identify herself with Bengali traditions and social attitudes. Deborah symbolizes American culture and its promise of freedom, but as a symbol she is devoid of human depth. Like Miranda with Dev, Usha does not confide in Deborah;

in "Hell-Heaven," as in "Sexy," the relationship with the adored racial other is characterized by silence. Both stories conflate transgressive sexuality and fabricated intimacy, suggesting an absence of genuinely close relationships among the characters as well as a need to fill such a void through interracial sex. Usha wants Deborah to offer the solace and guidance that her mother cannot provide in her distinctly American world. By imagining Deborah and her as both physically and emotionally intimate, Usha creates an impossible fantasy that is safely expressed only because it is focused upon unattainable Deborah.

Although Usha's feelings toward Deborah express lesbian desire, such a coupling is rendered impossible not only because of their age difference but also because the latter is engaged to Pranab. Nonetheless Usha's homosexual attraction to Deborah again situates interracial relationships as a site of taboo fantasy. Because Deborah exists outside the tight-knit Bengali community that includes Usha's family, she becomes an easy target for the projection of forbidden passions. Moreover, we might understand Usha's homoerotic and interracial attraction to Deborah as deeply connected, for, as Judith Butler notes, both desires "converge at and as the constitutive outside of a normative heterosexuality that is at once the regulation of a racially pure reproduction" (*Bodies that Matter*, 167). Usha's desire for Deborah represents a radical break from expectations of race and sexual practice. However, this escape from prescribed categories of identity remains unspeakable, too unsettling to even be fully imagined.

After twenty-three years of marriage, Pranab and Deborah get divorced. Significantly, it is not Deborah who instigates the separation but Pranab "who had strayed, falling in love with a married Bengali woman, destroying two families in the process" (81). The identity of Pranab's lover suggests that he always harbored unfulfilled longings for Aparna and that the pull toward his cultural origin was ultimately stronger than the American life represented by Deborah. In this way, his marriage to Deborah may be understood as adulterous or at least as no more than a distraction from his far deeper commitment to Aparna. Like Dev's dalliance with Miranda, Pranab was only experimenting with an interracial liaison when in fact his true loyalty remained with Aparna and the South Asian community. The dissolution of Pranab's marriage provides cautionary insight into Usha's own attraction toward Deborah as it implies that her girlhood crush was only a response to Aparna's overbearing love. Both Usha and Pranab seek out Deborah because they cannot reconcile themselves with the roles Aparna has set for them. Usha refuses to be an obedient Bengali daughter while Pranab cannot remain a platonic family friend. From this perspective, Deborah becomes a false object of desire whose power derives from the reactionary force Aparna inspires.

In a surprise turn, following the divorce Deborah seeks support from Aparna, calling her to help make sense of Pranab's betrayal. Usha notes the remarkable similarity between Deborah and her mother: "Their hearts had been broken by the same man, only my mother's had long ago mended" (81). The conversations between the two women offer the most meaningful interracial intimacy of the story. They serve to demystify Pranab's marriage as Deborah admits that "she had felt hopelessly shut out" of a part of her husband's life. Deborah also confesses her abiding insecurities to Aparna: "I was so horribly jealous of you back then, for knowing him, understanding him in a way I never could" (82). Though she encouraged him to maintain friendships with other Bengalis and even make peace with his parents who were outraged by his relationship with Deborah, Pranab resisted such efforts until he at last pursued an affair with his married Bengali lover. Deborah's attempts to reunite Pranab with his parents expose the fantasy of individual freedom Usha projected onto Deborah. There is no simplistic opposition between familial commitment and American identity; Deborah in all her Americanness worked to strengthen, not undermine, Pranab's ties to his South Asian family.

Despite the obvious similarities between Deborah and Aparna, the latter does not share the story of own heartache. Devastated by Pranab's marriage, Aparna prepared herself to commit sati, the South Asian practice of self-immolation by widows on their husband's funeral pyre. This action suggests that she understood herself to be Pranab's wife; in her fantasy, the two are married, and thus sati is an appropriate cultural response to express her grief. Although Aparna doused herself in lighter fluid and carefully pinned her sari to her underclothes so that it could not be easily removed, she did not go through with her suicide. Much like Miranda's botched attempt to write her name in Bengali, Aparna's sati indicates how misguided translations of language and culture fail to make sexual fantasies real. She is not Pranab's wife, nor is he dead, and the customs of another world do not provide meaning or solace in her American reality. Significantly, Aparna is saved by neither her daughter nor her husband, but by a neighbor, the American Mrs. Holcomb, who comes out to rake the leaves in her yard and comments to Aparna on the beautiful sunset. The casual, friendly gesture returns Aparna to her immediate reality and the responsibilities she has to her family. In this American world, there is no place for sati, no place for a fantasy of herself as a grieving widow.

Aparna confesses her aborted suicide only to her adult daughter who at last strikes some balance between her American and South Asian identities. Usha concludes the story by describing the peace she has made with her mother who "had accepted the fact that I was not only her daughter but a child of America as well. Slowly, she accepted that I dated one American man, and then another, and then yet another, that I slept with them, and even that I lived with one though we were not married. She welcomed my boyfriends into our home and when things didn't work out she told me I would find someone better" (81–82). Usha describes her identity as a "child of America" with respect to her sexual practices; she dates and sleeps with American men, and even lives with one out of wedlock. These are the key qualities that separate her from her mother. By framing her Americanness as a function of her sexuality, Usha makes her marginally trangressive sexual behavior the ultimate signifier of her separation from her South Asian roots. As "a child of America," Usha may be understood here as adopting a new racialized identity. She is becoming American in the ways once represented by Deborah, and, unlike Pranab, she may not return to her South Asian origins.

Due to Usha's history of failed relationships and one heartbreak in particular, Aparna tells her daughter how she nearly committed suicide following Pranab's marriage. By admitting her anguish over Pranab and expressing her fantasy to be his widow, Aparna attempts to empathize with her daughter's once taboo encounters with American men. Her tragic vision of herself as a grieving widow acts as the critical link to her daughter's interracial intimacies. As she gives voice to her fantasy, she finds commonality with Usha through their lasting heartache. Only through the shared pain of mother and daughter is a new language of intimate connection borne, one that depends upon the articulation of fantasy and illicit desire. By relating their stories to one another, they find a deeper bond that is cross-cultural if not cross-racial. This critical connection also implies that Pranab's marriage failed in part because he lacked such supportive networks, or he lacked more specifically a language within his family in which to speak of his love for Deborah. However, even as Lahiri leaves readers with the hopeful exchange between mother and daughter, other silences remain. Aparna never shares her story with Deborah or her husband, and Usha's earlier homoerotic attachment remains unexplored. These limitations expose barriers that are rooted not solely in distinctions of race but attest to persistent anxieties of gender and sexuality. The work of intimacy is hardly race-specific.

Making Fantasy Real: "A Choice of Accommodations"

The failed romantic relationships depicted in "Sexy" and "Hell-Heaven" might suggest that Lahiri is critical of the possibility of sustaining interracial love, but as Robin E. Field notes in his study of depictions of arranged and independently chosen marriages in *Interpreter of Maladies* and *The Namesake*, "Lahiri portrays both types of marriage in her fiction but ultimately privileges neither" ("Writing the Second Generation," 172). The demise of the interracial relationships analyzed here underscores the danger of mistaking desire for intimacy and projecting personal identity crises upon a cultural other. Lahiri appears less invested in demonstrating the impossibility of interracial relationships than in highlighting the unique challenges that they pose and the need for a language that communicates racial difference without making it a totalizing dynamic. "A Choice of Accommodations," from her most recent collection of stories, again explores the complexities of developing love across racial lines and provides the most hopeful portrait of marriage between a white and South Asian American. Once again adultery figures as an attendant trope to interracial relationships, but Lahiri interrogates the very foundation of erotic fantasy to discover an alternative to the false images of the racial other presented in "Sexy" and "Hell-Heaven."

As in "Hell-Heaven," no actual sexual transgression is committed in "A Choice of Accommodations," but the threat of adulterous exchange haunts the entire story. Amit and Megan leave their two young daughters to attend the marriage of Amit's adolescent friend Pam whom Amit describes

as "the most beautiful woman he had ever known" (103). Amit and Megan
have a committed though vaguely uneasy marriage that is marked by silence
and miscommunication. Most notably, Amit has failed to tell Megan about
his former love for Pam: "He had loved her, it was true, but because she'd
never been his girlfriend there had been nothing to explain" (88). His
logical but glaringly insufficient reasoning emphasizes the communication gap between them that is reiterated throughout the text in small,
telling exchanges. Amit must remind Megan that the wedding is to be held
at Langford, his former boarding school, and when she tells him of a burn
on her skirt, he wonders if Megan deliberately damaged her clothes to prevent them from going. Regarding his relationship with Pam, Amit believes
there is "nothing to explain" because he and Pam never had a physical
relationship and they never formally dated. His adherence to conventional
definitions of courtship belies his genuine heartache over his first real
love. As in "Sexy" and "Hell-Heaven" where failures of language generate
resentment and miscommunication, Amit does not speak about Pam to
his wife because their past relationship is not easily categorized. While
Miranda fails to fulfill the role of mistress and Usha cannot name her
homoerotic attraction to Deborah, Amit remains mute on the topic of
Pam. All three characters cannot name the terms of a defining interracial
relationship in part because they are unable to determine what role race
plays in these taboo dynamics. Moreover, for Amit to speak of Pam would
require him to admit his failure to woo and seduce her. What is most
unspeakable and, for Amit, even unnameable, is Pam's lack of interest in
him. It signifies his undesirability and the possibility that he is nobody's
fantasy.

Amit's silence concerning Pam is consistent with much of his misguided sense of intimacy. Rather than stay at Langford with the other wedding guests, Amit books a room at the Chadwick Inn, a pricey local hotel
that proves to be far less charming than expected. His attempt to create an
ideal weekend getaway for himself and Megan collapses once they enter
the disappointing lobby. This failure betrays his submerged guilt for taking
his wife to the wedding of someone he hardly keeps in touch with. Amit
recognizes "that on some level he had dragged her here, to an unfamiliar
place full of unfamiliar people, to a piece of his past that had nothing to do
with the life he and Megan shared" (88). Although Amit has left behind his

past at Langford (he does not keep in touch with former classmates and "had no nostalgia for the school" (86)), the memory of Pam continues to have a profound influence upon him. Though Megan has little sense of what Pam once meant to her husband, she puts up with his desires, trusting him despite his notable silence.

Amit's failure to connect his manufactured romantic getaway with Pam's wedding establishes the key opposition of the text, the difference between fantasy and reality. Pam is the ever beautiful and glamorous figure of his adolescent dreams while Megan defines the pragmatic reality of raising two daughters and paying a Manhattan mortgage. It is important to note that both of these women are white, which suggests that the difference between Amit's fantasy and reality is not solely defined by the allure of the racial other versus the Bengali wife his parents hoped he would marry. In fact, a Bengali wife would not necessarily constitute a familiar choice for Amit, who was born and raised in Massachusetts and is later sent to Langford when his parents move to India. Rather, the choice of a Bengali wife represents what his parents desire for him, not what is culturally relevant to Amit's life. He realizes that Megan is a disappointment to them, but, having endured the isolation of Langford, even as an adult "he refused to forgive them" (97).

The only South Asian student at the prestigious all-boys school, Amit does not tell anyone that he "was crippled with homesickness, missing his parents to the point where tears often filled his eyes, in those first months, without warning" (97). In effect, Amit is orphaned by his parents and consequently does not develop any meaningful loyalty or even identification with his cultural heritage. When he visits his parents, he stays at their house in New Delhi where he can hardly use his rudimentary Bengali and misses his relatives in Calcutta. Racially, Amit is Asian, but socially he is American. Like Usha, he has no peers with whom to share his experience, making him a cultural exile from both India and the United States. Although Amit resents his forcible move to Langford it is here that he meets Pam, the daughter of the headmaster. While at Langford, Amit "and all the other boys were in love with Pam" who was "the only girl on campus, the only girl, it had felt back then, in the world" (98). Amit and Pam become close as college students at Columbia though notably Pam initiates their relationship: "Suddenly, because she had decided so, they were friends"; then she defines the terms of their interaction, "He'd wondered at first if it was romantic but quickly realized that she was involved in affairs, that he was just a friend" (99).

Amit's passivity reflects his muffled outrage at being separated from his family and underscores his desire to find a new identity among his peers. Like Miranda, Amit looks to a racial other to provide himself with definition, but the largely white world of elite educational institutions is all he knows. Amit's desire for Pam underscores both his resentment at his parents and the immediate reality of his upbringing. However, rejection of his Bengali heritage is, essential to his later attraction to Megan whose face he admires as belonging to someone "living in a previous era, a simpler time, in an America that was oblivious to India altogether" (92–93). Amit's vision of a "simpler" America is as deluded and naive as Miranda's fantasies of elephants and floating pavilions. Both seek escape in false cultural images that conveniently disregard their own vexed origins. Even more than Pam, Megan represents a complete disavowal of Amit's cultural background and the expectations decreed by his parents' impressive careers. The youngest of five children, Megan worked two jobs after graduating from high school, eventually becoming a doctor while Amit dropped out of medical school. However, the allure of difference also shapes Megan's desire for Amit as he reflects, "were he not Indian, Megan would have probably avoided someone like him" (95). Amit's ability to separate himself from his Indian identity highlights his tenuous relationship to his cultural heritage. The "someone like him" is a person defined by the privilege of his elite education, not by his race. For both Amit and Megan, race was a significant factor in their initial attraction to one another, and yet this influence remains unacknowledged or at least unstated. Such racialized motives seem too crude to be mentioned even as they structure many of the couple's ensuing difficulties.

Amit's return to Langford for Pam's wedding does not represent a homecoming, but only emphasizes his prior alienation from the school, its inhabitants, and, most important, from Pam. He misidentifies a former classmate and is somewhat troubled by Pam's new husband, an older divorcee with children of his own. Amit's alienation from Pam parallels the more profound distance that has developed between Megan and him. When asked about the shift from having one child to two, Amit tells his dinner companion, "Actually, it was after the second that our marriage sort of . . . disappeared" (113–114). He subsequently realizes "there were times Amit felt as alone as he had first been at Langford" (114). Amit characterizes his entrance into "the world of parenting" as "exotic" (113) as if it were a foreign country. He rather mournfully describes the physical appearance of his children: "His daughters looked nothing like him, nothing like his family, and in spite of the distance Amit felt from his parents, this fact bothered him, that his mother and father had passed down nothing, physically, to his children. . . . They appeared fully American" (94). As with Usha's use of this term at the end of "Hell-Heaven," "American" can be understood as an occlusion of racial difference, but it likewise signals Amit's recognition that unlike his children he is not "fully American." Though born and raised in the United States, Amit identifies himself as something else. He never names that identification; his closest articulation of identity is expressed in the ambiguous characterization "someone like him." This failure of language underscores the multiple layers of Amit's racial and cultural difference from others: his alienation from his parents, his adolescence among the educated elite, his status as the only South Asian at Langford, and the absence of a stable community of any kind in his life.

Amit's ambivalence about his heritage and identity is not only projected onto his children but also frames his relationship with his wife. He is both attracted to a woman who represents the possibility of a world that exists without India and resents his failure to pass along a more substantial inheritance to his children. Like Miranda, Amit seeks definition externally and assumes a largely passive position in his relationships with others. Although Miranda could easily assume a submissive role in her affair with Dev, such a quality in a man is destabilizing. For example, Amit is haunted by the memory of his infant daughter choking on a piece of fruit. Despite his previous medical training, he was paralyzed by this simple emergency. The incident breeds nightmare scenarios in which "he saw himself surviving, the girls perishing under his supervision. Megan would blame him, naturally, and then she would divorce him, and all of it, his life with her and the girls, would end. A brief glance in the wrong direction, he knew, could toss his existence over a cliff" (91). Amit's fears reveal his fundamental insecurity concerning his relationship with

Megan as well as his own tenuous sense of self. For Amit there is an essential fragility to his family; it is ever vulnerable to catastrophe precipitated by his passivity and inadvertent neglect. The question that strangers pose to him when he is out with his daughters "Are they yours?" (94) characterizes the estrangement that Amit feels from his family. He does not belong, and thus he must be undesirable, even unworthy of those around him. Although Pam immediately asks about his daughters when she sees Amit at the wedding, he must admit that they have been left behind with their maternal grandparents. His children fit into neither the fantasy Amit has of Pam nor the fantasy of his alienated adolescence at Langford. His botched attempt to call the girls on the night of the wedding exposes his inability to establish a language that can meaningfully include them.

After passing out at the hotel in his futile search for the phone number of his in-laws, Amit awakens in the late morning to find Megan on the balcony of the hotel room having fulfilled her promise to stay up all night though she admits that "the sunrise wasn't visible today" (119). Amit's dream of a romantic weekend has collapsed, but Megan has at least made her fantasy real. The simplicity of her dream as well as its lack of a racialized component presents a striking contrast to Amit's inflated expectations. Before heading home, the two return to Langford in search of the wedding brunch. They arrive too late, and, as they wait for the rain to stop, they linger in a dorm room. Megan observes, "You know we should have just stayed here," noting that they would have saved money and she would have been spared the worry of his disappearance. Amit accepts the blame, "My fault for trying to have a romantic getaway" to which Megan replies, "But this is so much more romantic" (124). Megan's comment indicates that the richest fantasy lies not in the manufactured getaway of a weekend escape in an expensive hotel. Rather, the most romantic setting involves their own personal histories, the unfulfilled longings of youth that have come to structure their adult desires. In this way, the fantasy of Langford supplants all the artificial erotic visions apparent in Lahiri's stories. Miranda dreams of elephants and pavilions, creating a reality that is entirely removed from Dev's actual life; while she fantasizes about the Taj Mahal, he does not even bother to accompany his wife back to India. Pranab believes he can find lasting union with Deborah when in fact he is inexorably bound to his original love for Aparna who grew up in the same North Calcutta neighborhood of his youth. In "Sexy" and "Hell-Heaven" the exotic other is figured as no more than a mirage occluding the personal histories that animate our most basic desires. While "Hell-Heaven" may be read as evidence that true love is found only in a return to one's cultural community, "A Choice of Accommodations" indicates that the roots of romantic attachment are determined by childhood encounters that can be interracial.

Consequently, it is in the truly romantic dorm room that Amit and Megan can at last speak directly about Pam, for, as they discover, their sexual fulfillment depends upon intimate discourse. Megan begins by asking Amit, "Was it in a room like this that you had sex for the first time?" (124). Amit admits that he did not, and Megan pushes him further by asking about Pam, "Did you ever have sex with her?" Amit replies, "It was nothing, Meg. We were friends and for a while I had a crush on her. But nothing happened. Is that so terrible?" (125). Amit's relationship with Pam was "nothing" because they never dated, but, while there was no realization of his love for her, Pam became a powerful force of erotic fantasy. Amit does not verbally admit this to Megan, but he then closes the window blinds and kneeling on the floor, he presses his face against her jeans. With Amit now assuming an active, even aggressive role, the two have sex despite Megan's protest, "We can't do this here. . . . It's a dorm room, Amit. Kids live here" (126). Goaded by the excitement of getting caught, they both climax, and "for a few moments they remained together on the narrow bed in the little room, his heart beating rapidly, vigorously, plainly striking the skin of her palm" (127). The emphasis on the small space they occupy through reference to the "narrow bed" and the "little room" highlights the fragility of this union between fantasy and reality. In a story filled with missed connections and miscommunications, Amit and Megan at last find intimacy in the real world of Amit's past. Though cramped and unglamorous, the dorm room is charged with Amit's former love of Pam, but by having sex with Megan here Amit shares his history and perhaps deepest erotic fantasy with his wife. They make the unspeakable real.

Race and the Impurity of Love

Lahiri's stories suggest that all interracial sexual encounters must contend with fantasies associated with the racial other, for, as Nemoto contends, attraction and passion are bound to "a person's craving for certain social and cultural powers." As such, "intimacy is a cultural and social device of self-making" that reflects how "power and identity are constituted by race, class, and gender" (1). If the significations of race affect even our most personal interactions and impulses, how are love and genuine intimacy to develop? Do pervasive stereotypes inevitably mar interracial relationships by feeding sexual fantasies?

Obama certainly seemed to think so when as a young man he reflected upon the courtship between his white mother and Kenyan father. Obama's parents divorced when he was only a child. After Obama Sr. won a scholarship to pursue a Ph.D. at Harvard, Obama's mother, decided to remain in Hawaii where she raised her young son with the help of her parents. Throughout his childhood and adolescence, Obama had only intermittent contact with his father, who eventually moved back to Kenya and married again. As a result, Obama grew up surrounded by nearly mythic stories of his absent father, stories in which his father boldly confronts racists head-on or effortlessly charms rooms full of skeptical observers. There is a strong element of fantasy in these tales that as a child Obama intuits but cannot entirely grasp. Obama recalls how "the path of my father's life occupied the same terrain as a book my mother once bought for me, a book called *Origins*, a collection of creation tales from around the world" (10). The young Obama is unable to distinguish between the story of the earth's creation from the story of his own creation. Both involve invisible sources, larger than life characters, and an inheritance he can only barely comprehend.

As Obama reflects upon the confluence of his father's story with that of various creation myths, he notes how these puzzling narratives generated an array of questions that were equally ponderous and impossible to answer. He describes how he was troubled by such issues as "Why did an omnipotent God let a snake cause such grief?" and "Why didn't my father return?" but explains that "at the age of five or six I was satisfied to leave these distant mysteries intact, each story self-contained and as true as the next, to be carried into peaceful dreams" (10). This silence carries over into Obama's adult life, fostering a dangerous mythology as well as a critical absence of language to express the complexities of his difference from others.

It is difficult to gauge how much of the mythology, tending even toward fantasy, that surrounds Obama's father is racially tinged. The exotic allure of a racial other certainly influenced his mother's initial attraction toward Obama Sr. Only later in life does Obama come to understand the dynamic between his parents that led to their marriage. At first, the discovery of how race and sex collided in their courtship unnerves him because these two elements appear to be inseparable. While a student at Columbia University, Obama is visited by his mother who insists that they go see *Black Orpheus*, her first foreign film, and which she remembered as "the most beautiful thing I had ever seen" (123). Horrified by the movie's "depiction of childlike blacks," Obama concludes that these demeaning caricatures, "the reverse image of Conrad's dark savages, was what my mother had carried with her to Hawaii all those years before, a reflection of the simple fantasies that had been forbidden to a white middle-class girl from Kansas, the promise of another life: warm, sensual, exotic, different" (124).

Obama never approaches his mother with his suspicion that her attraction to his father was motivated by such crude racial fantasies. As in Lahiri's stories, the complexities and consequences of interracial romance prove to be unspeakable. Instead Obama draws his own troubling conclusions: "The emotions between the races could never be pure; even love was tarnished by the desire to find in the other some element that was missing in ourselves. Whether we sought out our demons or salvation, the other race would always remain just that: menacing, alien, and apart" (124). Obama suggests here that interracial love can never be pure because it cannot be divorced from the prejudices and projections bound to racial difference. His criticism that this love is always marred by the pursuit of "some element that was missing in ourselves" pertains to any love relationship, not just those that are interracial.

The strategic egoism of love is evident in Obama's own marriage. His nearly twenty-year marriage to his wife Michelle has received national attention as a model for the passion, hard work, and compromise necessary for any long-term relationship. Despite Obama's comments on the nature of impure love, it is difficult not to believe that he pursued his wife in part because she represented "some element that was missing" in himself. Born and raised in a strong African American community, Michelle Obama enjoyed a sense of rooted identity and community that long eluded her future husband. As he explains prior to his decision to transfer to Columbia, "And if I had come to understand myself as a black American, and was understood as such, that understanding remained unanchored to place. What I needed was a community" (115). Just as Obama's search for his father is inextricably tied to his identity as a black American, Obama's search for a life partner reflects his continued struggle to understand himself as part of a supportive community.

Love necessarily involves a search for the missing self in another. This is not a quality particular to interracial relationships. In that sense all love is "impure" because it is always bound to the egocentric needs of the lover. However, Obama's observation that race may mark another person as "menacing, alien, and apart" is apt. *Black Orpheus* and Lahiri's stories amply demonstrate the danger of racially tinged fantasies. Racial difference introduces images of escape, domination, and exceptionalism that do not adhere to intraracial relationships. The challenge is not to ignore or render them unspeakable but instead to explore how and why they operate as well as what affection and connection nonetheless remains.

Obama at last grants his mother a softer judgment after he hears her relate the story of his parents' first date. Obama's father was late in meeting Dunham at the library so she sat down on one of the benches and fell asleep. He arrived an hour later with a few of his friends, announcing, "You see, gentlemen. I told you that she was a fine girl, and that she would wait for me." Dunham may very well have been "that girl with the movie of beautiful black people in her head, flattered by my father's attention, confused and alone, trying to break out of the grip of her own parents' lives." However, Obama's father was also constructing a romantic fantasy of his own in which he brags how he can make a white girl wait for him. Obama does not ask his mother if she would have waited for his father had she not fallen asleep. Instead the young couple presumably succeeds in fulfilling one another's fantasies and from that "impure" beginning, the two work to develop something more. Obama explains of his mother:

> The innocence she carried that day, waiting for my father, had been
> tinged with misconceptions, her own needs. But it was a guileless
> need, one without self-consciousness, and perhaps that's how any
> love begins, impulses and cloudy images that allow us to break

across our solitude, and then, if we're lucky, are finally transformed into something firmer. What I heard from my mother that day, speaking about my father, was something that I suspect most Americans will never hear from the lips of those of another race, and so cannot be expected to believe what might exist between black and white: the love of someone who knows your life in the round, a love that will survive disappointment. (127)

Obama here recognizes that any love necessarily begins with need and misconceptions. Race complicates that premise, but it does not render the fulfillment of love impossible. His mother understood that Obama Sr. brought his own racially inflected fantasies to their relationship, and yet she loved him still.

4

Performing Intimacy

"Race-Specific, Race-Free Language" in Political Discourse

President Obama has proved to be our country's most adroit user of "race-specific, race-free language." However, because the race of participants upon the national stage is already known, such coded rhetoric operates apart from the experimental ambiguity of *Paradise* and "Recitatif," the deliberate isolation of the protagonist in *Apex Hides the Hurt*, and the intimate silences of Lahiri's characters. Instead, this discourse, when used for political purposes, paradoxically both preserves and elides racial difference according to various strategic ends. Although "race-specific, race-free language" has proved to be a powerful rhetorical tool for Obama, it poses complex challenges. Black critics like Michael Eric Dyson and Zadie Smith may admire how Obama invokes race without stating it explicitly, but this type of muted racialized language that is open to an array of interpretations can have problematic consequences. Race becomes an unstable signifier, apparent in seemingly innocuous comments that demonstrate highly contested reading practices.

During the 2008 campaign, Obama expertly invoked race without specifically mentioning it in order to solidify the broadest possible voting base. Some examples of his rhetorical nuance, however, have led to charges that he is more concerned with pleasing white audiences than with aiding communities of color. For example, when Obama urged black fathers to do more for their children and their families in his 2008 Father's Day speech, many read this as a concession to prospective white voters still wary that a black president might favor African American communities.

Ishmael Reed observed in his blog: "The talking heads also concluded that Obama's speech before a black congregation in which he scolded black men for being lousy fathers and missing in action from single parent households and being boys, etc., was clearly aimed at those white male Reagan democrats, who, apparently, in Obama and the media's eyes, provide the gold standard for fatherhood."[1] Was Obama's call for self-reliance and accountability among blacks a denial of abiding forms of racism?

Obama's rhetoric, like most public references to race, be they racist or well-meaning, are made through largely veiled language. W.E.B. Du Bois's veil, his symbol of black alienation, has moved from the face of the Negro to the site of racial encounters. "Race-specific, race-free language" and the ambiguity it generates puts the onus of interpretation on readers and listeners, often making intention no more than a guessing game and leading to exhausting bouts of racial paranoia. Richard Thompson Ford calls this "a new, postmodern idea of race" in which racism becomes "a product of interpretation, a symptom of the gaze" (*The Race Card*, 333). As a result, there is no fixed understanding of what constitutes racism— only discrete perspectives that argue for how race operates in contemporary life.[2]

As both a purveyor of "race-specific, race-free language" and a fraught symbol of national progress, Obama models racialized speaking and reading practices that call for unity though often at the expense of necessary racial particularity. In 2007 when then Senator Joe Biden referred to Obama in language that many read as racially offensive, "I mean, you got the first mainstream African-American who is articulate and bright and clean and a nice-looking guy," Obama responded by issuing a written statement that defused the testy situation: "I didn't take Sen. Biden's comments personally, but obviously they were historically inaccurate. African-American presidential candidates like Jesse Jackson, Shirley Chisholm, Carol Moseley Braun, and Al Sharpton gave a voice to many important issues through their campaigns, and no one would call them inarticulate."[3] By focusing on the African American presidential candidates who preceded him rather than on the condescension implicit in lauding a black candidate for being articulate and clean, Obama made Biden's gaffe not a racial jab but a failure in historical knowledge. Here Biden is not a prejudiced white man surprised that a black man can be so successful but a poor student of American history. Obama does not read racism into this situation and presumably the American public is to follow.

Obama's reply succeeded in moving away from Biden's explicit racialization toward "race-specific, race-free" discourse. Although he clearly aligned himself with other black presidential candidates, our future president did not identify race as the defining aspect of his campaign. By naming those African American politicians who ran before him, Obama effectively revised Biden's initial comments. He in fact is not the first bright, articulate, and clean African American to campaign for the presidency, and thus the excitement around him cannot be due to his race but to something else. The implication that race alone does not distinguish Obama suggests that to make sense of his impressive rise we must consider other aspects of his candidacy, such as his individual achievements, his hopeful vision for the country, or his specific policy positions. In this way, Obama roots himself in a race-specific history, but he is still free to move beyond the prejudices evident in Biden's comments. What remains unexpressed, however, is the history of white racism that Biden regrettably evoked. Obama focuses on the political pioneers who preceded him, neatly avoiding any discussion of the long-standing stereotypes about black inferiority that underscore Biden's remark. Here history is made of triumphant black leaders, not of culpable whites.

In confronting other racially charged incidents, Obama has not always been as savvy as in his reply to Biden. This may be in part a matter of form, for it is telling that Obama submitted his response to Biden's comment as a written document. Obama handles racial incidents best when he has the opportunity to craft language that strikes the perfect, fragile balance between acknowledging and occluding race. Such carefully constructed rhetoric is deliberately performative like Toni Morrison's own literary explorations of "race-specific, race-free language." She too has used such prose to political ends, as in her 2008 endorsement of Obama. Her letter to the then junior senator is emblematic of an increasingly popular form of communication between black intellectuals and politicians, the shared private epistle. These open letters showcase black speech as nonthreatening and welcoming, even as they depend upon obvious subterfuge. Like Obama's landmark speech on race, delivered at Constitution Center in 2008 following the Reverend Jeremiah Wright scandal, the letters offer comforting portraits of cross-racial intimacy and understanding. However, the nuance and insight of Obama's race speech has been impossible to mimic in the demanding twenty-four-hour news cycle of his young presidency. Obama has made significant missteps in dealing with such controversies as the arrest of Henry Louis Gates Jr. and the forced resignation of Shirley Sherrod, an official in the Department of Agriculture. These examples demonstrate both the possibilities and perils of "race-specific, race-free language" and the ongoing challenge to create words that capture the paradox of race.

Morrison's Letter to Obama

While Obama is the most obvious purveyor of "race-specific, race-free language" in the public sphere, Toni Morrison joined the discussion concerning his candidacy by issuing a letter endorsing the Illinois senator at the start of 2008. Morrison's letter stands as a critical example of how such prose can effectively operate and models the strategic advantages of performing intraracial intimacy. Although Morrison states that her support for Obama was not derived from racial preference, the letter has deep racial significance due in part to her vexed history with the term "black President." As an example of the shared private epistle, it illustrates the fundamental friction of "race-specific, race-free language" while also demonstrating the utility of such language to reach out to audiences of all races. This type of prose creates a new division between insider and outsider, a split that Morrison capitalizes on by positioning her readers as spectators to a seemingly private correspondence. By acknowledging that those who read the letter, regardless of race, are outside this direct exchange, Morrison creates a space in which the language of race can be disregarded because it is already known. Her audience is thus left to read race not as a series of identity categories, but as an intimacy that renders its specific reference obsolete. The discontinuity between her stated audience, Senator Obama, and her implicit audience, undecided voters, underscores the performative nature of this gesture while betraying the manufactured conceit of publicly produced "race-specific, race-free language."

In January 2008 while Obama and Senator Hillary Clinton were engaged in a fierce battle for the Democratic nomination for the presidency,

Morrison publicly issued a letter, addressed to Senator Obama, in support of his candidacy. The letter made national news and was printed in its entirety on various websites. Morrison begins by stating that this act "represents a first for me—a public endorsement of a Presidential candidate." She explains that she was motivated by the hope that her support may encourage others to vote for him; moreover, due to "the multiple crises facing us . . . this opportunity for a national evolution (even revolution) will not come again soon, and I am convinced you are the person to capture it."[4] Morrison is unclear as to what constitutes this "national evolution"—an evolution from white to black leadership? from Republican to Democratic control of the White House? from a series of baby-boomer presidents to a man who has now spawned his own "Obama Generation"? Here, as elsewhere in the 495-word letter, Morrison avoids directly naming race. The ambiguity concerning the nature of this imminent "national evolution" invites speculation and suggests that, while race is a major factor in the historic nature of Obama's presidency, it is not the only significant feature of his compelling candidacy. Consistent with the nature of "race-specific, race-free language," we may read a racial meaning here, but that interpretation falls upon readers. Race is thus both present and absent, fully dependent upon how the reader understands Obama's significance. As in Obama's speeches, Morrison's elusive reference to a "national evolution" performs a form of double consciousness by making race apparent only to the discerning reader.

Morrison's endorsement likely did little to increase individual support for Obama's campaign, especially as it was announced the same day that three members of the Kennedy family backed the Illinois senator rather than Clinton. Obama was collecting weekly endorsements from celebrities of far greater political influence than Morrison, and there is little precedent for a literary figure to publicly support a presidential campaign. The week before, Maya Angelou published a poem entitled "State Package for Hillary Clinton" in the British newspaper the *Observer*, but Angelou's endorsement failed to make national headlines in the United States.[5] Why then did Morrison issue her letter?

Morrison's opening description of her long admiration for Senator Clinton must be understood as a way to acknowledge her well-known esteem for former President Clinton. Like Georgia congressman John Lewis who, switching allegiance from Clinton to Obama, stated that he did not "want to be on the wrong side of history," Morrison may also have been motivated by a desire to publicly support the man who would become the nation's first indisputably black president.[6] In a short essay published in the *New Yorker* Morrison famously referred to Bill Clinton ten years earlier as "our first black President."Her controversial claim was premised upon the assumption of guilt applied to Clinton at the start of the Lewinsky investigation as well as upon her observation that "Clinton displays almost every trope of blackness: single-parent household, born poor, working-class, saxophone-playing, McDonald's-and-junk-food-loving boy from Arkansas." Obama's impressive candidacy and Kenyan heritage threatened to demolish Morrison's claim that Clinton was "blacker than any actual black person who could ever be elected in our children's life-time" (152). Obama was well on his way to making the impossible possible and to bringing an inarguable blackness to the White House. Morrison's characterization of Clinton as black would now be read as no more than a convoluted bit of sophistry, the worst kind of intellectual handiwork.

A presidential contender who defines himself as a "black American" was about to secure the nomination of the Democratic Party even as the echo of "our first black President" was still attached to Clinton. Significantly, other prominent African Americans continued to apply this term to Clinton; for example, former Atlanta mayor and civil rights icon Andrew Young declared in 2007 that Clinton was "every bit as black" as Obama.[7] Young told a public audience that he knew this because he had seen the former president moonwalk like Michael Jackson. Given such powerful and long-lasting associations, might Clinton's wife be perceived as an appropriate substitute, a woman black enough for African American voters or at least sufficiently sensitive to black culture as to make race incidental? Irrespective of the specific merits of the two competing sena-tors, Morrison's declaration of Clinton as the first black president might suggest that race was not an issue in the 2008 election. Because Senator Clinton and Senator Obama have substantial connections to the African American community, both could be perceived as "black" in some regard. This troubling conclusion might undermine the significance of Obama's eventual success. Moreover, Morrison's *New Yorker* piece adheres to a pessimism concerning black achievement that reeks of resignation and despair. Was Bill Clinton really the best that black America could do in our lifetime, in the lifetime of our children? While Obama's call for hope and change was galvanizing the country and inspiring supporters of all races, Morrison was about to be caught among those without the courage and conviction to make a black presidency real. Like Congressman Lewis, the only African American Nobel laureate was in danger of being on "the wrong side of history."

It is impossible to read Morrison's letter to Obama apart from her *New Yorker* essay, especially as they chart a movement from deeply raced language to one nearly stripped bare of direct racial references. Morrison injected race into national discussions of Clinton and his treatment following the Lewinsky scandal, but within her support of Obama (minus her opening avowal—"nor do I care much for your race[s]") race is neatly elided. Morrison's use of brackets in this phrase indicates that she recognizes Obama as a possibly multiracial figure. The brackets perform ambiguity; readers can choose to understand Obama as someone with one race or many. By allowing for both interpretations, Morrison seemingly disregards the importance of race. Whatever Obama may be is incidental to the grounds of her endorsement. Whereas Bill Clinton was proclaimed "black," Obama's race is more uncertain and presumably less important. Its very ambiguity serves to defuse the significance of race altogether.

Following this brief reference, Morrison avoids specific mention of race. There's no need to name it when Obama's race is so obviously a factor in his biography. This difference between Morrison's comments on President Clinton and her letter to Obama indicates that race requires discussion when it remains the unrecognized element in national discourse. Such was the case with Clinton's treatment during the Lewinsky scandal and with the two other occasions in which Morrison entered national debates. She edited two collections of scholarly essays, one on the Clarence Thomas/Anita Hill hearings and another on the O. J. Simpson trial. In these two widely scrutinized events, race was the factor that should not matter; both Thomas and Simpson deserved objective hearings as citizens, not as black men, publicly indicted for crimes that play on tropes with long racial histories. But as Morrison argued in the introductions to both books, racial stereotypes fundamentally shape public perspective and the very nature of national spectacles situated upon black bodies. In these two cases, Morrison made race visible and speakable, but in her letter to Obama she works to occlude race by performing a kind of intraracial intimacy. Although race is still a powerful force in her endorsement of Obama, it has moved underground, a signifier not legible to everyone.

Between the publication of her *New Yorker* piece and her endorsement of Obama, Morrison was notably silent on public issues, suggesting that the two pieces are best read together rather than as discreet interventions. Obama's impressive rise offers yet another case in which race should not matter; Obama should be judged upon his merits, not upon his race. However, while Morrison focuses intently upon defining blackness and its attendant tropes in the *New Yorker* essay, her letter to Obama praises qualities in the young senator that seem to operate apart from race: "in addition to keen intelligence, integrity and a rare authenticity, you exhibit something that has nothing to do with age, experience, race or gender and something I don't see in other candidates. That something is a creative imagination which coupled with brilliance equals wisdom."

Morrison supports Obama not because he is the black candidate, but because he possesses wisdom. And what defines this noble quality? Morrison explains, "Wisdom is a gift; you can't train for it, inherit it, learn it in a class, or earn it in the workplace—that access can foster the acquisition of knowledge, but not wisdom." Apparently, one cannot provide examples of it either because beyond this stirring description, Morrison does not cite moments in Obama's biography that exemplify this most important quality. Morrison's conception of wisdom suggests an innate quality, something bestowed rather than acquired and hence something biological rather than social. Though Morrison is not voting for Obama because he is the black candidate, she supports him because of some inherent aspect to his being. Wisdom, if not race, is an essential quality and the basis of Morrison's endorsement.

Typically, wisdom is associated with old age and experience, both traits that Obama at forty-six and, at the time of the letter's publication, with less than a full term in the Senate was notably lacking. My concern here is not to determine if Obama is wise or not, but I seek instead to examine what is at stake in Morrison's characterization of him as such. By disavowing race as a consideration yet affirming the oddly innate quality of wisdom, Morrison sidesteps allegiance based on race alone while also expressing some essential pull toward his candidacy. Morrison's previous comments on the nature of wisdom provide further insight into her characterization of Obama.

In "Rootedness: The Ancestor as Foundation," Morrison, outlining key qualities of black literature, extrapolates in particular on the presence of an ancestor. As noted before, she explains that ancestors are "not just parents, they are sort of timeless people whose relationships to the characters are benevolent, instructive, and protective, and they provide a certain kind of wisdom" (2289). Morrison's purpose in this essay is to distinguish the unique attributes of black literature and thus the ancestor comes to signify a specifically African American figure. The wisdom that Morrison perceives in Obama suggests that he has internalized an ancestral presence, and thus he is rooted to a fundamental and necessary part of black identity.

Morrison's reference to wisdom in her letter to Obama is not to be read as a synonym for blackness, but it does signify the slippery tension that exists when black intellectuals enter the public sphere. Morrison's letter is notable as an example of how the language of race is elided in public discourse even as it operates as a driving force. This articulation of "race-specific, race-free language" is emblematic of the continued friction between black intellectuals and the black community. Morrison has long stated that she writes fiction for a specifically black audience, but her readership includes the entire world. And when rallying support for a presidential candidate during a time of national upheaval, the widest audience must be addressed. Although Morrison certainly aims to generate as many votes for Obama as possible, it is useful to consider that readership for her novels is predominantly white and female. Presumably those who know and admire Morrison's fiction will be most influenced by her endorsement, and hence we may understand her letter as a direct play for what had been Senator Clinton's most important base.

While Morrison emphasizes her hope to inspire others to support Obama, her letter does not directly appeal to those anonymous voters. She writes instead to "Senator Obama" and describes the qualities she sees in him that make him best suited to become the next president of the United States. Because Obama hardly needs to be convinced of the case for his own candidacy, there is an obvious dissonance in this address. Morrison leaves out the very people she seeks to move; they must read the message

as outsiders viewing a private exchange. For a writer who has long emphasized the practice of "participatory reading" in which literature should
"make you feel something profoundly . . . to behave in a certain way, to
stand up and to weep and to cry and to accede or change and to modify"
(2287), Morrison's specified audience, Senator Obama, belies the readers
she intends to address. This somewhat evasive rhetorical move highlights
the abiding conflict of the black intellectual—that is, the relationship
between the black intellectual and the black community. In his widely
cited essay, "The Dilemma of the Black Intellectual," Cornel West claims
that the "choice of becoming a black intellectual is an act of self-imposed
marginality; it assures a peripheral status in and to the black community"
("The Dilemma of the Black Intellectual," 110). According to West, "the
Afro-American who takes seriously the life of the mind inhabits an isolated
and insulated world" (109).

Superficially, Morrison's address to Obama seems to secure her
"peripheral status" because she does not directly name the black community in her letter. I argue, however, that Morrison's letter changes the
terms of West's dilemma in important ways. Morrison seems to specifically
embrace West's "isolated and insulated world" of the intellectual by crafting her letter as a singular address to Obama. This is not to suggest that
she remains within her "self-imposed marginality." Rather, by publishing
her letter, she welcomes others into her "life of the mind" even as she
upholds its borders. Morrison effectively inverts West's formulation; while
as a black intellectual she indeed chooses a life apart from others, she
allows readers access to that world. However, this access is notably third-
hand. Readers of Morrison's letters are figured as outsiders upon a private
correspondence. The letter is not for them. It is intended for Senator
Obama, and consequently we are quiet intruders to this exchange. As such,
the letter remains firmly within the black community, both addressed and
written by notable black public figures. Yet the audience for the letter is
not limited to the black community at large, thus revealing its attempt to
influence Americans of all races.

Morrison's strategy in her letter to Obama has precedent in her fiction.
The opening line of *The Bluest Eye*, "*Quiet as it's kept, there were no marigolds
the fall of 1941*" (5), divulges a type of secret knowledge. The narrator speaks
in a hushed voice to an audience that is figured as a confidant, someone

who is worthy of the trust necessary to comprehend the tragic story of a little girl's demise. As with her letter to Obama, the reader of *The Bluest Eye* is an intruder upon a private affair. In "Unspeakable Things Unspoken," Morrison elaborated on the tone she sought to capture in this opening sentence: "First, it was a familiar phrase, familiar to me as a child listening to adults; to black women conversing with one another; telling a story, an anecdote, gossip about some one or event within the circle, the family, the neighborhood. . . . In some sense it was precisely what the act of writing the book was: the public exposure of a private confidence" (2313). Morrison here explains that the use of the phrase "Quiet as it's kept" is racialized. It is meant to refer specifically to the private conversations of black women, and yet Morrison does not use the language of color to make this association. Race is encoded in the text without obvious reference to black culture or community life; here again we have "race-specific, race-free language."

The public exposure of a private confidence is precisely what Morrison achieves in her letter to Obama. In both texts, readers are invited to listen in on intimate black speech. Audience members can be of any race; in neither work is there a direct appeal to African Americans. The racial ambiguity of the intruding reader underscores how the epistolary form capitalizes upon "race-specific, race-free language." The effect is inclusive, allowing readers of all races to feel, as Morrison aspired for the audience of *The Bluest Eye*, "in on things." Our nation's only living Nobel laureate in literature may exist in West's "self-imposed marginality," but she allows all of us to read her private correspondence. Within this sphere of intimacy, albeit one that is decidedly manufactured, reference to race is not necessary; race would actually be intrusive, even as it is critical to the foundation of this exchange. Moreover, this approach reveals the latent didacticism of Morrison's fiction. She explains in the afterword of *The Bluest Eye* that her objective in the novel was to lead readers "into an interrogation of themselves" (211) for the destruction of Pecola Breedlove. To this end, she does not condemn readers for maintaining damaging conceptions of beauty or identifying blackness with inferiority; instead, she exposes how Pecola becomes convinced of her own ugliness. That process is to serve as the means by which readers are to consider their own culpability in Pecola's tragedy. As in her letter to Obama, Morrison seeks to persuade through indirection and the construction of shared intimacy.

Although her letter is figured as a private correspondence, significantly Morrison imparts no private information to Obama. He already knows he is a worthy candidate, and her endorsement only has value in the public realm. Instead the confidence that is passed is one between text and audience. By entrusting readers with such private matters, Morrison constructs them as therefore worthy to make the right decision about which candidate to support. The letter enacts a type of performed intimacy. Her address to Obama is a rhetorical ruse made to create the illusion of a private correspondence. But, in fact, we are not intruders upon a confidential exchange; the letter is written for the public. This subterfuge allows readers to believe that Morrison's decidedly manufactured "race-specific, race-free language" is the language of home, the language of intimacy, the language that makes readers of any race feel like an insider.

Blackness Revealed: Private Epistles Made Public

Morrison is not alone among black intellectuals in adopting the epistolary form as a way to gain a broad national audience while also preserving black community identity. James Baldwin opens *The Fire Next Time* (1963) with a dedicatory letter to his nephew and namesake James, entitled "On the One Hundredth Anniversary of the Emancipation" which advises the young boy to accept and love white people because they are "still trapped in a history which they do not understand" (8). The letter is thick with condescension, but, by addressing his words to his nephew, Baldwin forgoes a direct attack upon ignorant and misguided whites, who are as much his audience as his nephew. Baldwin was always convinced that meaningful social change would only come from the efforts of both whites and blacks.

In the run-up to the 2008 presidential election, there was a spate of private letters made public by black intellectuals and politicians. In an op-ed entitled "Jesse Jr. to Jesse Sr.: You're Wrong on Obama, Dad," published in December 2007, Jesse Jackson Jr. responded to his father's condemnation of Obama for ignoring the primary concerns of African Americans. Harold Ford Jr., the current chairman of the Democratic Leadership Council who lost a close Senate race in 2006 due to flagrant race-baiting, published an essay in *Newsweek* in June 2008 called, "Go Meet Them, Senator," which urged Obama to meet with rural and working-class people. Alice Walker offered her own endorsement of Obama in March 2008 as a public address to "my sisters who are brave" as well as a November 2008 letter to "Brother Obama," which provides advice to the new president. The book *Go, Tell Michelle: African American Women Write to the New First Lady*, published in January 2009, collects advice and reflections from scholars, activists, artists, and other publicly engaged black women.[8]

Why is the epistle the preferred form for black intellectuals and politicians to communicate ideas to and about Obama? What is at stake in making private correspondence public, especially when all of these letters come from and are addressed to members of the black community? The example of Jesse Jackson Jr.'s letter to his father exemplifies the intimate dynamics at play here and the critical need to affirm contrary opinions among African Americans. There is no single black voice, suggests Jackson Jr.; Jackson Sr. is not to be understood as the mouthpiece of the African American community, for there are contentions even within his family. These letters read as adamant claims to the diversity of black opinion. Obama does not simplistically represent the group because here are voices of opposition and criticism even as they also articulate support and hope for his endeavors. Moreover, with the possibility of a black man in the Oval Office becoming ever more real, these letters appear to provide a necessary window on the inner workings of the black community. They implicitly counter suspicion that a President Obama will cause radical change or undermine the safety and livelihood of non-black citizens. In the nonthreatening tones of "race-specific, race-free language," race becomes the context, not the subject of the exchange, perhaps even fading into invisibility.

The use of race-neutral language was key to Obama's success in the 2008 presidential campaign. He has repeatedly deemphasized race and racial identification in favor of a broader perspective on national issues and voter constituencies. For example, he was significantly criticized for not attending the 2008 State of the Black Union, and in a public letter to conference host Tavis Smiley, Obama explained that he was most needed on the campaign trail where he was speaking to voters about "the causes that are at the heart of my campaign and the State of the Black Union forum such as affordable healthcare, housing, economic opportunity, civil rights and foreign policy." Obama emphasized that he was "committed to touching every voter, and working to earn their vote"—every voter, but perhaps not every black voter.[9] Obama's use of the epistolary form again demonstrates the broad scope of his audience. He was writing to a group that included far more than Tavis Smiley, a readership of all the voters he had yet to win.

Alice Walker's November 2008 letter to Obama is unique in that it deploys explicitly racialized language. As the author of the first and best-known African American epistolary novel, *The Color Purple* (1982), Walker is especially attuned to literary effects upon eavesdropping readers. Writing to "Brother Obama" in *Newsweek,* Walker begins by stating, "You have no idea, really, of how profound this moment is for us. Us being the black people of the Southern United States." Walker presumes Obama's ignorance of this profundity despite conceding that, "You think you know, because you are thoughtful, and you have studied our history." Apparently such knowledge is impossible for Obama because he is not a black person of the South. Do blacks of the North feel the profundity of this moment less than those of the South? Walker's categorization of "black people of the Southern United States" casts doubt on Obama's racial authenticity. He cannot know of the significance of his victory because he did not partici-pate in southern history. Walker explains, "But seeing you deliver the torch so many others before you carried, year after year, decade after decade, century after century, only to be struck down before igniting the flame of justice and of law, is almost more than the heart can bear."[10] That Walker was hardly a witness to centuries of oppression does not exclude her from claiming this history as her own. Regardless, it certainly does not belong to Obama.

Walker's identification as writing from an "us" defined as "the black people of the Southern United States" demonstrates the pitfalls of utilizing race-specific, but not race-free language in the public sphere. As with Ferraro's comment about Obama, the effect is divisive. Race creates obvious and insurmountable barriers—an us and a them that makes history and legacy sites of exclusive possession. The fact that Walker uses such lan-guage to alienate Obama, a black man, indicates that specifically racialized language can be detrimental both within and between racial communi-ties. Nonetheless, Walker's support for Obama is fundamentally based upon her trust in his ability to speak with others. In her March 2008 letter of endorsement, she praises Obama's ability to converse with anyone: "I can imagine Obama sitting down and talking, person to person, with any leader, woman, man, child or common person, in the world, with no baggage of past servitude or race supremacy to mar their talks."[11] Walker ultimately envisions Obama capable of a type of freedom to speak with others that she apparently does not possess herself as the "baggage" of the past mars her conception of how Obama understands the profundity of his election. And yet Walker recognizes that it is Obama's talent for communication, his use of language that affirms both difference and inclusion, which ultimately enabled his success.

The Dangers of Private Black Speech

Like Walker, the Reverend Jesse Jackson has also exhibited concern about Obama's relationship to black America though he did so not through a public epistle but in shockingly crude language. According to many black leaders, Jackson, a long-time crusader for civil rights and two-time presidential candidate, resented Obama's rise as well as his apparent distance from many of the concerns most relevant to the African American community. In July 2008, Jackson was caught on an open microphone disparaging Obama for "talking down to black people" and while making a gesture with his hand he said, "I wanna cut his nuts out." Notwithstanding his outrageous invective, Jackson was angered by comments Obama made to black communities in which he emphasized the need for greater personal responsibility. As David Remnick observed, "What seemed to irritate Jackson was the double discourse, the way that Obama's rhetoric was, by design, being overheard by white audiences that might understand it not as brotherly sympathy but, rather, as lofty reproach."[12]

Jackson's ire was derived from his sense that Obama was not actually addressing black audiences when speaking to them about personal responsibility but was instead pandering to whites concerned about how a black president might favor African Americans once in office.[13] Jackson here assumes that Obama's address to blacks, to some extent a private exchange that has been made public, is actually a message to whites promising a mild approach to race relations. Unfortunately this valid concern about the deceptions of Obama's "race-specific, race-free language" was expressed in a private exchange that should very much have remained

private. While the publication of seemingly private letters only manufactures intimacy, the fact that Jackson directed his comments to a nearby
companion and not to Obama himself underscores the constructed nature
of such intimacy. His remarks reveal that there are private communica-
tions between black politicians and intellectuals to which the public is not
privy, and, if they are anything like Jackson's comments, such truly private
intraracial correspondence is violent and frightening. Ironically, however,
Jackson's crude remark does not expose hostility toward white Americans
but instead poses a threat to the most celebrated black politician of our
time. Intimate black speech does not rage against white America; it rages
against seemingly inauthentic rhetoric.

Although Jackson expressed his contention with Obama in a wholly
inappropriate way, this episode represents one of the few times in which
Obama has been called out for the dangers of his racially ambiguous
rhetoric. Jackson later explained his concern with how Obama addressed
black audiences:

> Barack would go to various groups and spell out public policy. . . .
> He'd go to Latino groups and the conversation would be about the
> road to citizenship and immigration policy. He'd go to women and
> talk about women's rights, *Roe v. Wade*. But he'd gone to several
> black groups, talking about responsibility, which is an important
> virtue that should be broadly applied, but, given our crisis, we need
> government policy, too. African-Americans are No. 1 in voting for him,
> because he excited people. But we're also No. 1 in infant mortality,
> No. 1 in shortness of life expectancy, No. 1 in homicide victims.[14]

Jackson's anger over Obama's approach to black audiences stems from
justifiable concern that the latter's coded rhetoric may at last exclude
African Americans, that Obama is only performing black intimacy. However, this is a concern that Obama never had to counter because Jackson's
inflammatory remark negated any reasonable foundation for his anger.
His legitimate contention was simply overshadowed by the fact that one
of the most important black leaders in America wanted to castrate the
Democratic presidential nominee. Jackson was roundly criticized for his
remarks, including a sharp rejoinder from his own son, and soon after he
apologized to Obama.

Jackson's comment inevitably summoned the long, vicious history of lynching in the United States, positioning Obama as the victim to Jackson's deranged fantasy. In this confounding dynamic, Obama only becomes more fully aligned with the African American community while Jackson appears as an irrational nut. It is difficult if not impossible to understand why Jackson expressed his anger in such historically loaded terms. The desire to castrate another signals jealousy and profound vulnerability, but it may also speak to Walker's concern that Obama is not counted among the "black people of the Southern United States." I do not mean to imply that lynching was only a crime of the South or only enacted upon black people. However, Jackson's standing as one of the most vital black leaders from the civil rights movement positions him as part of what Obama has termed "the Moses generation," men and women who marched and sacrificed for the rights we all enjoy today. Jackson's comment might thus be read as a reminder of the history that Obama does not fully bear, the fact that, while he has faced racial discrimination and the outrages of injustice, he most likely has never confronted the possibility of physical violence, such as Jackson mentioned.

None of these issues was discussed in the aftermath of Jackson's comment. Instead as Julian Bond noted, "Jesse provided Obama that sort of Sister Souljah moment."[15] Obama was able to establish distance from Jackson's anger and his far more left-leaning politics while also appearing magnanimous for accepting Jackson's apology. He reassured voters that when attacked, he will not rise to the bait, will not play the race card even when he is provoked by other blacks. Obama identifies himself as part of a new "Joshua generation" and despite the fact that his father is from Kenya, not Kentucky, he absolutely claims the legacy of the Moses generation as foundational to both his success and his very existence. Speaking of his parents at a commemoration for the Selma Voting Rights March in March 2007, he explained:

> There was something stirring across the country because of what happened in Selma, Alabama, because some folks are willing to march across a bridge. So they got together and Barack Obama Jr. was born. So don't tell me I don't have a claim on Selma, Alabama. Don't tell me I'm not coming home to Selma, Alabama. I'm here because somebody marched. I'm here because you all sacrificed

for me. I stand on the shoulders of giants. I thank the Moses generation; but we've got to remember, now, that Joshua still had a job
to do.[16]

According to Obama, the work of the Joshua generation is to fulfill the
legacy of the pioneers of the civil rights movement, "to cross over to the
other side" and into the promised land. Obama's language of home and
paradise return us to Morrison's concern with the architecture of racism
that has defined so much of American history. In identifying Selma as his
home, Obama stresses the conditions of equality that made the marriage
of his parents possible. Home becomes not a geographic place but the
foundation of transformative politics that is passed on through story.
Obama suggests that by learning that "some folks are willing to march
across a bridge" his parents had the courage to marry and have a child.
Home is where those inspiring stories derive, a flawed place necessarily
rooted in conflict while paradise is the union we make more perfect.

Although the job of the Joshua generation is to complete the vision of
the Moses generation, this work will no doubt be done in another kind of
language. The race-specific approach of Jackson and Walker has passed. It
is too exclusionary in its conception of what race signifies for individuals.
However, the "race-specific, race-free language" of Morrison and Obama
presents new challenges for enunciating and understanding how race
still impacts American society. The figure of the outsider listening in on
a publicly aired private exchange becomes an empty vessel of racial
identification. This is especially evident in another private letter made
public that Obama issued in January 2009.

On the Sunday before his inauguration, Obama printed an address
to his daughters Malia and Sasha in *Parade* magazine. Obama begins by
explaining why he decided to run for president and notes that the turning
point of his life was their birth: "I soon found that the greatest joy in my life
was the joy I saw in yours. And I realized that my own life wouldn't count
for much unless I was able to ensure that you had every opportunity for
happiness and fulfillment in yours. In the end, girls, that's why I ran for
President: because of what I want for you and for every child in this
nation."[17] These comments provide an easy segue into a description of
Obama's vision for America—increased educational opportunities, ample

employment, health care, a cleaner environment, and international relations based upon diplomacy rather than war. Obama urges his daughters to embrace his commitment to the United States, reminding them "that with the great privilege of being a citizen of this nation comes great responsibility." They are bound to follow his example of public service "Not just because you have an obligation to give something back to this country that has given our family so much . . . But because you have an obligation to yourself." For Sasha and Malia to achieve their "true potential" they must dedicate themselves to something larger than themselves.

As in Morrison's letter, Obama avoids the language of race and instead connects with his daughters through the notion of citizenship. As citizens of a country that has provided opportunities for their diverse family members, they are obligated to nurture such opportunities for others. Citizenship here becomes a category without race, and, as Obama invokes his white mother who read the opening lines of the Declaration of Independence to him, it is shown to be an identification that is transferable across race. He explains: "She helped me understand that America is great not because it is perfect but because it can always be made better—and that the unfinished work of perfecting our union falls to each of us. It's a charge we pass on to our children, coming closer with each new generation to what we know America should be." Obama envisions an America with imperfections that are necessary because they provide critical opportunity for unity across all social boundaries. Once again race is implicit in his words, but his emphasis lies on more inclusive modes of self-definition—as citizen, son, and father. However, as with all of these private epistles made public, an element of subterfuge exists. Obama addresses his daughters, but he is effectively writing to the nation. Through this letter of paternal advice and expectation, race becomes incidental; all may relate to and admire the values this exemplary father imparts to his children. Blackness has no secrets the letter suggests; intimate black exchange does not harp on race, does not seethe with anger and hostility—it is familiar. And yet the reader remains an outsider. White, black, or something else, we are only listening in on this exchange.

Obama, Morrison, and other black public figures refuse to identify their true audience in these letters, not because we are without race but because we embody them all. "Race-specific, race-free language" welcomes us each as listeners, and as such it has profound consequences for building interracial political coalitions. As either readers of black private epistles made public or as listeners to Obama's racially inclusive rhetoric, we may believe in the intimacy of such speech, imagining that we are insiders to language made just for us. And yet this powerful rhetorical strategy depends upon the invisibility of its audience. The language is race-specific and race-free, but we are raceless.

Our Storyteller in Chief

Throughout the prolonged 2008 presidential election, Obama often seemed to present himself as raceless as he sought to balance what Gwen Ifill identified as the delicate task of "putting whites at ease without alienating blacks" (*The Breakthrough*, 189–190). The necessity of this double objective caused candidate Obama to elide clearly racialized language until he was forced to confront the issue directly following the widely publicized clips of the Reverend Jeremiah Wright Jr.'s incendiary remarks.[18] "A More Perfect Union," delivered in March 2008, marks a significant departure from Obama's previous approach to race. On the campaign trail he most often spoke of race through coded signs that appealed to the broadest possible base of support. However, when clips of Reverend Wright began running endlessly on news programs and the Internet, Obama had to put aside his "race-specific, race-free language." He was obliged to explain his connection to the man who presided over his marriage and baptized his children, and yet repeatedly exclaimed "God damn America" in front of hundreds of congregants.

In jettisoning his signature race-neutral rhetoric, Obama adopted a form of address that emphasizes storytelling. His deft use of narrative is a primary reason for his impressive success in American politics. As John Dickerson observed during the 2008 campaign, Obama repeatedly "told stories about a transaction—the moment inspiration jumps from one person to another. It was this transaction, repeated thousands of times, that turned the Obama candidacy into a movement."[19] Understanding Morrison's claim from her Nobel Lecture that "narrative is radical, creating us at the very moment it is being created" (*What Moves at the Margin*, 205), Obama recognizes that listeners naturally place themselves within the stories of others. In this way, Obama creates his audience through stories, telling us who we are or who we can be if we follow his mandate for change and share his optimistic vision of America. However, as he exploits the political potential of storytelling, Obama must maintain a racially ambiguous address that calls upon listeners not as racially identified individuals but rather as raceless citizens.

Obama chose the location of his speech on race carefully: Constitution Center in Philadelphia. Physically invoking the document that begins his speech, Obama tells the story of America: "'We the people, in order to form a more perfect union.' Two hundred and twenty-one years ago, in a hall that still stands across the street, a group of men gathered and, with these simple words, launched America's improbable experiment in democracy" (*The Speech*, 237). More than forty years earlier at the steps of the Lincoln Memorial, Martin Luther King Jr. began his "I Have a Dream" speech also by telling the story of a people and citing a document that changed history. King referred to the Emancipation Proclamation, "This momentous decree came as a great beacon light of hope to millions of Negro slaves who had been seared in the flames of withering injustice" and then lamented how "one hundred years later, the Negro is still not free" (*I Have a Dream*, 102). Rather than chart the history of black America from slavery to the fight for civil rights to his own momentous campaign, Obama begins his speech with the founding of the Constitution at the 1787 convention in Philadelphia. Unlike King's conception of American history, the Emancipation Proclamation neither inaugurates Obama's vision of our nation's past nor heralds its future. The freedom of African Americans is not his goal; instead, he looks to the creation of "a more perfect union." This is a startling beginning also because it transfers emphasis from the Declaration of Independence to the collective work of the Constitutional Convention as the founding moment of America. "We the people," though once signifying only certain white men, now stands for a citizenry of all races.

Obama's speech on race is not about blackness or the journey from bondage to freedom; it is a speech about the totality of America. When King spoke about his dream, he stated, "if America is to be a great nation, this must become true" (105). Obama instead emphasizes that America needs its citizens to become great, that the Constitution is a dream we must fulfill. From this perspective, King's dream is already present in the promise offered by the Constitution. However, the work to achieve this "more perfect union" is ongoing, and in his final lines, Obama explains that the work begins with neither the founding of the Constitution nor any moment of national history; rather, the challenge begins, as he concludes the story of campaign worker Ashley Baia, in "that single moment of recognition between that young white girl and that old black man" (250). The force of change takes root through personal encounters; inspiration is specific, not abstract. While King spoke of "little black boys and black girls" joining hands with "little white boys and white girls" (105), Obama describes actual people united not in simple harmony but in purposeful cause. For Obama, racial difference is not the obstacle to overcome; racial difference is the context for a battle for better health care, better schools, better jobs, and a cleaner environment. Racial union is the means by which we can achieve a more perfect America; it is not a singular end in itself. King's vision of harmony will come only through collective struggle.

Obama ends his speech on race by telling the story of Ashley Baia, a twenty-three-year-old white woman who worked for his campaign in Florence, South Carolina. Obama presents her with a writer's sensibility for terse but telling prose:

> She had been working to organize a mostly African-American community since the beginning of this campaign, and one day she was at a roundtable discussion where everyone went around telling their story and why they were there.
>
> And Ashley said that when she was nine years old, her mother got cancer. And because she had to miss days of work, she was let go and lost her health care. They had to file for bankruptcy, and that's when Ashley decided that she had to do something to help her mom.
>
> She knew that food was one of their most expensive costs, and so Ashley convinced her mother that what she really liked and really wanted to eat more than anything else was mustard and relish sandwiches. Because that was the cheapest way to eat.
>
> She did this for a year until her mom got better, and she told everyone at the roundtable that the reason she joined our campaign was so that she could help the millions of other children in the country who want and need to help their parents too. Now Ashley

might have made a different choice. Perhaps somebody told her along the way that the source of her mother's problems were blacks who were on welfare and too lazy to work, or Hispanics who were coming into the country illegally. But she didn't. She sought out allies in her fight against injustice.

Anyway, Ashley finishes her story and then goes around the room and asks everyone else why they're supporting the campaign. They all have different stories and reasons. Many bring up a specific issue. And finally they come to this elderly black man who's been sitting there quietly the entire time. And Ashley asks him why he's there. And he does not bring up a specific issue. He does not say health care or the economy. He does not say education or the war. He does not say that he was there because of Barack Obama. He simply says to everyone in the room, "I am here because of Ashley." (249–250)

As demonstrated here and in his first book, *Dreams from My Father*, Obama proves masterful at finding indelible details that make people like Ashley real (the "mustard and relish" sandwiches that she swore were her favorite) and relating her decision in simple, almost inevitable strokes ("Ashley decided that she had to do something to help her mom"). Obama speaks candidly about Ashley's race. She is a white woman who has likely heard common stereotypes about other racial groups—that blacks are on welfare, that Hispanics are most likely illegals, and that the problems incurred by both groups contribute to her mother's difficulties. But here Obama frames such prejudice against Ashley's agency by establishing an opposition between the passivity of accepting racial stereotypes and the far more difficult work of changing her life and the lives of those around her. "Ashley might have made a different choice," he explains; she might have caved to prejudice and focused her efforts on attacking others, but instead "she sought out allies in her fight against injustice." The word "allies" quietly invokes racial difference in part because Ashley has been working in African American communities and she tells her story at a meeting for Obama campaign workers. But Obama's careful juxtaposition of her choice to be a community organizer against her choice not to concede to racism transforms the lazy blacks and illegal Hispanics of the previous sentence into people who also struggle against injustice. More-over, the racially ambiguous "allies" implies the inclusion of other whites who share Ashley's cause. "Allies" is a word that unites those who fight for change and against injustice without referencing race; this is precisely what Obama seeks from his audience.

Ashley's story might very well end there; she has chosen to agitate for change and establish coalitions among racially diverse communities. In this narrative arc of challenge and resolution, it is easy to draw a simple identi-fication between Obama and Ashley. Both work as community organizers because they want to change existing inequalities, and both find allies across racial lines in their struggle against injustice. Obama, however, pushes the story further to include the elderly black man's response to Ashley and thus profoundly changes how we read the story. By emphasizing that the black man does not "say that he was there because of Barack Obama," a critical distance is established between Obama and Ashley. Obama is not the force behind his own campaign; he does not directly moti-vate the thousands of people who made his campaign a success. Instead, it is Ashley who inspires others. In this crucial shift, Obama becomes linked not with Ashley but with the elderly black man who remains nameless in order to encourage the audience's identification with him. As he speaks the black man's words, "I am here because of Ashley," Obama speaks his own truth as well. He is here, campaigning for the presidency and addressing the entire nation in Philadelphia, because of Ashley.

Obama ends his momentous speech on race not drawing upon the legacy of the leaders of the civil rights movement—at no point does he mention the work of Martin Luther King Jr. or any other familiar hero—but by focusing on the work of a young white woman.[20] Obama reverses the very expectations of a race speech as well as numerous abiding social dichotomies. Here the young inspire the old, the white inspire the black, the woman inspires the man. Obama's speech on race is ultimately a speech about national unity, and to that end he highlights the challenges facing Americans, both white and black. As Remnick noted, commenting on Obama's speech following his victory in the Iowa caucus, which defini-tively proved that he was viable in a white-dominated state, "What the African-American left once referred to as the 'black freedom struggle' becomes, in Obama's terms, an American freedom struggle."[21] The "black freedom struggle" was and is a battle against racism, but, by transforming that effort into an "American freedom struggle," Obama does not make racism the focus of this other national battle. Anger over racial conflict is not what brought Ashley Baia to organize for Obama's campaign. Her original objective was to help her mother, to ensure better health care for the poor, and, in pursuit of that battle, she found multiracial allies. Like the women of Morrison's novels, struggle makes racism a frivolous impediment. Racial unity comes not by dreaming of a diverse utopia but by forging coalitions necessary to achieve such goals as universal health care, quality public education, and a sustainable environment—goals that do not necessarily have a racial component. The more perfect union that Obama envisions is one made perfect by interracial allies, not one made perfect because such allies merely exist.

Obama Unscripted

As demonstrated in "A More Perfect Union" and countless other occasions, Obama has proved to be a brilliant rhetorician. His speeches are remarkable for their nuance and literary sensibility, and he delivers them with power and passion. Speeches, however, are premeditated affairs that allow Obama to find the perfect word, the one that will resonate precisely and in multiple ways. While candidate Obama was generally successful at defusing racial confrontations, President Obama has made some notable missteps due in part to the spontaneous performances required of his office. He cannot easily escape into the transcendent possibilities of "race-specific, race-free" discourse when called to immediately address racially charged matters as in his now infamous July 2009 press conference. The president was then asked about the arrest of Harvard professor Henry Louis Gates Jr. at his home in Cambridge, Massachusetts. After returning home from an overseas trip, Gates discovered that his front door was jammed. With the help of his driver, he forced open the door. A neighbor saw what appeared to be a break-in and called the police. When Sergeant James Crowley arrived he asked Gates to come outside. Gates refused, showing his identification, and a confrontation ensued resulting in Gates's arrest for disorderly conduct.

Gates was later released, but the conflict generated a media firestorm. Was Crowley a racist? Or had Gates overreacted when he exclaimed to the arresting officer, "Is this how you treat a black man in America"?[22] Why was one of America's most distinguished public intellectuals arrested in his own home? Although Obama admitted to not knowing all of the facts leading up to Gates's arrest, when asked about the matter he replied:

> I think it's fair to say, number one, any of us would be pretty angry; number two, that the Cambridge Police acted stupidly in arresting somebody when there was already proof that they were in their own home; and number three, what I think we know separate and apart from this incident is that there is a long history in this country of African Americans and Latinos being stopped by law enforcement disproportionately. That's just a fact.[23]

Obama's response is notable in that he does not refer to any of the specific individuals involved. He begins first by universalizing Gates's anger; anybody arrested under these circumstances would be incensed, regardless of their race. By claiming that the Cambridge Police "acted stupidly," rather than referring to Sergeant Crowley specifically, Obama places blame on an institution, not an individual. Obama frames the incident abstractly, distancing himself from the messy details of human interaction and limiting the occurrence to the absurdity of being arrested in your own home. In his final comment, he speaks generally about the abiding injustice of racial profiling. Obama's response makes clear that he perceives race to be a significant factor in what happened between Crowley and Gates, but by not referring to the actual people involved he refrains from identifying both a victim and a perpetrator of racism. Race indeed played a role here, but what roles were played by specific individuals remains unclear or at least unspeakable. Obama is on dangerous ground here; he agrees that race "still haunts us," yet he is unable to level a definitive accusation. Like Ferraro commenting on his success as a candidate, Obama recognizes that race is important to what happened, but he cannot draw conclusions beyond that point.

Following his press conference, cops around the country expressed their displeasure with Obama's characterization of the Cambridge Police Department. Republican Congressman Thaddeus McCotter threatened to issue a resolution to the House of Representatives demanding that Obama apologize to Crowley. Only 29 percent of the country approved of Obama's "handling of the situation," and his support from white voters slipped from 53 to 46 percent.[24] The president placed a personal call to Crowley and invited the sergeant as well as Gates to join him for a beer at the White House. Referring to his press conference comments, Obama publicly admitted that he "could have calibrated those words differently" and conceded, "Professor Gates probably overreacted as well."[25] The criticism Obama received for his initial response to Gates's arrest stemmed from how our "post-racial" president had become alarmingly racialized. As Arica L. Coleman observed, "Obama transgressed polite politics before a majority white audience as he gave voice to the current dilemma of the abuse of police authority in minority communities," becoming an "advocate . . . for those at the bottom of the racial food chain."[26] Even Katharine Q. Seelye of the *New York Times*, gauging Obama's response, observed that "the incident had struck a raw nerve with the president."[27] Obama spoke to the nation as a black man, accustomed to the humiliations of racial profiling and attentive to the specific afflictions facing communities of color. With the sudden collapse of the illusion of our post-racial president, the backlash was inevitable.

On July 30, Obama hosted Gates and Crowley at the White House where they shared a beer along with Vice President Biden. Both Gates and Crowley described the encounter as pleasant and agreed to meet later on their own for lunch. The image of the four men relaxing together as well as public calls to transform the incident into a "teachable moment" seemed to ease some of the media-generated tension. But the aftermath of the controversy was most evident in Obama's response to the next racially charged encounter of his presidency, Congressman Joe Wilson's outburst at Obama's September address to a joint session of Congress. Wilson exclaimed "You lie!" after Obama stated that his health care reform initiative would not insure illegal immigrants. Wilson was heavily criticized by both Democratic and Republican leaders and issued an apology to the president that same night. Obama accepted the apology and seemed ready to put the incident behind him. Although many noted that a white president would be unlikely to receive such boorish treatment, Obama refused to comment on how race may have influenced Wilson's outburst. Having learned the danger of naming race, Obama would not accuse Wilson of racism as Gates had done of Crowley only months earlier. America had proved that it was ready for a black president, but not one who spoke about what it was like to be a black president.

When days later former President Jimmy Carter explicitly named racism as a root cause of the vehement protests against Obama, emblematized by Congressman Wilson's outburst, Obama immediately distanced himself from such claims.[28] Unlike the Gates controversy, Obama did not personally comment on the matter, but instead press secretary Robert Gibbs explained that the president "does not believe that criticism comes based on the color of his skin."[29] Obama knew that to address Carter's comments explicitly would only encourage more media attention and that racial issues are best left unspoken or at least addressed in carefully scripted language. While candidate Obama glittered with the promise of racial unity, President Obama was in danger of becoming voiceless on matters of race.

This limitation again became apparent in the aftermath of the misguided ousting of Shirley Sherrod, a black bureaucrat in the Georgia office of the Agriculture Department during the summer of 2010. The media frenzy that ensued is especially instructive for how it reveals persistent anxieties about private black speech. Sherrod was fired after a videoclip of her 1986 speech to the NAACP was posted online by conservative blogger Andrew Breitbart. The clip suggested that she had discriminated against a white farmer in her capacity as a USDA official. As an example of private black speech, that is, a nonpublic address by a black official to a black organization, it seemed to confirm the hidden racism of the NAACP. Unlike the nonthreatening tenor of the shared private epistles between black politicians and intellectuals that appeared throughout the 2008 campaign, Sherrod's remarks were not manufactured performances, but evidence of real intraracial discourse and apparently of real racism.

Days after Sherrod was forced to resign, the full video of her speech was circulated, vindicating her of all charges of racism. Her story about the white farmer actually demonstrated her commitment to working across racial divides. Following an apology from Agriculture Secretary Tom Vilsack, Sherrod was offered a new job and, at her request, received a personal call from President Obama. Sherrod asked that cameras be turned off for her seven-minute conversation with the president. At last intraracial black speech would be private—private and assuredly familiar, for, just as Obama championed racial reconciliation through work toward common goals in his 2008 speech on race, Sherrod offered the same message in her decades old address to the NAACP.

A week after the Sherrod incident dominated national headlines, Obama delivered a speech to the National Urban League for the Centennial Conference of the historically black civil rights organization. Although the speech was initially billed as a major statement on education reform, Obama took the time to discuss what happened to Shirley Sherrod. He recognized the mistakes made by members of his administration and emphasized the necessity of listening to the full story of quiet crusaders like Sherrod. Although Obama's administration was notably silent when the week before such influential black academics as Charles Ogletree Jr. and Ward Connerly urged Obama to convene a national conference on race, the president called on Americans to begin a dialogue of their own:

> We should all make more of an effort to discuss with one another, in a truthful and mature and responsible way, the divides that still exist—the discrimination that's still out there, the prejudices that still hold us back—a discussion that needs to take place not on cable TV, not just through a bunch of academic symposia or fancy commissions or panels, not through political posturing, but around kitchen tables, and water coolers, and church basements, and in our schools, and with our kids all across the country.[30]

Obama's reference to "a bunch of academic symposia or fancy commissions or panels" reads as a direct rejoinder to Clinton's failed race initiative. Where Clinton convened a formal discussion of race, Obama asks all Americans to "have that conversation in [your] own lives" so that "we can move forward together and make this country a little more perfect than it was before." Obama's approach differs from Clinton's in that it places responsibility for these discussions on ordinary citizens, not distinguished scholars. But perhaps, more important, it emphasizes storytelling.

Noting that Sherrod's story "is exactly the kind of story we need to hear in America," Obama implies a structure to the conversation he envisions for the country. It is not to be an airing of racial grievances or even a debate about racially charged issues like affirmative action and immigration; instead, the discussion must be an exchange of stories. Notably,

Sherrod's speech to the NAACP was an account of her personal history, including reference to the murder of her father by white farmers and her struggle to form multiracial coalitions. Like Obama's speech on race, Sherrod's NAACP address is an exercise in storytelling. The failure of all those who initially denounced Sherrod—including Breitbart and his followers, the NAACP, and Secretary Vilsack—reveals the obvious effects of a media environment that values sound bites, not narratives. When Morrison envisioned home as "a world-in-which-race does-*not*-matter," she imagined a sleepless woman wandering through the night. She established a narrative to express a place of simultaneous freedom and safety. The story of her sleepless woman is what allows Morrison's use of "race-specific, race-free language" to function as a meaningful form of discourse. The intimacy embedded in such prose requires that we take the time to hear one another's stories. The foundation of Morrison's racial home is narrative. To that end, we may understand literature as the basis of this political vision.

Obama ended his address to the Urban League by drawing from a letter he recently received from ten-year-old Na'Dreya Lattimore of Covington, Kentucky. Lattimore, describing the difficulties she faced in school, urged the president to improve the education system. He then quoted directly from the letter, "One more thing . . . You need to look at us differently. We are not black, we're not white, biracial, Hispanic, Asian, or any other nationality. . . . We are the future." Following the fury of the Sherrod incident and its multiple accusations of racism, Obama closes the affair by again returning to an example of intimate black speech. Like all the black writers and politicians who penned such open letters, Lattimore confirms that private black discourse is nonthreatening and shares the universal goals of the nation. But in a long line of politically motivated epistles, Lattimore's missive is exceptional for being sincerely private. Unlike Morrison, Walker, Jackson Jr., Obama, and others, the straight-A student, angry about America's dysfunctional school system, does not perform intimacy; she assumes it.

Conclusion

The Demands of Precious

Lee Daniels's 2009 film, *Precious: Based on the Novel by Sapphire*, begins with the appearance of the words "LE DANS TINMIN" written in a red scrawl at the bottom right of a black screen. A moment later "(Lee Daniels Entertainment)" emerges in a standard font below the original phrase. Both titles are replaced by another pair, "IN ASHLAN WIT SMOKWD TINMANT," again in the uneven red lettering and then "(in association with Smokewood Entertainment)." Once these two fade, the film's title, "PRECIOUS," appears in red, followed closely by "(BASE ON NOL BY SAF)," and finally, "(Based on the novel 'Push' by Sapphire)" again in standard font.

The considerable critical discussion that *Precious* generated largely focused on the representation of its protagonist, Claireece "Precious" Jones, an overweight African American teenager who is pregnant for the second time by her father. However, the movie begins as a study in language whereby the script juxtaposes the idiosyncratic vocabulary of its functionally illiterate title character against standard English. The red print is the language of Precious, a kind of contemporary eye dialect or language that looks like dialect but does not necessarily sound different. George Knapp, who first defined the term in *The English Language in America* (1925), noted, "The convention violated is one of the eyes, not of the ear" (228). I emphasize this definition of eye dialect because, as the movie subsequently demonstrates, Precious speaks in standard, easily comprehended English. However, although her language is aurally familiar, the opening titles make her speech visually distinct. Unstable, tentative, and private, this is language that may have no intimate listener. Its uneven spelling—note the difference between "TINMIN" and "TINMANT"—suggests that no one can comprehend it without resorting to the parenthetical translations.

Precious assumes that its audience will be disoriented by the language of its protagonist. Unlike Obama who speaks in coded tropes such that listeners can either read race in his speeches or instead hear calls for a generalized national unity, the movie's opening titles instruct audience members how to read. The juxtaposed lines declaim: this is the language of Precious, and this is your language. Although Precious speaks familiar English, her printed speech encodes difference. Without the parenthetical translations, it is impenetrable. The sharp contrast between the paired lines may seem to invite a simplistic mapping of racial duality, but we cannot easily assume that the written language of Precious is black and its translation is white. To do so returns us to the racism "Recitatif" teases its readers to impose. Instead, the film's opening titles announce the necessity of translation for audience members of all racial backgrounds. To see the words of Precious is to recognize her difference, a difference that marks her not as black but as lacking an audience fluent in her language. Precious combines seemingly every trope of otherness; she is black, female, overweight, dark-skinned, HIV-positive, and a victim of incest and physical abuse, but what the opening titles make most explicit is that she is a person without intimates. No one can understand the opening titles without the parenthetical translations.

While Obama reaches out to audiences through the ambiguity of "race-specific, race-free language," Precious's written speech marks her as completely isolated from others. She cannot read her own translation, much less understand a world beyond the circumscribed streets of Harlem in the 1980s. If Obama performs intimacy to draw audiences of all racial backgrounds, Precious represents the absence of intimacy—not the unifying possibilities of blackness, but the abiding isolation of abjection. Released approximately one year after the 2008 election, *Precious,* in its sharp repudiation of the post-racial narrative attached to Obama, indicts racial transcendence as a narrow privilege if not a complete fiction. While he soared to victory, she seems to wallow in the intractable shackles of otherness, mired in speech that is barely comprehensible. However, just as Obama makes blackness safe by revealing familiar, affirming speech, Precious is also a study in the development of intimacy. The key difference between them is that while Obama constructs his listeners, no matter their particular racial identity, as already intimate, already fluent in his unifying rhetoric, *Precious* assumes that its audience is estranged from the experiences of its protagonist. Nothing about her language is familiar; nothing is safe and reassuring. Obama unified the country (if only briefly) through strategic ambiguity; he encouraged listeners to project their own desires onto his call for hope and change. By contrast, Precious poses a far more difficult challenge—to create intimacy where no common language even exists.

The emphasis given by the film's opening titles to the impenetrability of Precious's language effectively disappeared following Oprah Winfrey's widely publicized declaration, "We are all Precious."[1] This universalizing statement fostered a popular conception of the film that runs counter to Daniels's representation of Precious as uniquely alone, but, with Winfrey's exuberant endorsement and the financial backing of media mogul Tyler Perry, the independent movie reached a broad national audience and was debated on the pages of every major American newspaper and magazine. Though it opened in only eighteen theaters, the film generated an astonishing $1.8 million in its first weekend. Winfrey's description of the film's title character was echoed by numerous other critics such as Lynn Hirschberg, who wrote, "Precious is a stand-in for anyone—black, white, male, female—who has ever been devalued or underestimated."[2] In an essay printed in *Newsweek*, former first lady Barbara Bush urged readers to see the film because "there are kids like Precious everywhere. Each day we walk by them: young boys and girls whose home lives are dark secrets."[3] Even if Bush did not herself identify with Precious, she like many others regarded Precious's story as an accurate reflection of real circumstances.

Hirschberg's cover story for the *New York Times Magazine*, "The Audacity of Precious," asked "Is America ready for a movie about an obese Harlem girl raped and impregnated by her abusive father?" The article's title with its reference to Obama's bestselling campaign treatise, *The Audacity of Hope: Thoughts on Reclaiming the American Dream* (2006), draws a necessary connection between our young president and a figure that seemed to be his absolute antithesis. In addition to their obvious gender and class differences, while Obama looks like a model gazing confidently from the cover of *The Audacity of Hope*, the dark-skinned Precious barely makes eye contact with others, relishing fantasies that she is either a thin white woman or a red-carpet celebrity. Obama is cosmopolitan, educated, and often cited for his unflappable cool. By contrast, Precious steals a bucket of fried chicken for breakfast and notes that her teacher and her lesbian lover "talk like TV channels I don't watch." The light-skinned boyfriend with nice hair that Precious dreams of having could be Obama; both are handsome, camera-ready gallants vested with transformative power. But the reality of Obama is still decades away for Precious who in the novel by Sapphire tends toward the strident rhetoric of Louis Farrakhan. Precious's fantasies as much as her brutal reality attest to a world in which nothing is race-free.

Director Lee Daniels recognized the stark opposition between our inspirational president and his title character but suggested that the two are nonetheless intimately related. "Precious is so not Obama," he stated, noting, "As African-Americans, we are in an interesting place. Obama's the president, and we want to aspire to that. But part of aspiring is disassociating from the face of Precious." For Daniels, the movie represents an effort to bring together the contested dualities of black representation. Describing the election of Obama as liberatory, Daniels observes "because of Obama, it's now O.K. to be black. I can share that voice. I don't have to lie. I'm proud of where I come from. And I wear it like a shield. 'Precious' is part of that." Daniels claims that Obama's victory allows Precious to be represented, facilitating a reconciliation among the broad range of black experience. He explains, "I am so used to having two faces. A face that I had for black America and a face for white America. When Obama became president, I lost both faces. Now I only have one face."[4] Daniels understands Obama as making Precious possible, and through that pairing he finds the possibility of a single face for himself.[5] More important, Daniels does not claim that he is either Precious or Obama. And here we must be wary of conflating the publicity for the movie, which includes Winfrey's widely repeated endorsement, with the vision of its director. Daniels did not set out to create a simplistic identification between viewer and protagonist. Describing the process of making the film, Daniels observed, "I learned so much about myself, and I hope that people will walk away with the same sort of growth that I had."[6] Daniels's growth is having found "one face"—not Obama's, not Precious's, but his own.

Daniels understands Obama as opening the door to other representations of black life by guaranteeing the reality of African American achievement. Presumably, without Obama, Precious cannot exist; he ensures that she is not representative, but unique. Thus the experiences of the most degraded members of the black community can be explored without the expectation that such images are emblematic of the group as a whole. This purportedly new freedom in fact recalls Stuart Hall's declaration concerning "the end of the innocent notion of the essential black subject" that involves "the recognition of the extraordinary diversity of subjective positions, social experiences and cultural identities which compose the category 'black'" ("New Ethnicities," 224–225). More than twenty years have passed since Hall heralded the arrival of this new phase in the representation of black culture, but responses to both Obama and *Precious* indicate that the singular meaning attached to blackness nevertheless persists as does the burden of representation for black artists to promote positive racial images.

Henry Louis Gates Jr. has written that "the burden of representation is an illusion" yet "it follows you everywhere like your own shadow. It isn't a thing of your making, and it won't succumb to your powers of unmaking—not yet, anyway" (*Thirteen Ways*, xvii). Despite Daniels's best attempts to explore rather than define the contours of black life, the critical response to *Precious* largely involved judgments concerning its realism. Critics frequently referred to the film as if it were a documentary rather than a work of fiction, causing many to mistake Gabourey Sidibe, the actress who plays Precious, as the character herself. Sidibe said of the press, "They try to paint the picture that I was this downtrodden, ugly girl who was unpopular in school and in life, and then I got this role and now I'm awesome. But the truth is that I've been awesome, and then I got this role."[7] Daniels has explained that he chose Sidibe largely because she is so different from the wary, angry Precious: "I felt that if I had hired one of the girls that I was trying to be authentic with, that would have been exploiting them. Really not putting on a movie, but rather just exploiting this girl . . . and it would have been a documentary, as opposed to acting."[8] Daniels's goal was never factual representation; rather he sought to produce a piece of creative imagination. In fact, he understands too much reliance on real experience as exploitative, a deeply ironic concern given the critical outcry surrounding his movie. Moreover, the contrast between Sidibe and Precious undermines the claim to the latter's universality. How can we all be Precious when Precious isn't even herself Precious?

Daniel's vision requires that *Precious* be understood as neither a sociology text nor a political message movie but as art. However, discussions of the film revolved almost entirely around issues of authenticity as critics responded directly to the question, "Are you Precious?" In her scathing denunciation, entitled "She Ain't Me, Babe," author Jill Nelson wrote, "I don't eat at the table of self-hatred, inferiority, or victimization. I haven't bought into notions of rampant Black pathology or embraced the overwrought, dishonest, and black people hating pseudo-analysis too often passing as post-racial cold hard truths."[9] Nelson engages the film entirely as a personal indictment, listing the "Top 10 Ways to Know If You Are Precious"; number ten reads, "You order the 10 piece chicken bucket when you're dining alone." Her criticism of the movie's "arc of hype" is based upon her scorn of Winfrey, Perry, and the actress Mo'Nique who "legitimize the movie" by "attesting to their own sexual abuse." For Nelson, the film fails because it is not an accurate representation of reality. Armond White concurred, noting "Perry and Winfrey naively treat *Precious*' exhibition of ghetto tragedy and female disempowerment as if it were raw truth. . . . Not since *The Birth of a Nation* has a mainstream movie demeaned the idea of black American life as much as *Precious*."[10] White conflates his distaste for the movie with the promotion it received from Winfrey and Perry. Notably, White indicts them, not Daniels, for treating the film "as if it were raw truth." He proves unable to distinguish the film from its representation in the media, much like observers of Obama who could not always parse the hype from the man.

While Oprah effectively universalized Precious, she is also partly responsible for the exaggerated adulation surrounding Obama. During the beginning of the Democratic primary season in 2007, she joined him on the campaign trail. In rallies in New Hampshire, Iowa, and South Carolina, Winfrey introduced Obama with the astounding pronouncement, "He is the one." For some, this announcement resonated with biblical import; Obama was a messiah who would save the nation from quickening financial collapse, two desperate wars abroad, and its floundering reputation as the world's last superpower. For a younger generation galvanized by Obama's savvy use of the Internet to generate support for his candidacy, Winfrey's pronouncement echoed the language of the blockbuster films, *The Matrix Trilogy* (1999); Obama, like Neo, played by fellow Hawaiian Keanu Reeves, would awaken us from our numbing reality to a vivid new reality of multi-cultural cooperation and freedom.[11]

Unlike Morrison's endorsement, which seemed to have little effect on influencing voters, there was a discernible rise in support for Obama following Winfrey's announcement.[12] But perhaps more important than the voters Winfrey persuaded was her inauguration of a powerful narrative concerning Obama: that he is our nation's savior.[13] Obama effortlessly reconciled many of the oppositions that have long vexed our nation's identity. With his mixed racial heritage, a family history rooted in both the rural heartland and the immigrant's dream of a better life, as well as an Ivy League education coupled with unglamorous years as an urban community organizer, Obama seemed uniquely poised to bring America into the twenty-first century. "He is the one," Winfrey declared, and her failure to subsequently clarify which one he may be proclaimed its own a priori value. "He is the one" requires no elaboration from Winfrey because its fulfillment comes in the dreams and hopes that individual listeners project onto Obama. Obama thus becomes the one we each desire.

Wary critics mocked such lofty characterizations of Obama and warned against what Adolph Reed Jr. called "Obama's style of being all things to all people."[14] Writing in the *Los Angeles Times*, David Ehrenstein linked Obama's exalted image in the media to a familiar racial stereotype. He called the then aspiring junior senator a "Magic Negro" who is "there to assuage white 'guilt' (i.e., the minimal discomfort they feel) over the role of slavery and racial segregation in American history, while replacing stereotypes of a dangerous, highly sexualized black man with a benign figure for whom interracial sexual congress holds no interest."[15] Obama, like countless black characters from movies such as *The Defiant Ones* (1958) and *Driving Miss Daisy* (1992), would fix the world and leave white audiences with a lesson well-learned and racial hierarchies still firmly in place.

Enhrenstein's critique is less an attack on Obama than it is an indictment of how the young politician was represented. Enhrenstein admires Obama's "talk of uniting rather than dividing," calls it a "praiseworthy goal," but argues that ultimately the latter's appeal resides in how he fulfills a familiar white fantasy. This power depends upon the fictionalization of Obama, for, as Enhrenstein notes, "as with all Magic Negroes, the less real he seems, the more desirable he becomes. If he were real, white America couldn't project all its fantasies of curative black benevolence on him." For Obama to succeed he must function as an imaginative fiction, a mythical, transcendent "one." Even Morrison's letter to Obama, which emphasizes his "wisdom" rather than his political experience or his specific positions on critical issues, contributes to a conception of Obama as preternaturally gifted and destined for greatness. Both Winfrey and Morrison's endorsements reinforce familiar tropes of blackness, and, although they don't go so far as to call Obama "magic," they describe him in extraordinary terms. Their support of his candidacy is inextricable from troubling conceptions of racial signification. Although we might understand this as a form of strategic representation, by promoting Obama in racialized terms albeit in language that is "race-specific, race-free," they maintain existing structures of racial meaning.

Is Obama "the one"? His first two years in office, which failed to deliver on so many of his campaign promises—the closing of the Guatanamo Bay detention camp, the removal of combat brigades from Iraq, not to mention the concessions made on his health care proposal—clearly demonstrate that he is as human as every other man who has occupied the Oval Office. Because discussions about whether Obama is the one are obviously futile, it is imperative instead to consider what allows such a narrative to take hold. Obama's plummeting approval rates midway through his presidency indicate that he has paid a significant price for the inflated expectations established by the narrative of his campaign. Winfrey's coronation of Obama as "the one" certainly helped him win the election, but trading in unrealistic descriptions does not lead to sustainable and meaningful leadership.

Unlike his white peers, during and since the presidential campaign Obama was subjected to racialized representations that both vilified and validated his candidacy.[16] The pictures of Obama as an African witchdoctor or smiling in whiteface like the Joker from the most recent Batman film, *The Dark Knight* (2008), are vested in the same fraught field of contemporary racial discourse that also yielded his designation as "the one." Just as Senator John McCain could never be depicted as a monkey or half naked with a bone through his nose, there is not a single white politician who could ever be called "the one" because whiteness trades in specificity, not abstraction. Richard Dyer observes in his essay "White": "Power in contemporary society habitually passes itself off as embodied in the normal as opposed to the superior. This is common to all forms of power, but it works in a peculiarly seductive way with whiteness" (127). In defining what constitutes the "normal," white candidates shape narratives of themselves that function independent of race, crafting identities based on geographic region, professional or military experience, as well as on their relationship to preexisting political networks. In such cases, race functions through its absence, for whiteness continues to be the comfortable standard in the political sphere. However, this standard of whiteness means that George W. Bush or Bill Clinton could never construct a campaign built on the premise that either is "the one." In these contexts, the claim becomes absurd, a distasteful and even ridiculous display of pomposity. For all their privileges and gifts, they are men, not magic.

And yet, while many warned against generating impossible expectations for Obama's presidency, few beyond Enhrenstein perceived Obama's messianism in racial terms.[17] This may in part be due to the fact that it was Winfrey, the most powerful black woman in America, who named him "the one." Presumably, a fellow African American would not trade in racialized depictions, would not capitalize upon stereotypes that reinforce racial hierarchies. Obama can be construed as "the one" not simply because of his considerable talents and powerful vision of America but also because his blackness signifies beyond the boundaries of himself as a single person, transforming him from man to fetish. Although Winfrey's declaration might be read as an escape from damaging stereotypes of African American pathology, it ultimately enforces the very otherness of blackness. Obama is not like us, not the guy you want to have a beer with, but the guy who has to stage a "beer summit" because consorting with average Americans is not natural to this messiah man.[18]

Assessing the huge gap between Obama and Precious, Erin Aubry Kaplan argues that the film offers a necessary antidote to "the Obama era, which urges us to believe in the president as a symbol of success for blacks everywhere."[19] Echoing Oprah's twin characterizations of Obama and Precious, Kaplan understands Obama as the exception to the abiding reality of girls like Precious. If he is the "one," the one who speaks to and realizes our deepest fantasies of a racially harmonious America, then she is representative of suppressed "real-life." And yet Obama is the real-life person, and Precious is the fiction. If we are all Precious, then we are all fused to a fantasy of her abuse that erases the material conditions of her abjection in order to privilege our own individual forms of suffering. The racism, sexism, and classism that contribute to Precious's appalling circumstances become no more than metaphors for personal moments of difficulty that may be far removed from the problems Precious confronts. To identify with Precious and her exhausting list of social stigmas is to trivialize the specific consequences of her identity and her circumstances. If we are all Precious, then we all suffer from the same oppressive institutions, and we all triumph in a satisfying narrative of individual uplift. And if Obama is "the one," then we are all excluded from his achievements. Just as the universalizing impulse behind the promotion of Precious erases difference, the particularism applied to Obama makes difference irrelevant.

The ways in which Obama and Precious were each treated by the media demonstrate opposite trajectories of representation. Obama is made singular and exceptional while Precious is universalized; her story reflects the lives of everyone. We are all made to identify with her alienation and abuse, even if our lives are nothing like hers; struggle, whatever its contours, is familiar. But Obama stands alone, gifted and unique. These starkly contrasting descriptions are best understood through the distinction that while Obama's characterization requires fantasy, Precious must be rooted to reality. Obama becomes a fiction with messianic qualities. Precious becomes a girl who exists either within us or in the underbelly of America's urban core. From this perspective, Obama's success reads as so abnormal as to be beyond human. His achievements do not mark a new standard but signify the heights of an exceptional individual. Precious, by contrast, is evidence of ignored, uncomfortable truths. The inversion that occurs in placing representations of a mythical Obama against a hyper-real Precious demonstrates the overwhelming persistence of blackness as a trope of abjection and poverty as well as the ways in which black women continue to be read as the ultimate symbol of degradation. To maintain the familiar significations of racial meaning, we fictionalize the real and treat art as reality. A black man is president, and yet the meaning of blackness has changed not at all.

Might "race-specific, race-free language" free us from the ways in which race continues to signify? Can it allow us to signify race not simply through new forms but in order to fundamentally shift what concepts like black and white have come to mean? This necessitates a transformation not of signifiers but of signifieds so that racial symbols may be attached to alternative kinds of meaning such that blackness does not equate with otherness, be it super-human or subaltern. It requires judging a film like *Precious* not through the measure of its representational veracity and understanding the title character not as a reflection of oneself, but as part of a comprehensive artistic vision. Consequently, we might perceive the overwhelming circumstances of Precious's life—the morbidly obese teenager who is sexually abused by both her parents, mother of a Down syndrome child, and HIV-positive—not as a testament of reality, but as a reflection on blackness itself and its troubling conflation with pathology. Despite sustaining seemingly endless forms of abuse, Precious is not a predictable character. In a welcome departure from the novel, which depicts its protagonist as markedly more passive and introverted, the Precious of Daniels's film is wry, combative, and funny. She rises from her desk to beat an unruly student when her math teacher is unable to bring order to the classroom. In response to her principal's exasperated query of how at sixteen she is pregnant yet again, Precious replies deadpan, "I had sex, Mrs. Lichtenstein." Tired of answering questions about her home life, Precious begins asking her social worker about her own relationship to her parents. "Really, I am here to help you," she states in quietly amused mockery. "It's a safe environment." These exchanges move beyond any simplistic depiction of black pathology and abjection.

In fact, the film addresses the overwhelming nature of Precious's life, offering another kind of realism to substitute for the excesses of "reality" decried by critics. In a scene that does not include Precious, her teacher, Ms. Rain, asks two fellow students, "What do I mean when I say the author describes her protagonist's circumstances as unrelenting?" This exchange, which does not appear in the novel (though the reference to a female author can be read as an allusion to Sapphire), is clearly designed as a preemptive response to critiques of the film as providing little more than a litany of abuses suffered by a young black woman. Prior to this scene the students are shown struggling to master the alphabet, and thus the type of literary discussion that Ms. Rain initiates here seems well beyond the scope of students enrolled not in a GED class, but a pre-GED class. The first student, Rita, says that she does not know the answer to Ms. Rain's question, but her companion, Rhonda, provides a telling response. In heavily accented Jamaican patois that parallels the disorienting language of the opening credits, Rhonda explains that if Rita were to do something but then was somehow hindered she would persist and keep "going and going." Gazing at Ms. Rain, Rhonda concludes, "Relentless, un."

Rhonda's response provides an accurate description of what "unrelenting" means, but it is important to note that she does not actually answer Ms. Rain's question. Rhonda shifts the descriptor, "unrelenting," from Ms. Rain's concern with "the protagonist's circumstances" to the example of Rita, framing her as relentless. Circumstances are not unrelenting; Rita is. Rhonda's reply to Ms. Rain's question can thus be understood to counter claims like those of White who described *Precious* as "an orgy of prurience."[20] White's characterization emphasizes Precious's circumstances over her will to flourish. However, the most unrelenting aspect of the film is not the onslaught of abuses that Precious faces but her own determination to strive for a better life. Critics would be better served by debating the realism of that aspect of Precious, rather than the accuracy of her unrelenting circumstances. For Rhonda and her fellow classmates, judging the nature of their social conditions is irrelevant. The issue is not how bad things are, but what they must do to move beyond those circumstances. This scene effectively instructs audience members how to understand the film by emphasizing a kind of reading practice that stresses individual agency, not social circumstances. From this perspective, the film posits an important parallel between Obama and Precious; both achieve remarkable heights through fierce resolve and a loving network of support. Daniels presents his protagonist not as an inversion of Obama, but rather as his determined predecessor.

Another common criticism of the film involves its seemingly colorist approach to its cast. Characters who operate as agents of positive change, including Ms. Rain (Paula Patton), the social worker Ms. Weisz (Mariah Carey), and Nurse John (Lenny Kravitz), are all played by light-skinned actors. By contrast, as Jim Downs observed, "The dark-skinned characters, from boys on the street to Precious's mother (who are, by contrast, unredeemed and unredeemable by virtue of their undeniable African-ness) are marked as villains."[21] Downs overstates the debasing power of "African-ness"; the dark-skinned Precious is the most obvious counter example to this claim, and in the climatic scene involving Precious's mother, played by Mo'Nique, Ms. Weisz, and Precious, Mo'Nique is whitened with make-up as if to further the contrast between Precious and her. Although the characters do generally fall on a colorist spectrum that seems to value white skin, the film ultimately undermines conventional associations of black as evil and white as good.

When Precious first appears at the alternative school, "Each One Teach One," run by Ms. Rain, she has to take a diagnostic test. As she struggles through the multiple-choice questions, Precious comments, "There is always something wrong with these tests. These tests paint a picture of me with no brain." Among the questions that troubles Precious is one that reads, "There are dark clouds. It looks dark. It is: a) sunny b) funny c) happy d) raining." Precious marks "c) happy." She associates darkness with happiness, a somewhat unusual connection that counters the simplistic color binary that Downs observes in the film. Precious here unsettles the conventional meaning assigned to blackness. Oddly, the question does not have a clear answer. Although the dark clouds may portend rain, they do not guarantee that it is actually raining. Both "funny" and "happy" are subjective descriptions, and as such it is possible to view dark clouds as either one. The question has no obvious answer, indicating the failures of standardized tests and the arbitrary meanings assigned to color.

Understanding the test as ultimately an attack on her very self, Precious erases her answer and at last leaves the question blank. She knows that her conception of blackness will be judged as wrong; her approach to the world will not be validated by the test, which leaves her, as she describes, "ugly black grease to be wiped away." Blackness remains a mark of degradation, and in fact the people that Precious encounters largely justify that conception. The most supportive and caring characters are light-skinned. The conventions of racial meaning abide through this casting. The challenge for Precious to value herself is all the more acute as a result. She is not like Ms. Rain, Ms. Weisz, or Nurse John; she does not and will never have the privilege of their skin tone. In effect, they are not Precious, and thus any simplistic claim that "We are all Precious" is here under-mined by the film's representation of an abiding color hierarchy.

"Race-specific, race-free language" might provide a refuge from such color-based inequalities as it invokes the possibility of race without racism. Such prose, however, operates by making its audience raceless. In this way, it is in danger of imposing a new kind of racial standard akin to how whiteness often continues to function. Just as whiteness long operated as the default standard of identification, racelessness appears ready to assume that position. "Race-specific, race-free language" may lay the grounds for critical forms of interracial communication, but it does not guarantee the mutual recognition of racial identity that is necessary for meaningful exchange and intimacy. For a black presidential candidate this kind of language is a political necessity even as it poses other problems for the articulation of identity. Morrison's vision of a home as "a-world-in-which-race-does-*not*-matter" demands the enunciation of race, not its dissolution. Among the many striking contrasts to Obama that Precious poses is her demand for an audience that remains not in the safety of ambiguity but that claims a racial identification. In her penultimate session with her social worker, Precious asks Ms. Weisz, "So you Italian, what color are you, anyway? You some type of black or Spanish?" Ms. Weisz equivocates, replying, "What color do you think I am?" Precious remains silent, and Ms. Weisz asks again, "I'd like to know, what color do you think I am?" Precious at last refuses to respond, stating, "My throat is dry."

The question is not for Precious to answer, and Ms. Weisz's refusal to identify herself racially undermines the trust that has slowly emerged between them. Their conversations offer some hope that Precious's once impenetrable language may at least be understood. While Ms. Weisz goes to get them both sodas, Precious raids her files, stealing her own. This theft acts as an indictment of Ms. Weisz's embrace of racial ambiguity. Precious's blackness has always been clear and undeniable, and consequently Ms. Weisz's evasion regarding her own racial identity represents the impossibility of their intimacy. Ms. Weisz can only become race-free once she acknowledges racial specificity, thereby becoming a worthy audience for Precious's story, for, as Precious tells her in their final encounter, "I like you too but you can't handle me, you can't handle none of this." We must understand "race-specific, race-free language" not as an invitation to hide from race but as a demand to articulate it. Intimacy depends upon an answer to Precious's question.

NOTES

INTRODUCTION

1. This phrase has also been linked to the Hopi Elders. However, its first print publication is ascribed to Jordan's poem "Poem for South African Women," in *Passion: New Poems, 1977–80* (Boston: Beacon Press, 1980), 42–43. Obama used the phrase in his address on Super Tuesday 2008, http://www.barackobama .com/2008/02/05/remarks_of_senator_barack_obam_46.php.

2. Richard Cohen, "The Election that LBJ Won," *Washington Post*, November 4, 2008, http://www.washingtonpost.com/wpdyn/content/article/2008/11/03/AR 2008110302609.html.

3. "President Elect Obama," *Wall Street Journal*, November 5, 2008, http://online .wsj.com/article/NA_WSJ_PUB:SB122586244657800863.html

4. News anchor Chris Matthews's comment that he "forgot" Obama was black during the president's first State of the Union address in January 2010 is emblematic of how racial identity is figured as a quality best erased from mainstream consciousness.

5. David Theo Goldberg, who has written extensively on the distinction between "racial conception and racism" (4), emphasizes that antiracism should not be conflated with antiracialism, which involves "take(ing) a stand, instrumental or institutional, against a concept, a name, a category, a categorizing" (*The Threat of Race* [Malden Mass.: Wiley-Blackwell, 2009], 10).

6. Fred Moten, "The Case of Blackness," *Criticism* 50, no. 2 (Spring 2008): 204.

7. Eduardo Bonilla-Silva, in *Racism without Racists* (Lanham, Md.: Rowman & Littlefield, 2003), identifies "color-blind racism" as the prevailing form of racism in contemporary American society. He explains, "Whereas Jim Crow racism explained blacks' social standing as the result of their biological and moral inferiority, color-blind racism avoids such facile arguments. Instead, whites rationalize minorities' contemporary status as the product of market dynamics, naturally occurring phenomena, and blacks' imputed cultural limitations" (2).

8. Philip D. Carter, "Another of the 'New Souths,'" *Washington Post*, October 10, 1971.

9. In "Post-Feminism and Popular Culture," *Feminist Media Studies* 4:3 (2004): 255–264, Angela McRobbie writes, "post-feminism positively draws on and

invokes feminism as that which can be taken into account, to suggest that equality is achieved, in order to install a whole repertoire of new meanings which emphasize that it is no longer needed, it is a spent force" (255).

10. See Henry Louis Gates Jr., *The Signifying Monkey: A Theory of African-American Literary Criticism* (New York: Oxford, 1988).

11. Ferraro's comments were first reported in the *Daily Breeze*. Jim Farber, "Geraldine Ferraro lets her emotions do the talking," *Dailybreeze.com*, March 7, 2008, http://www.dailybreeze.com/lifeandculture/ci_8489268.

12. Many politicians have used race as a political tool by stoking racial prejudice. George H. W. Bush successfully exploited white fears of black criminality through his "Revolving Door" campaign ad, which attacked the 1988 Democratic presidential nominee, Michael Dukakis, for his support of a weekend furlough program used by convicted felon Willie Horton. Horton committed assault, armed robbery, and rape while on furlough.

13. Harry Reid, quoted in John Heilemann and Mark Halperin, *Game Change: Obama and the Clintons, McCain and Palin, and the Race of a Lifetime* (New York: HarperCollins, 2010), 36.

14. Anthony Appiah identifies racialism in *In My Father's House* (New York: Oxford, 1993), as the view that "there are heritable characteristics, possessed by members of our species, which allow us to divide them into a small set of races." Though racialism may endorse a kind of "racial essence," Appiah notes, "racialism is not, in itself, a doctrine that must be dangerous" (13).

15. In November 2009, Michael Luo reported for the *New York Times*: "Various academic studies have confirmed that black job seekers have a harder time than whites." For in-depth discussion of abiding inequalities in communities of color, see "Barack Obama, White Denial, and the Reality of Racism," in Tim Wise's *Between Barack and a Hard Place: Racism and White Denial in the Age of Obama* (2009).

16. Bakhtin explains in "Discourse in the Novel" from *The Dialogic Imagination* (Austin: University of Texas Press, 1981): "What is hybridization? It is a mixture of two social languages within the limits of a single utterance, an encounter, within the arena of an utterance, between two different linguistic consciousnesses, separated from one another by an epoch, by social differentiation or by some other factor" (358).

17. When asked by Bill Moyers in 1989, "Does the public now expect you to write only about black people?" Morrison cited this scene in *Beloved* as an example of her commitment to writing about black people though she "won't identify them as such." She elaborates, "There are two moments in *Beloved* when I tried to do just that. I set up a situation in which two people are talking—two black people—and some other people enter the scene. They're never identified as either black or white, but the reader knows instantly, and not because I use the traditional language of stereotype. One moment comes Paul D and Sethe are walking down the street, and he touches her shoulder to lead her off the sidewalk onto the ground because three women are walking this way. That's all.

But you know who they are. . . . What I really want to do, and expect to do, is not identify my characters by race. But I wont be writing about white people. I'll be writing about black people. It will be part of my job to make sure readers aren't confused. But can you think what it would mean for me and my relationship to language and to texts to be able to write without having to always specify to the reader the race of the characters?" (265–266). "A Conversation with Toni Morrison," interview by Bill Moyers, in *Conversations with Toni Morrison*, ed. Danille Taylor-Guthrie (Jackson: University Press of Mississippi, 1994), 262–274.

18. Obama does not employ what John Russell Rickford and Russell John Rickford term "Spoken Soul" or African American Vernacular English, which is defined by its own vocabulary, grammar, and phonology (see *Spoken Soul: The Story of Black English* [2000]). We might, however, understand Obama's language as conforming to what James Baldwin calls "Black English," which he defined as "the creation of the black diaspora" in "If Black English Isn't a Language, Then Tell Me, What Is?" http://www.nytimes.com/books/98/03/29/specials/baldwin-english.html. The difficulty in defining Obama's language as black or not demonstrates the ambiguity of both racial and linguistic categories, an interpretive gap that Obama maximizes to his own advantage.

19. U.S. Society & Values: Electronic Journals of the U.S. Information Agency, *Toward One America: A National Conversation on Race* (Washington, D.C.: U.S. Information Agency, August 1997), 9.

20. Assessing the Presidential Initiative on Race, Linda Faye Williams, in *The Constraint of Race* (University Park: Pennsylvania State University Press, 2004), writes: "For the most part, the dialogue on race never really seemed to take off; never really seemed to break new ground; never seemed enough to shake up the bulk of Americans, complacent about race relations or indifferent to them; never seemed enough to arouse what Martin Luther King had termed 'creative tension' in thoughtful people; never seemed enough to challenge the views of even those who were explicitly and openly racist" (327).

21. Frances Fox Piven observed, "Presidential advisory bodies are not ordinarily created to craft genuinely new policy recommendations. . . . And sometimes, as seems to be the case with the Advisory Board to the President's Initiative on Race, the intention is merely to adorn with serious studies and lofty thoughts a government determined to do nothing of consequence" ("Escaping Clinton's Control," 2001, 318).

22. Angela Oh, quoted in Frank H. Wu, *Yellow: Race in America Beyond Black and White* (New York: Basic Books, 2002), 34.

23. John Hope Franklin, quoted in Wu, *Yellow*, 34.24. Mary Frances Berry, "Color Codes: Moving Beyond Clinton's Race Initiative Means Facing Black-White Reality and Building Bridges," *Emerge*, January 31, 1999, 55.

25. William Clinton, Commencement Speech, University of California at San Diego, June 14, 1997, http://www.whitehouse.gov/Initiatives/OneAmerica/announcement.html.

26. In "Seven Lessons from President Clinton's Race Initiative" Patricia A. Sullivan and Steven R. Goldwiz write, "If Clinton was truly intent upon creating One America and achieving the desired racial reconciliation, more attention might have been paid to the relation between race, class, and the economy" (159) and note that "taboo topics as such as white privilege, class and the new resegregation occurring in America" (157) were excluded from discussion (Westport, Conn.: Praeger, 2003).

27. Felicia R. Lee, "The Honest Dialogue That Is Neither," *New York Times*, December 7, 1997, late edition. Even advisory chair Franklin admitted a degree of defeat, writing in the *New York Times*, "We have learned how difficult it is to hold productive discussions about race under the glare of television lights and cameras, in large meetings among relative strangers, and among people who expect more than an advisory board can reasonably deliver."

28. Toni Morrison, letter to Obama, January 28, 2008, http://firstread.msnbc.msn.com/archive/2008/01/28/614795.aspx.

29. For further description of recent changes in the black community, see William Jelani Cobb's *The Substance of Hope: Barack Obama and the Paradox of Progress* (New York: Walker, 2010) and Gwen Ifill's *The Breakthrough: Politics and Race in the Age of Obama* (New York: Doubleday, 2009). Thelma Golden, in the introduction to *Freestyle (New York: The Studio Museum in Harlem, 2001), 14–15,* is largely credited with first using the term "post-black" to describe a new generation of artists "who were adamant about not being labeled as 'black' artists, though their work was steeped, in fact deeply interested, in redefining complex notions of blackness" (14).

30. Michael Eric Dyson, "His Way With Words Begins at the Pulpit," *Washington Post*, January 18, 2009, http://www.washingtonpost.com/wp-dyn/content/article/2009/01/16/AR2009011602312.html.

31. As Dyson notes, this line, "You've been hoodwinked. You've been had. You've been took. You've been led astray, led amok. You've been bamboozled," became best known to contemporary audiences through Spike Lee's film about the life of Malcolm X; ibid.

32. While Ta-Nehisi Paul Coates concluded in an article for *Time* magazine entitled "Is Obama Black Enough?" in February 2007 that "Barack Obama's real problem isn't that he's too white—it's that he is too black," Stanley Crouch wrote in the *New York Daily News*, "Obama makes it clear that, while he has experienced some light versions of typical racial stereotypes, he cannot claim those problems as his own—nor has he lived the life of a black American." Coates, http://www.time.com/time/nation/article/0,8599,1584736,00.html and Crouch, http://www.amren.com/mtnews/archives/2006/11/what_obama_isnt.php.

33. Christopher Beam, "The Fallacy of False Choices: Why Obama's favorite rhetorical tic can be misleading," *Slate*, December 10, 2009, http://www.slate.com/id/2238074/.

34. Zadie Smith, "Speaking in Tongues," *New York Review of Books*, February 26, 2009, http://www.nybooks.com/articles/22334.

35. Morrison explains that the first word immigrants to the United States learn is "okay." Bonnie Angelo, "The Pain of Being Black: An Interview with Toni Morrison," in *Conversations with Toni Morrison*, ed. Danille Taylor-Guthrie (Jackson: University Press of Mississippi, 1994), 255.

36. Toni Morrison, interview by Timehost, *Time.com*, January 21, 1998, http://www.time.com/time/community/transcripts/chattr012198.html.

CHAPTER 1   VIOLENCE AND TONI MORRISON'S RACIST HOUSE

1. Toni Morrison, "Toni Morrison Finds *A Mercy* in Servitude," interview by Michelle Norris, NPR (October 27, 2008).

2. "Minha mãe" translates as "my mother" in Portuguese.

3. Michiko Kakutani, "Worthy Women, Unredeemable Men," review of *Paradise* by Toni Morrison, *New York Times*, January 6, 1998, http://www.nytimes.com/1998/01/06/books/books-of-the-times-worthy-women-unredeemable-men.html?n=Top/Features/Books/Book%20Reviews.

4. David Gates, "Trouble in Paradise," review of *Paradise* by Toni Morrison, *Newsweek*, January 12, 1998, 62. Brook Allen, "The Promised Land," review of *Paradise* by Toni Morrison, *New York Times Book Review*, January 11, 1998, sec. 7, 6.

5. Louis Menand, "The War between Men and Women," review of *Paradise* by Toni Morrison, *New Yorker*, January 12, 1998, 78.

6. Toni Morrison, interview by Timehost, *Time.com*, January 21, 1998, http://www.time.com/time/community/transcripts/chattr012198.html.

7. Sarah Appleton Aguiar, in "'Passing On' Death," *African American Review* 38:3 (2004): 513–519, provides an innovative reading of the discrepancy among the women found at the Convent. She claims that "several subtleties suggest that at least some of the women are dead before the Ruby posse attacks" (515). Aguilar does not specifically identify which of the Convent women are dead, but instead she argues that they all have intimate relationships with death.

8. Julia Kristeva, "Revolution in Poetic Language," in *The Kristeva Reader*, ed. Toril Moi (New York: Columbia University Press, 1986), 89–135.

CHAPTER 2   HIDING THE INVISIBLE HURT OF RACE

1. Harris-Lacewell goes on to suggest "that the folksy interventions of Sarah Palin were a desperate attempt to reclaim and redefine whiteness as a gun-toting ordinariness that eschews traditional and elite markers of achievement." "Black by Choice," *The Nation*, April 15, 2010, http://www.thenation.com/article/black-choice.

2. Toni Morrison, quoted in Jamin Brophy-Warren, "A Writer's Vote," *Wall Street Journal*, November 7, 2008, Books & Authors section.

3. Morrison has elaborated on her concerns regarding mid-twentieth-century black male writers: "Ralph Ellison and Richard Wright—all of whose books I admire enormously—I didn't feel were telling me something. I thought they were saying something about it or us that revealed something about us to you, to others, to white people, to men." Charles Ruas, "Toni Morrison," in *Conversations with Toni Morrison*, ed. Danille Taylor-Guthrie (Jackson: University Press of Mississippi, 1994), 96.

4. Pam Houston, "Pam Houston Talks with Toni Morrison," in *Toni Morrison: Conversations*, ed. Carolyn C. Denard (Jackson: University Press of Mississippi, 2008), 236.

5. Ibid., 253.

6. Michaels perceives America's fixation with race as generating a stalled debate. He writes, "Where contemporary liberalism's antiracism argues that we can solve our problems by respecting racial difference, contemporary conservatism's antiracism maintains we can solve our problems only by eliminating or ignoring it." Apex's vision of racial harmony partakes of both sides of this conflict; it superficially respects racial difference through the multicolored bandages, but it also ignores racial difference by stressing the commonality of wound and emblematizing physical injury rather than emotional or historical trauma. Michaels concludes, "The problem with this debate (or, looked at another way, the virtue of this debate) is that, from the standpoint of economic inequality, it doesn't matter which side you're on and it doesn't matter who wins. Either way, economic inequality is untouched" (75). Within the context of Whitehead's novel, the ultimate success of Apex's ad campaign is to sell more products to people of all races.

7. Bakhtin wrote, "No speaker is after all, the first speaker, the one who disturbs the eternal silence of the universe." Quoted in Kenneth J. Gergen, *An Invitation to Social Construction* (Thousand Oaks, Calif: Sage, 1999), 130.

8. Reflecting on the nature of his invisibility, Ellison's protagonist explains, "you often doubt if you really exist. . . . You ache with the need to convince yourself that you do exist in the real world, that you're a part of all the sound and anguish, and you strike out with your fists, you curse and you swear to make them recognize you. And, alas, it's seldom successful" (4).

9. Although beyond the scope of this analysis, the protagonist's wounded toe can be productively read as a mark of castration. His self-cultivated isolation prevents him from engaging in sexual relationships. While in Winthrop he twice finds himself attracted to women (Regina and Beverley, the town librarian) and in both cases he fails to make a move. As a psychic wound that manifests itself through the body, his injured toe might also be understood as a sign of hysteria, a further challenge to his masculinity.

10. This vision poses a striking contrast to the glib rhetoric of his predecessor, George W. Bush, who declared an end to major combat in Iraq in 2003 under a banner reading, "Mission Accomplished." Though the contexts of these two

speeches differ radically, both point to a critical contrast between Obama and Bush. Notwithstanding the fact that guerilla warfare markedly increased in Iraq following the "Mission Accomplished" speech, Bush moves to celebrate the final conclusion of our nation's work by staking victory in what has been, not what must be.

CHAPTER 3   THE UNSPEAKABLE LANGUAGE OF RACE AND
              FANTASY IN THE STORIES OF JHUMPA LAHIRI

1. Numerous sources identify Obama's poet friend as Frank Marshall Davis, a well-known author and civil rights activist.

2. Obama's description of how his mother taught him about black American history suggests a highly romanticized vision of blackness: "Every black man was Thurgood Marshall or Sidney Poitier; every black woman Fannie Lou Hamer or Lena Horne. To be black was to be the beneficiary of a great inheritance, a special destiny, glorious burdens that only we were strong enough to bear" (*Dreams from My Father: A Story of Race and Inheritance* [New York: Three Rivers Press, 2004], 51).

CHAPTER 4   PERFORMING INTIMACY

1. Ishmael Reed, "Obama Scolds Black Fathers, Gets Bounce in Polls," http://www.counterpunch.org/reed06242008.html.

2. Ford approaches these matters as a legal scholar, charting evolving conceptions of what constitutes racial discrimination: "even judges don't always know racism when they see it. The courts employ several methods to define discrimination, but these don't really identify a specific thing—a prohibited state of mind or distinct wrongful action. Instead they define a set of duties and obligations in an attempt to balance the goal of social justice against other considerations, such as privacy, productivity, and freedom of expression" (*The Race Card* [New York: Picador, 2008], 264).

3. Joe Biden and Barack Obama quoted in Xuan Thai and Ted Barrett, "Biden's Description of Obama Draws Scrutiny," CNN.com, February 9, 2007, http://www.cnn.com/2007/POLITICS/01/31/biden.obama/.

4. Toni Morrison, letter to Obama, January 28, 2008, http://firstread.msnbc.msn.com/archive/2008/01/28/614795.aspx.

5. Maya Angelou, "State Package for Hillary Clinton," *The Observer*, January 20, 2008, http://www.guardian.co.uk/world/2008/jan/20/usa.poetry.

6. John Lewis, interview by Tavis Smiley, *Tavis Smiley Late Night on PBS*, August 28, 2008.

7. Andrew Young, quoted in Gwen Iffil, *The Breakthrough: Politics and Race in the Age of Obama* (New York: Doubleday, 2009), 34.

8. Jesse Jackson Jr., "Jesse Jr. to Jesse Sr.: You're Wrong on Obama, Dad," *Chicago Sun-Times*, December 3, 2007, http://www.suntimes.com/news/commentary/

letters/678092,CST-EDT-vox03.article; Harold Ford Jr., "Go Meet Them, Senator," *Newsweek*, June 2, 2008, http//www.newsweek.com/id/138511; Alice Walker, "Lest We Forget: An Open Letter to My Sisters Who Are Brave," *Root*, March 27, 2008, http://www.theroot.com/views/lest-we-forget-open-letter-to-my-sisters-who-are-brave; Alice Walker, "White House Advice," *Newsweek*, January 19, 2009, http://www.newsweek.com/id/180457; and Barbara Seals Nevergold and Peggy Brooks-Bertram, *Go, Tell Michelle: African American Women Write to the New First Lady* (Albany: State University of New York Press, 2009).

9. Barack Obama, "Sen. Barack Obama's Letter to Tavis Smiley," *Chicago Sun-Times*, February 14, 2008, http://blogs.suntimes.com/mitchell/2008/02/sen_barack_obamas_letter_to_ta_1.html.

10. Alice Walker, "White House Advice."

11. Alice Walker, "Lest We Forget: An Open Letter to My Sisters Who Are Brave."

12. David Remnick, "The Joshua Generation: Race and the Campaign of Barack Obama," *New Yorker*, November 17, 2008, http://www.newyorker.com/reporting/2008/11/17/081117fa_fact_remnick?currentPage=all.

13. This is a concern that has also been voiced by Tim Wise: "Obama has issued a challenge to black folks to be more responsible for the problems in their communities—in part a message he sincerely believes, of course, but also one intended to make whites more comfortable with his candidacy" (Between Barack and a Hard Place [San Francisco: City Lights, 2009], 12).

14. Jesse Jackson, quoted in Remnick, "The Joshua Generation."

15. Julian Bond, quoted in Remnick, "The Joshua Generation."

16. Barack Obama, "Selma Voting Rights March Commemoration," March 4, 2007, http://www.barackobama.com/2007/03/04/selma_voting_rights_march_comm.php

17. Barack Obama, "What I Want for You—and Every Child in America," *Parade*, January 18, 2009, http://www.parade.com/export/sites/default/news/2009/01/barack-obama-letter-to-my-daughters.html.

18. The most controversial statements made by the Reverend Wright are derived from two sermons he delivered in September 2001 and April 2003. In the first he characterized the 9/11 terrorist attacks as indicative that "America's chickens are coming home to roost." In the second, he stated, "No, no, no, not God Bless America. God damn America—that's in the Bible—for killing innocent people. God damn America, for treating our citizens as less than human. God damn America, as long as she tries to act like she is God, and she is supreme. The United States government has failed the vast majority of her citizens of African descent." Wright later claimed that his comments were taken out of context. For detailed discussion of the Wright scandal, see Richard Wolffe, *The Renegade: The Making of a President* (New York: Random House, 2009).

19. John Dickerson, "The Storyteller," *Slate*, January 17, 2009, http://www.slate.com/id/2208776.

20. Obama does mention Martin Luther King's birthday since he spoke on that day at King's home church, Ebenezer Baptist and also told the story of Ashley Baia there.

21. David Remnick, "The Joshua Generation."

22. The police report, Incident Report #9005127 from the Cambridge Police Department, can be viewed online at http://www.thesmokinggun.com/documents/crime/henry-louis-gates-jr-police-report.

23. Barack Obama quoted in Katharine Q. Seelye, "Obama Wades into a Volatile Racial Issue," *New York Times*, July 23, 2009, http://www.nytimes.com/2009/07/23/us/23race.html.

24. The Pew Research Center for the People & the Press reported these findings on July 30, 2009. http://people-press.org/report/532/obamas-ratings-slide.

25. Barack Obama quoted in "I Could Have Calibrated Those Words Differently," *New York Times*, July 25, 2009, http://query.nytimes.com/gst/fullpage.html?res=9F04E4DC163AF936A15754C0A96F9C8B63

26. Arica Coleman, "What's Been Missing from Obama's Response to the Arrest of Henry Louis Gates," *L.A. Progressive*, July 30, 2009, http://www.laprogressive.com/rankism/obamas-beer-summit/.

27. Katharine Q. Seelye, "Obama Wades into a Volatile Racial Issue."

28. Carter said, "I think an overwhelming portion of the intensely demonstrated animosity toward President Barack Obama is based on the fact that he is a black man, that he's African-American. I live in the South, and I've seen the South come a long way, and I've seen the rest of the country that shred the South's attitude toward minority groups at that time, particularly African-Americans. And that racism inclination still exists. And I think it's bubbled up to the surface because of the belief among many white people, not just in the South, but around the country, that African-Americans are not qualified to lead this great country." Jimmy Carter quoted in "Carter Again Cites Racism as Factor in Obama's Treatment," CNN.com, September 17, 2009, http://www.cnn.com/2009/POLITICS/09/15/carter.obama/index.html.

29. Robert Gibbs quoted in "Back and Forth on Race: Sept.13–19," *New York Times*, September 20, 2009, http://query.nytimes.com/gst/fullpage.html?res=940CE6D81239F933A1575AC0A96F9C8B63.

30. Barack Obama, Speech to the Urban League, July 29, 2010, http://blogs.suntimes.com/sweet/2010/07/obama_urban_league_speech_sher.html.

CONCLUSION

1. The film's website uses Oprah's declaration as its address. See www.weareallprecious.com.

2. Lynn Hirschberg, "The Audacity of Precious," *New York Times Magazine*, October 21, 2009, http://www.nytimes.com/2009/10/25/magazine/25precious-t.html.

3. Barbara Bush, "A Precious Moment," *Newsweek*, December 3, 2009, http://www.newsweek.com/2009/12/02/a-precious-moment.html.

4. Daniels quoted in Hirschberg, "The Audacity of Precious."

5. Daniels followed up his comments about now having a single face by stating, "But old habits die hard, and sometimes I can't remember who I'm supposed to be," suggesting the abiding struggle involved in producing and maintaining racial identity; quoted in ibid.

6. Lee Daniels, interview by Reshma Gospaldas, November 11, 2009, http://blogs .myspace.com/index.cfm?fuseaction=blog.view&friendId=252682909&blogId= 518071881.

7. Gabourey Sidibe quoted in Tim Murphy, "Living the Life," *New York Magazine*, September 25, 2009, http://nymag.com/movies/profiles/59419/.

8. Lee Daniels, interview by Nathan Rabin, *The A.V. Club*, November 5, 2009, http://www.avclub.com/articles/lee-daniels-and-gabby-sidibe,34991/.

9. Jill Nelson, "She Ain't Me Babe," December 9, 2009, http://www.niaonline.com/ ggmsblog/?p=3934.

10. Armond White, "Pride & Precious," *New York Press*, November 4, 2009, http:// www.nypress.com/article-20554-pride-precious.html.

11. In *The Matrix* (1999), the first film in the trilogy, Neo is named "the one" by a character known as the Oracle, played by African American actress Gloria Foster. By calling Obama "the one," Winfrey positions herself as the Oracle, a familiar figure of black wisdom who facilitates the transformation of a typically white protagonist. In this way, her endorsement strategically traffics in a series of preestablished racialized images though Obama's blackness makes him an unusual focal point.

12. In "The Role of Celebrity Endorsements in Politics: Oprah, Obama, and the 2008 Democratic Primary," Craig Garthwaite and Timothy J. Moore conclude, "Winfrey's endorsement was responsible for approximately 1,000,000 additional votes for Obama." http://www.econ.umd.edu/~garthwaite/ celebrityendorsements_garthwaitemoore.pdf.

13. Timothy Noah of Slate.com collected examples of the media's representation of Obama as the country's savior online at "The Obama Messiah Watch," http://www.slate.com/id/2158578.

14. Adolph Reed Jr., "Obama No," *The Progressive*, May 2008, http://www .progressive.org/mag_reed0508.

15. David Ehrenstein, "'Magic Negro' Returns," *Los Angeles Times*, March 19, 2007, http://articles.latimes.com/2007/mar/19/opinion/oe-ehrenstein19.

16. In a related manner, Hillary Clinton was subjected to gendered representations that her fellow male candidates entirely escaped.

17. David Brooks diagnosed "Obama Comedown Syndrome" in the inevitable letdown following his inauguration in "When the Magic Fades," *New York Times*, February 19, 2008, http://www.nytimes.com/2008/02/19/opinion/19brooks .html.

18. During the presidential campaign, Republicans sought to capitalize on this aspect of Obama, positing "Joe the Plumber," Samuel Joseph Wurzelbacher, as a symbol of everyday middle-class Americans and notably a white male. His ordinariness is inextricable from his whiteness.

19. Erin Aubry Kaplan, "'Precious' in the Age of Obama," *Salon*, November 9, 2009, http://www.salon.com/entertainment/precious/index.html?story=/ent/movies/feature/2009/11/09/precious_feature.

20. Ibid.

21. Jim Downs, "Are We All Precious?" *Chronicle of Higher Education*, December 13, 2009, http://chronicle.com/article/Are-We-All-Precious-/49458/.

BIBLIOGRAPHY

Aguiar, Sarah Appleton. "'Passing On' Death: Stealing Life in Toni Morrison's *Paradise*." *African American Review* 38:3 (2004): 513–519.

Allen, Brook. "The Promised Land." Review of *Paradise* by Toni Morrison. *New York Times Book Review*, January 11, 1998, sec. 7, 6.

Angelou, Maya. "State Package for Hillary Clinton." *The Observer*, January 20, 2008. http://www.guardian.co.uk/world/2008/jan/20/usa.poetry.

Appiah, Anthony. *In My Father's House: Africa in the Philosophy of Culture*. New York: Oxford University Press, 1993.

Bakhtin, M. M. *The Dialogic Imagination: Four Essays*. Edited by Michael Holquist. Translated by Caryl Emerson and Michael Holquist. Austin: University of Texas Press, 1981.

Baldwin, James. *The Fire Next Time*. New York: Vintage, 1992.

———. "If Black English Isn't a Language, Then Tell Me, What Is?" *New York Times*, July 29, 1979. http://www.nytimes.com/books/98/03/29/specials/baldwin-english.html.

Beam, Christopher. "The Fallacy of False Choices: Why Obama's Favorite Rhetorical Tic Can be Misleading." *Slate*, December 10, 2009. http://www.slate.com/id/2238074/.

Berlant, Lauren. *The Queen of America Goes to Washington City: Essays on Sex and Citizenship*. Durham, N.C.: Duke University Press, 1997.

Berry, Mary Frances. "Color Codes: Moving Beyond Clinton's Race Initiative Means Facing Black-White Reality and Building Bridges." *Emerge*, January 31, 1999, 55.

Bhabha, Homi K. *The Location of Culture*. London: Routledge, 1994.

Bonilla-Silva, Eduardo. *Racism without Racists: Color-Blind Racism and the Persistence of Racial Inequality in the United States*. Lanham, Md.: Rowman & Littlefield, 2003.

Bronson, Po, and Ashley Merryman. *NurtureShock: New Thinking About Children*. New York: Twelve, Hatchette Book Group, Inc., 2009.

Brooks, David. "When the Magic Fades." *New York Times*, February 19, 2008. http://www.nytimes.com/2008/02/19/opinion/19brooks.html.

Brophy-Warren, Jamin. "A Writer's Vote." *Wall Street Journal*, November 7, 2008, Books & Authors section.

Bush, Barbara. "A Precious Moment." *Newsweek*, December 3, 2009. http://www.newsweek.com/2009/12/02/a-precious-moment.html.

Butler, Judith. *Bodies that Matter: On the Discursive Limits of Sex*. New York: Routledge, 1993.

Carcasson, Martin, and Mitchell F. Rice. "The Promise and Failure of President Clinton's Race Initiative of 1997–1998: A Rhetorical Perspective." *Rhetoric & Public Affairs* 2:2 (Summer 1999): 243–274.

Carter, Jimmy. Quoted in "Carter Again Cites Racism as Factor in Obama's Treatment." CNN.com, September 17, 2009. http://www.cnn.com/2009/POLITICS/09/15/carter.obama/index.html.

Carter, Philip D. "Another of the 'New Souths.'" *Washington Post*, October 10, 1971.

Cheng, Anne Anlin. *The Melancholy of Race: Psychoanalysis, Assimilation, and Hidden Grief.* New York: Oxford University Press, 2001.

Clinton, William. Commencement Speech, University of California at San Diego. June 14, 1997. http://www.whitehouse.gov/Initiatives/OneAmerica/announcement.html.

Coates, Ta-Nehisi Paul "Is Obama Black Enough?" *Time*, February 1, 2007. http://www.time.com/time/nation/article/0,8599,1584736,00.html.

Cobb, William Jelani. *The Substance of Hope: Barack Obama and the Paradox of Progress.* New York: Walker & Company, 2010.

Cohen, Richard. "The Election that LBJ Won." *Washington Post*, November 4, 2008. http://www.washingtonpost.com/wpdyn/content/article/2008/11/03/AR2008110302609.html.

Coleman, Arica. "What's Been Missing from Obama's Response to the Arrest of Henry Louis Gates." *L.A. Progressive*, July 30, 2009. http://www.laprogressive.com/rankism/obamas-beer-summit/.

Crouch, Stanley. "What Obama Isn't: Black Like Me." *New York Daily News*, November 2, 2006. http://www.amren.com/mtnews/archives/2006/11/what_obama_isnt.php.

Daniels, Lee. Interview by Nathan Rabin. *The A.V. Club*, November 5, 2009. http://www.avclub.com/articles/lee-daniels-and-gabby-sidibe,34991/.

———. Interview by Reshma Gospaldas, November 11, 2009. http://blogs.myspace.com/index.cfm?fuseaction=blog.view&friendId=252682909&blogId=518071881.

Denard, Carolyn C., ed. *Toni Morrison: Conversations.* Jackson: University of Mississippi Press, 2008.

Dickerson, John. "The Storyteller." *Slate*, January 17, 2009. http://www.slate.com/id/2208776.

Downs, Jim. "Are We All Precious?" *Chronicle of Higher Education*, December 13, 2009. http://chronicle.com/article/Are-We-All-Precious-/49458/

Du Bois, W.E.B. *The Souls of Black Folk.* A. C. McClurg & Co.: Cambridge, Mass., 1903. Reprint, New York: Dover Publications, 1994.

Duvall, John N. *The Identifying Fictions of Toni Morrison: Modernist Authenticity and Postmodern Blackness.* New York: Palgrave, 2000.

Dyer, Richard. "White." In *The Matter of Images: Essays on Representation*, 126–148. London: Routledge, 2002.

Dyson, Michael Eric. "His Way with Words Begins at the Pulpit." *Washington Post*, January 18, 2009. http://www.washingtonpost.com/wpdyn/content/article/2009/01/16/AR2009011602312.html.

Ehrenstein, David. "'Magic Negro' Returns." *Los Angeles Times*, March 19, 2007. http://articles.latimes.com/2007/mar/19/opinion/oe-ehrenstein19.

Ellison, Ralph. *Invisible Man*. New York: Vintage International, 1990.

Farber, Jim. "Geraldine Ferraro lets her emotions do the talking." *Dailybreeze.com*, March 7, 2008. http://www.dailybreeze.com/lifeandculture/ci_8489268.

Field, Robin E. "Writing the Second Generation: Negotiating Cultural Borderlands in Jhumpa Lahiri's *Interpreter of Maladies* and *The Namesake*." *South Asian Review* 25:2 (2004): 165–177.

Ford, Harold Jr. "Go Meet Them, Senator." *Newsweek*, June 2, 2008. http//www.newsweek.com/id/138511.

Ford, Richard Thompson. *The Race Card: How Bluffing About Bias Makes Race Relations Worse*. New York: Picador, 2008.

Franklin, John Hope. "Talking, Not Shouting, About Race." *New York Times*, June 13, 1998. http://www.nytimes.com/books/99/08/15/specials/franklin.html.

Garthwaite, Craig, and Timothy J. Moore. "The Role of Celebrity Endorsements in Politics: Oprah, Obama, and the 2008 Democratic Primary." http://www.econ.umd.edu/~garthwaite/celebrityendorsements_garthwaitemoore.pdf.

Gates, David. "Trouble in Paradise." Review of *Paradise* by Toni Morrison. *Newsweek*, January 12, 1998, 62.

Gates, Henry Louis Jr. *The Signifying Monkey: A Theory of African-American Literary Criticism*. New York: Oxford University Press, 1988.

———. *Thirteen Ways of Looking at a Black Man*. New York: Random House, 1997.

Gauthier, Marni. "The Other Side of Paradise: Toni Morrison's (Un)Making of Mythic History." *African American Review* 39:3 (2005): 395–414.

Gergen, Kenneth, J. *An Invitation to Social Construction*. Thousand Oaks, Calif.: Sage, 1999.

Gibbs, Robert. Quoted in "Back and Forth on Race: Sept. 13–19." *New York Times*, September 20, 2009. http://query.nytimes.com/gst/fullpage.html?res=940CE6D81239F933A1575AC0A96F9C8B63.

Goldberg, David Theo. *The Threat of Race: Reflections on Racial Neoliberalism*. Malden, Mass.: Wiley-Blackwell, 2009.

Golden, Thelma. Introduction to *Freestyle*, 14–15. New York: The Studio Museum in Harlem, 2001.

Hall, Stuart. "New Ethnicities." In *The Post-Colonial Studies Reader*, edited by Bill Ashcroft, Gareth Griffiths, and Helen Tiffin, 223–227. London: Routledge, 1995.

Harris-Lacewell, Melissa. "Black by Choice." *The Nation*, April 15, 2010. http://www.thenation.com/article/black-choice.

Heilemann, John, and Mark Halperin. *Game Change: Obama and the Clintons, McCain and Palin, and the Race of a Lifetime*. New York: HarperCollins, 2010.

Hirschberg, Lynn. "The Audacity of Precious." *New York Times Magazine*, October 21, 2009, http://www.nytimes.com/2009/10/25/magazine/25precious-t.html.

Hollinger, David. *Postethnic America: Beyond Multiculturalism*. New York: BasicBooks, 1995.

Holloway, Karla F. C. *BookMarks: Readings in Black and White*. New Brunswick, N.J.: Rutgers University Press, 2006.

———. *Codes of Conduct: Race, Ethics, and the Color of Our Character*. New Brunswick, N.J.: Rutgers University Press, 1995.

hooks, bell. "Eating the Other: Desire and Resistance." In *Media and Cultural Studies Keyworks*, edited by Meenakshi Gigi Durham and Douglas M. Kellner, 424–438. Malden, Mass.: Blackwell Publishing, 2001.

Ifill, Gwen. *The Breakthrough: Politics and Race in the Age of Obama*. New York: Doubleday, 2009.

Jackson, Jesse Jr. "Jesse Jr. to Jesse Sr.: You're Wrong on Obama, Dad." *Chicago-Sun Times*, December 3, 2007. http://www.suntimes.com/news/commentary/letters/678092,CST-EDT-vox03.article.

Johnson, James Weldon. *The Autobiography of an Ex-Colored Man*. Edited by William L. Andrews. Boston: Sherman, French & Company, 1912. Reprint, New York: Penguin Books, 1990.

Jordan, June. *Passion: New Poems, 1977–80*. Boston: Beacon Press, 1980.

Kakutani, Michiko. "Worthy Women, Unredeemable Men." Review of *Paradise* by Toni Morrison. *New York Times*, January 6, 1998. http://www.nytimes.com/1998/01/06/books/books-of-the-times-worthy-women-unredeemable-men.html?n=Top/Features/Books/Book%20Reviews.

Kaplan, Erin Aubry. "'Precious' in the Age of Obama." *Salon.com*, November 9, 2009. http://www.salon.com/entertainment/precious/index.html?story=/ent/movies/feature/2009/11/09/precious_feature.

King, Martin Luther Jr. "I Have a Dream." In *I Have a Dream: Writings and Speeches That Changed the World*, edited by James M. Washington, 101–106. New York: HarperCollins, 1992.

Knapp, George. *The English Language in America*. New York: Century Co., 1925.

Kristeva, Julia. "Revolution in Poetic Language." In *The Kristeva Reader*, edited by Toril Moi, 89–135. New York: Columbia University Press, 1986.

Lahiri, Jhumpa. *The Interpreter of Maladies*. New York: Houghton Mifflin Company, 1999.

———. *The Namesake*. New York: Houghton Mifflin, 2003.

———. *Unaccustomed Earth*. New York: Alfred A. Knopf, 2008.

Larsen, Nella. *Quicksand and Passing*. Edited by Deborah E. McDowell. New Brunswick, N.J.: Rutgers University Press, 1986.

Lee, Felicia R. "The Honest Dialogue That Is Neither," *New York Times*, December 7, 1997, late edition.

Lewis, John. Interview by Tavis Smiley. *Tavis Smiley Late Night on PBS*, August 28, 2008.

Lorde, Audre. *Sister Outsider: Essays and Speeches*. Freedom, Calif.: The Crossing Press Feminist Series, 1984.

Luo, Michael. "In Job Hunt, College Degree Can't Close Racial Gap." *New York Times*, November 30, 2009. http://www.nytimes.com/2009/12/01/us/01race.html?scp=1&sq=In%20Job%20Hunt,%20College%20Degree%20Can%E2%80%99t%20Close%20Racial%20Gap.%E2%80%9D%20&st=cse.

McRobbie, Angela. "Post-Feminism and Popular Culture." *Feminist Media Studies* 4:3 (2004): 255–264.

Menand, Louis. "The War between Men and Women." Review of *Paradise* by Toni Morrison. *New Yorker*, January 12, 1998, 78–82.

Michael, John. *Identity and the Failure of America: From Thomas Jefferson to the War on Terror*. Minneapolis: University of Minnesota Press, 2008.

Michaels, Walter Benn. *The Problem with Diversity: How We Learned to Love Identity and Ignore Inequality*. New York: Metropolitan Books, 2006.

Morrison, Toni. *Beloved*. New York: A. A. Knopf, 1987.

———. *The Bluest Eye*. New York: Plume, 1994.

———. "A Conversation with Toni Morrison," interview by Bill Moyers. In *Conversations with Toni Morrison*, edited by Danille Taylor-Guthrie, 262–274. Jackson: University Press of Mississippi, 1994.

———. "Home." In *The House that Race Built: Black Americans, U.S. Terrain*, edited by Waheema Lubiano, 3–12. New York: Pantheon Books, 1997.

———. Interview by Timehost, *Time.com*, January 21, 1998. http://www.time.com/time/community/transcripts/chattro12198.html.

———. Letter to Obama. January 28, 2008, http://firstread.msnbc.msn.com/archive/2008/01/28/614795.

———. *A Mercy*. New York: A. A. Knopf, 2009.

———. "The Nobel Lecture in Literature." In *What Moves at the Margin: Selected Nonfiction, Toni Morrison*, edited by Carolyn C. Denard, 198–207. Jackson: University Press of Mississippi, 2008.

———. "Pam Houston Talks with Toni Morrison," interview by Pam Houston. In *Toni Morrison: Conversations*, edited by Carolyn C. Denard, 228–259. Jackson: University Press of Mississippi, 2008.

———. "The Pain of Being Black: An Interview with Toni Morrison," interview by Bonnie Angelo. In *Conversations with Toni Morrison*, edited by Danille Taylor-Guthrie, 255–261. Jackson: University Press of Mississippi, 1994.

———. *Paradise*. New York: A. A. Knopf, 1997.

———. "Recitatif." In *Before Columbus Foundation Fiction Anthology: Selections from the American Book Awards 1980–1990*, edited by Ishmael Reed, Kathryn Trueblood, and Shawn Wong, 445–464. New York: W. W. Norton, 1992.

———. "Rootedness: The Ancestor as Foundation." In *The Norton Anthology of African American Literature*, 2d ed., edited by Henry Louis Gates Jr. and Nellie Y. McKay, 2286–2290. New York: W. W. Norton, 2004.

———. *Song of Solomon*. New York: Plume, 1977.

———. "The Talk of the Town." In *What Moves at the Margin: Selected Nonfiction, Toni Morrison*, edited by Carolyn C. Denard, 149–153. Jackson: University Press of Mississippi, 2008.

———. "Toni Morrison," interview with Charles Ruas. In *Conversations with Toni Morrison*, edited by Danille Taylor-Guthrie, 93–118. Jackson: University Press of Mississippi, 1994.

———. "Toni Morrison Finds *A Mercy* in Servitude." Interview by Michelle Norris, NPR, October 27, 2008.

———. "Unspeakable Things Unspoken: The Afro-American Presence in American Literature." In *The Norton Anthology of African American Literature*, 2d ed., edited by Henry Louis Gates Jr. and Nellie Y. McKay, 2299–2322. New York: W. W. Norton, 2004.

Moten, Fred. "The Case of Blackness." *Criticism* 50:2 (Spring 2008): 177–218.

Murphy, Tim. "Gabby Sidibe's Astonishing Debut in *Precious*." *New York Magazine*, September 25, 2009. http://nymag.com/movies/profiles/59419/.

Nelson, Dana. *The Word in Black and White: Reading "Race" in American Literature, 1638–1867*. New York: Oxford University Press, 1992.

Nelson, Jill. "She Ain't Me Babe." December 9, 2009, http://www.niaonline.com/ggmsblog/?p=3934.

Nemoto, Kumiko. *Racing Romance: Love, Power, and Desire among Asian American/White Couples*. New Brunswick, N.J.: Rutgers University Press, 2009.

Nevergold, Barbara Seals, and Peggy Brooks-Bertram, eds. *Go, Tell Michelle: African American Women Write to the New First Lady*. Albany: State University of New York Press, 2009.

Nicol, Kathryn. "Visible Differences: Viewing Racial Identity in Toni Morrison's *Paradise* and 'Recitatif.'" In *Literature and Racial Ambiguity*, edited by Teresa Hubel and Neil Brroks, 209–232. Amsterdam, The Netherlands: Rodopi B.V., 2008.

Noah, Timothy. "The Obama Messiah Watch." *Slate*, January 29, 2007. http://www.slate.com/id/2158578.

Obama, Barack. *The Audacity of Hope: Thoughts on Reclaiming the American Dream*. New York: Crown Publishers, 2006.

———. *Dreams from My Father: A Story of Race and Inheritance*. New York: Three Rivers Press, 2004.

———. "Keynote Address by Barack Obama to the Democratic Convention on July 27, 2004." In *Dreams from My Father: A Story of Race and Inheritance*, 443–453. New York: Three Rivers Press, 2004.

———. Quoted in "I Could Have Calibrated Those Words Differently." *New York Times*, July 25, 2009. http://query.nytimes.com/gst/fullpage.html?res=9F04E4DC163AF936A15754C0A96F9C8B63

———. "Sen. Barack Obama's Letter to Tavis Smiley." *Chicago Sun-Times*, February 14, 2008. http://blogs.suntimes.com/mitchell/2008/02/sen_barack_obamas_letter_to_ta_1.html.

———. "A More Perfect Union." In *The Speech: Race and Barack Obama's "A More Perfect Union,"* edited by T. Denean Sharpley-Whiting, 237–251. New York: Bloomsbury, 2009.

———. "Remarks of Senator Barack Obama: Super Tuesday," February 5, 2008. http://www.barackobama.com/2008/02/05/remarks_of_senator_barack_obam_46.php.

———. Speech to the Urban League. July 29, 2010. http://blogs.suntimes.com/sweet/2010/07/obama_urban_league_speech_sher.html.

———. "What I Want for You—and Every Child in America." *Parade*. January 18, 2009. http://www.parade.com/export/sites/default/news/2009/01/barack-obama-letter-to-my-daughters.html.

Patell, Cyrus R. K. *Negative Liberties: Morrison, Pynchon, and the Problem of Liberal Ideology*. Durham, N.C.: Duke University Press, 2001.

Piven, Frances Fox. "Escaping Clinton's Control." In *Challenges to Equality: Race and Poverty in America*, edited by Chester W. Hartman, 318. Armonk, N.Y.: M. E. Sharpe, 2001.

Precious: Based on the Novel by Sapphire. DVD. Directed by Lee Daniels. Lee Daniel Entertainment, 2009.

Price, Hugh. Quoted in *Conversations: William Jefferson Clinton: From Hope to Harlem*, edited by Janis F. Kearney, 345. Chicago: Writing Our World Press, 2006.

Read, Andrew. "'As if word magic had anything to do with the courage it took to be a man': Black Masculinity in Toni Morrison's *Paradise*." *African American Review* 39:4 (2005): 527–540.

Reed, Adolph Jr. "Obama No." *The Progressive*, May 2008. http://www.progressive.org/mag_reed0508.

Reed, Ishmael. "Obama Scolds Black Fathers, Gets Bounce in Polls," http://www.counterpunch.org/reed06242008.html.

Remnick, David. "The Joshua Generation: Race and the Campaign of Barack Obama." *New Yorker*, November 17, 2008. http://www.newyorker.com/reporting/2008/11/17/081117fa_fact_remnick?currentPage=all.

Rickford, John Russell, and Russell John Rickford. *Spoken Soul: The Story of Black English*. New York: Wiley Publishers, 2000.

Roediger, David R. *How Race Survived U.S. History: From Settlement and Slavery to the Obama Phenomenon*. New York: Verso, 2008.

Romero, Channette. "Creating the Beloved Community: Religion, Race, and Nation in Toni Morrison's *Paradise*." *African American Review* 39.3 (2005): 415–430.

Seelye, Katharine Q. "Obama Wades into a Volatile Racial Issue." *New York Times*, July 23, 2009. http://www.nytimes.com/2009/07/23/us/23race.html.

Smith, Zadie. "Speaking in Tongues." *New York Review of Books*, February 26, 2009. http://www.nybooks.com/articles/22334.

Stanton, Domna. "Language and Revolution: The Franco-American Dis-Connection." In *The Future of Difference*, edited by Hester Eisenstein and Alice Jardine, 73–87. Boston: G. K. Hall, 1980.

Stave, Shirley A. "The Master's Tools: Morrison's *Paradise* and the Problem of Christianity." In *Toni Morrison and the Bible: Contested Intertextualities*, edited by Shirley A. Stave, 215–231. Peter Lang: New York, 2006.

Sullivan, Patricia A., and Steven R. Goldwiz. "Seven Lessons from President Clinton's Race Initiative: A Post-Mortem on the Politics of Desire." In *Images, Scandal, and Communication Strategies of the Clinton Presidency*, edited by Robert E. Denton Jr. and Rachel L. Holloway, 143–171. Westport, Conn.: Praeger, 2003.

Tally, Justine. *Paradise Reconsidered: Toni Morrison's (Hi)stories and Truths*. FORECAST 2. Hamburg: Lit Verlag, 1999.

Taylor-Guthrie, Danille, ed. Conversations with Roni Morrison. Jackson: University of Mississippi Press, 2008.

Tettenborn, Eva. "Jhumpa Lahiri's *Interpreter of Maladies*: Colonial Fantasies in 'Sexy.'" *Notes on Contemporary Literature* 32.4 (September 2002): 11–12.

Thai, Xuan, and Ted Barrett. "Biden's Description of Obama Draws Scrutiny." CNN.com, February 9, 2007, http://www.cnn.com/2007/POLITICS/01/31/biden.obama/.

Updike, John. *Rabbit Novels*, Vol. 1: *Rabbit Run and Rabbit Redux*. New York: Ballantine Books, 2003.

U.S. Society & Values: Electronic Journals of the U.S. Information Agency. *Toward One America: A National Conversation on Race.* Washington, D.C.: August 1997.

Walker, Alice. *The Color Purple.* New York: Washington Square Press, 1982.

———. "Lest We Forget: An Open Letter to My Sisters Who Are Brave." *Root*, March 27, 2008. http://www.theroot.com/views/lest-we-forget-open-letter-to-my-sisters-who-are-brave.

———. "White House Advice," *Newsweek*, January 19, 2009, http://www.newsweek.com/id/180457.

Wall Street Journal. "President Elect Obama." November 5, 2008. http://online.wsj.com/article/NA_WSJ_PUB:SB122586244657800863.html

Washington, Elsie B. "Talk with Toni Morrison." In *Conversations with Toni Morrison*, edited by Danille Taylor-Guthrie, 234–238. Jackson: University Press of Mississippi, 1994.

West, Cornel. "The Dilemma of the Black Intellectual." *Cultural Critique* 1 (Autumn 1985): 109–124.

White, Armond. "Pride & Precious." *New York Press*, November 4, 2009. http://www.nypress.com/article-20554-pride-precious.html.

Whitehead, Colson. *Apex Hides the Hurt.* New York: Anchor, 2006.

Wiegman, Robyn. *American Anatomies: Theorizing Race and Gender.* Durham, N.C.: Duke University Press, 1995.

Williams, Linda Faye. *The Constraint of Race: Legacies of White Skin Privilege in America.* University Park: Pennsylvania State University Press, 2004.

Wise, Tim. *Between Barack and a Hard Place: Racism and White Denial in the Age of Obama.* San Francisco: City Lights Books, 2009.

Wolffe, Richard. *The Renegade: The Making of a President.* New York: Random House, 2009.

Womack, Ytasha. *Post Black: How a New Generation Is Redefining African American Identity.* Chicago: Lawrence Hill Books, 2010.

Wu, Frank H. *Yellow: Race in America Beyond Black and White.* New York: BasicBooks, 2002.

Wynter, Leon E. *American Skin: Pop Culture, Big Business, and the End of White America.* New York: Random House, 2002.

INDEX

2008 presidential campaign, 1–2, 5–7, 9–10, 17, 19–23, 28–29, 134–158, 169–171, 186n12, 188n12, 189n18

2008 presidential election, 1–2, 4, 31, 139, 165

affirmative action, 6

African American Review, 183n7

Aguiar, Sarah Appleton, 183n7

Allen, Brook, 45, 183n4

American dream, 17, 35, 82–83

American identity, 116–122, 125–127, 132, 154, 157–158

ancestor, 71, 90–91, 98, 142

Angelou, Maya, 138, 185n5

antiracialist, 14

Appiah, Anthony, 180n14

A.V. Club, The, 188n8

Bacon's Rebellion, 33–34

Bakhtin, Mikhail, 10, 88, 180n16, 184n7

Baldwin, James, 100–101, 145, 181n18

Beam, Christopher, 22, 182n33

Berlant, Lauren, 80

Berry, Mary Frances, 16, 181n23

Bhabha, Homi, 11

Biden, Joe, 135–136, 160, 185n3

biraciality, 21, 100–101, 163

Birth of a Nation, The (film), 169

black intellectual, 142–143, 146

blackness, 11, 25–27, 29, 31–33, 38–42, 44, 88, 167–169, 172, 176, 185n2; as chosen or disavowed identity, 68–79, 183n1; connection to ancestor, 90, 142; and Obama, 2–3, 5–6, 12–13, 18, 21, 68, 100–101, 177, 182n32; as performed intimacy, 137–154, 162–163; as trope, 17–18, 139–141, 165, 173–174; and violence, 47, 53–54, 64–67, 93, 95

Black Orpheus (film), 131–132

black speech, 12, 18, 20, 28–29, 136, 144, 148–149, 161, 163, 181n18

Bond, Julian, 150, 186n15

Bonilla-Silva, Eduardo, 179n7

Braun, Carol Moseley, 135

Breitbart, Andrew, 161, 163

Bronson, Po, 29

Brooks, David, 188n17

Brooks-Bertram, Peggy, 186n8

Brown v. The Board of Education, 83

Bush, Barbara, 166, 187n3

Bush, George H. W., 180n12

Bush, George W., 172, 184–185n10

Butler, Judith, 120

Carcasson, Martin, 16

Carey, Mariah, 175

Carter, Jimmy, 161, 187n28

Carter, Philip D., 3, 179n8

Cheng, Anne Anlin, 27, 94–95

Chisholm, Shirley, 135

Chronicle of Higher Education, 189n21

civil rights movement, 4, 11, 150–151, 154, 157

Clinton, Hillary, 5, 137–139, 142, 185n5, 188n16

Clinton, William Jefferson, 15–19, 68, 138–140, 162, 172, 181n25, 182n26; 1997 race initiative (*see* "One America in the 21st Century")

Coates, Ta-Nehisi Paul, 182n32

Cobb, William Jelani, 182n29

coded racial discourse, 1–2, 5, 11, 18, 23–24, 28, 134, 144, 149, 153

Cohen, Richard, 2, 179n2

Coleman, Arica, 160, 187n26

color blindness, 3, 5–7, 10, 14, 29, 70, 74, 79 82, 179n7

color-line, 4–5, 7, 24

Connerly, Ward, 162

Constitution, U.S., 9, 98–99, 153

Crouch, Stanley, 182n32

Crowley, James, 158–160

Daniels, Lee, 29, 167–169, 188nn4–6, 188n8; *Precious: Based on the Novel by Sapphire*, 29, 164–169, 172–177, 187nn1–3, 188nn4–10, 189nn19–21

ABOUT THE AUTHOR

STEPHANIE LI is an assistant professor of English at the University of Rochester. Her first book, *Something Akin to Freedom: The Choice of Bondage in Narratives by African American Women*, won the 2009 First Book Prize in African American Studies from SUNY Press. She has also published a short biography of Toni Morrison as well as essays in *Callaloo, American Literature, Legacy*, and *SAIL*.